Stephen Walther

Windows® 8.1 Apps
with HTML5 and JavaScript

UNLEASHED

SAMS | 800 East 96th Street, Indianapolis, Indiana 46240 USA

Windows® 8.1 Apps with HTML5 and JavaScript Unleashed

ISBN-13: 978-0-672-33711-6
ISBN-10: 0-672-33711-8

Library of Congress Control Number 2013951680

Printed in the United States on America

First Printing December 2013

Trademarks

Warning and Disclaimer

Special Sales

For information about buying this title in bulk quantities, or for special sales opportunities (which may include electronic versions; custom cover designs; and content particular to your business, training goals, marketing focus, or branding interests), please contact our corporate sales department at corpsales@pearsoned.com or (800) 382-3419.

For government sales inquiries, please contact governmentsales@pearsoned.com.

For questions about sales outside the U.S., please contact international@pearsoned.com.

Editor-in-Chief
Greg Wiegand

Executive Editor
Neil Rowe

Development Editor
Mark Renfrow

Managing Editor
Kristy Hart

Project Editor
Elaine Wiley

Indexer
Tim Wright

Proofreader
Charlotte HKughen

Technical Editors
Jeff Burtoft
James Boddie

Publishing Coordinator
Cindy Teeters

Senior Compositor
Gloria Schurick

Contents at a Glance

Table of Contents

Contents

Contents

Contents

Contents

About the Author

Formerly a Senior Program Manager at Microsoft, **Stephen Walther** now runs his own consulting and training company www.SuperexpertTraining.com. He flies to companies and provides hands-on training on building Windows Store apps.

Stephen was completing his Ph.D. at MIT and teaching classes on metaphysics at MIT and Harvard when he abruptly realized that there is no money in metaphysics. He dropped out to help found two successful Internet startups. He created the Collegescape website, a website used by more than 200 colleges, including Stanford, Harvard, and MIT, for online college applications (sold to ETS). He also was a founder of CityAuction, which was one of the first and largest auction websites (sold to CitySearch).

Dedication

This book is dedicated to Jon Robert Walther, who is a Jedi ninja.

Acknowledgments

Yikes, it takes too much work to write a technical book—don't ever do it! I would like to blame my editor Neil Rowe for talking me into writing another book. I also want to blame my wife Ruth Walther for failing to talk me out of it. Finally, I want to blame my technical editors Jeff Burtoft and James Boddie for doing such a careful job of coming up with ways to improve the book and forcing me to spend even more time working on the book.

We Want to Hear from You!

As the reader of this book, *you* are our most important critic and commentator. We value your opinion and want to know what we're doing right, what we could do better, what areas you'd like to see us publish in, and any other words of wisdom you're willing to pass our way.

You can email or write me directly to let me know what you did or didn't like about this book—as well as what we can do to make our books stronger.

Please note that I cannot help you with technical problems related to the topic of this book, and that due to the high volume of mail I receive, I might not be able to reply to every message.

When you write, please be sure to include this book's title and author as well as your name and phone or email address. I will carefully review your comments and share them with the author and editors who worked on the book.

Email: feedback@samspublishing.com

Mail: Neil Rowe
Executive Editor
Sams Publishing
800 East 96th Street
Indianapolis, IN 46240 USA

Reader Services

Visit our website and register this book at informit.com/register for convenient access to any updates, downloads, or errata that might be available for this book.

Introduction

If you want to build a software application and reach the largest possible market of customers and make the most money then it makes sense for you to build a Windows 8.1 app.

Microsoft Windows is the most popular operating system in the world. Windows accounts for more than 90 percent of the operating system market. More than 100 million licenses for Windows 8 were sold in its first six months of release. The size of the Windows market dwarfs the size of every other marketplace for software applications (including the iPhone and Android markets).

I want to own a toilet made of solid gold, Nathan Myhrvold's jet, and a Tesla Roadster (orange). These are modest goals, and I know that many of you reading this book share the same goals. The most likely way for you or me (hopefully me) to reach these goals is to build Windows 8.1 apps.

When you build a Windows 8.1 app, you can sell your app right within Windows 8.1 itself. Windows 8.1 includes the Windows Store (shown in Figure I.1) where you can list your app for anywhere between free and $999.99. You can sell a variety of different types of apps including productivity apps (think task lists and time trackers) and games (think Angry Birds and Cut the Rope).

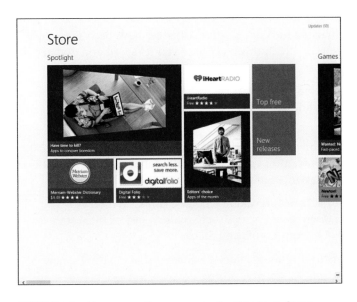

FIGURE I.1   You can sell your app in the Windows Store.

This book is all about building Windows apps that you can sell in the Windows Store. In particular, you learn how to build Windows apps using JavaScript and HTML5.

Why JavaScript and HTML5? You can build Windows apps using other technologies such as C# and XAML or C++, but this book focuses exclusively on building Windows apps with JavaScript and HTML5.

The advantage of building Windows apps with JavaScript and HTML5 is that you can leverage your existing skills building websites to build Windows applications. If you are already comfortable programming with JavaScript, HTML, and Cascading Style Sheets then you should find it easy to build Windows apps.

This book covers everything you need to know to build Windows apps. You learn how to use the Windows Library for JavaScript (WinJS) to create JavaScript applications. In particular, you learn how to use WinJS controls such as the `Rating`, `Menu`, `Repeater`, and `ListView` controls.

You also learn how to work with the Windows Runtime. By taking advantage of the Windows Runtime, you can access Windows 8.1 functionality to do things that you could not normally do in a pure web app, such as capture video and sound and convert text to speech.

By the end of this book, you will understand how to create Windows apps, such as game apps and productivity apps. In Chapter 15, "Graphics and Games," you learn how to create a simple arcade game—the Brain Eaters game. And, in Chapter 16, "Creating a Task List App," you learn how to build a productivity app—the MyTasks app.

Read this book, build a Windows app, sell lots of copies, and buy a jet.

Updated for Windows 8.1

This book has been extensively updated for Windows 8.1. Changes have been made to every chapter. All of the code associated with this book has been reviewed and updated to be compatible with Windows 8.1.

Windows 8.1 includes several important new controls, including the `Hub`, `Repeater`, `ItemContainer`, `SearchBox`, `WebView`, and `NavBar` controls. This book covers all of these new controls in depth.

Windows 8.1 ships with a new version of the Windows Library for JavaScript (WinJS 2.0). This new version has significant new features such as the WinJS Scheduler. I discuss the new WinJS Scheduler in Chapter 2, "WinJS Fundamentals."

Windows 8.1 includes important backwards breaking changes. Unlike Windows 8, Windows 8.1 no longer supports discrete view states such as a snapped or filled state. I discuss these changes in Chapter 11, "App Events and States."

Finally, I added four new chapters to this book. I added a chapter that covers the new `ItemContainer` and `Repeater` controls (Chapter 7, "Using the `ItemContainer`, `Repeater`, and `FlipView` Controls"), a chapter devoted to using Windows Azure Mobile Services (Chapter 10, "Storing Data with Windows Azure"), a chapter on implementing share and search (Chapter 13, "Creating Share and Search Contracts"), and a chapter on building a productivity app (Chapter 16).

Prerequisites for This Book

If you can build a website using JavaScript, HTML, and Cascading Style Sheets then you have the skills that you need to read and understand this book.

There are two software requirements for building Windows apps and using the code from this book.

First, you must build a Windows 8.1 app on the Windows 8.1 operating system. Let me repeat this: You must have Windows 8.1 installed on your computer to use the code from this book.

Second, in order to use the code from this book, you need Microsoft Visual Studio 2013. There is a free version of Visual Studio 2013—Microsoft Visual Studio Express 2013 for Windows—which you can download from the Microsoft.com website.

Source Code

You can download all of the source code associated with this book from GitHub: https://github.com/StephenWalther/Windows8.1AppsUnleashed

Click the Downloads link to download the latest version of the code in a zip file.

CHAPTER 1

Building Windows Store Apps

In this chapter, I introduce you to the basics of building Windows Store apps. I start off by explaining how a Windows Store app differs from a traditional Windows desktop application. You learn what makes a Windows Store app a Windows Store app.

Feeling fearless and bold, and hoping that *you too* feel fearless and bold, I next guide you through building your first Windows store app. You learn how to take advantage of the features of Microsoft Visual Studio 2013 to build, run, and debug a Windows Store app.

Next, we dive into a discussion of the fundamental elements of a Windows Store app. You learn how a Windows Store app is forged out of HTML5, JavaScript, the Windows Library for JavaScript, and the Windows Runtime.

Finally, we get to the money part. I explain how you can publish your Windows Store app to the Windows Store and start collecting those dollars.

What Is a Windows Store App?

I can still remember the first time that I used an iPhone. When you scroll the screen on an iPhone, the screen actually bounces! And when you add an email to the trash, the email gets sucked into the trashcan! It's as if there is a little universe inside an iPhone and it follows our physical laws.

For some reason—that I have not explored and that I do not completely understand—this illusion that there is a second universe inside my iPhone makes me happy. It makes interacting with an iPhone fun.

Now we come to Windows. Except for the dancing card thing in Windows Solitaire, I can't think of anything in Windows that has ever created this same sense of fun. I can't remember the last time that Windows made me laugh or brought me joy.

With Windows Store apps, Microsoft has finally acknowledged that user experience matters—in a big way. The heart of Windows Store apps is a set of user experience principles named the *Microsoft design style principles*. By embracing the Microsoft design style principles, you can create Windows Store apps that seem more alive and that are a pleasure to use.

Microsoft Design Style Principles

The Microsoft design style principles is a set of user experience design principles developed by Microsoft in the context of building the Windows Phone, Xbox Live, and the (now defunct) Zune. You also can see the Microsoft design principles applied to Microsoft websites such as Microsoft SkyDrive and the Windows Azure Portal. Get ready. Here they are:

1. **Show pride in craftsmanship**

   ▶ Devote time and energy to small things that are seen often by many.

   ▶ Engineer the experience to be complete and polished at every stage.

2. **Do more with less**

   ▶ Solve for distractions, not discoverability. Let people be immersed in what they love and they will explore the rest.

   ▶ Create a clean and purposeful experience by leaving only the most relevant elements on screen so people can be immersed in the content.

3. **Be fast and fluid**

   ▶ Let people interact directly with content, and respond to actions quickly with matching energy.

   ▶ Bring life to the experience, create a sense of continuity and tell a story through meaningful use of motion.

4. **Be authentically digital**

   ▶ Take full advantage of the digital medium. Remove physical boundaries to create experiences that are more efficient and effortless than reality.

   ▶ Embrace the fact that we are pixels on a screen. Design with bold, vibrant and crisp colors and images that go beyond the limits of real-world material.

5. **Win as one**

  ▶ Leverage the ecosystem and work together with other apps, devices and the system to complete scenarios for people.

  ▶ Fit into the UI model to reduce redundancy. Take advantage of what people already know to provide a sense of familiarity, control, and confidence.

NOTE

The Microsoft design style principles were originally known as *Metro design principles*. This list of Microsoft design style principles was taken from http://msdn.microsoft.com/en-us/library/windows/apps/hh464920 and http://msdn.microsoft.com/en-us/library/windows/apps/hh465424.aspx.

When I first read these principles, my initial reaction was that they seemed overly abstract and squishy. Exactly the type of principles that would be created by beret-wearing user experience guys.

But then, when I saw how the principles were applied in practice—when building actual Windows Store apps—I started to develop a better appreciation for these principles.

Take the "Do more with less" design principle. One of the distinctive features of a Windows Store app is the lack of chrome. Ironically, a Windows Store app is a Windows app without the window. Windows Store apps are full-screen apps.

This lack of chrome makes it easier to concentrate on the content of the application. For example, Windows 8 includes two version of Internet Explorer: a desktop version and a full-throated Windows 8 version that follows the Microsoft design style principles.

I really prefer using the Windows 8 version of Internet Explorer over the desktop version. When using the Windows 8 version, all you see is the web page, which is the point of the application in the first place.

Or consider the "Be fast and fluid" principle. The reason that I like interacting with my iPhone so much is the illusion of motion, and this illusion is created by the judicious use of animations: On an iPhone, objects bounce and wobble.

When building a Windows Store app, you are encouraged to take advantage of animations. For example, if you use the standard ListView control—which we discuss in detail later in this book—then you get animations when you add or remove items. When you add an item to a ListView, it not only appears, it glides into place. When you remove an item, it doesn't just disappear, items above and below it collapse into place.

Common Features of Windows Store Apps

Windows Store apps are applications that follow the Microsoft design style principles. Furthermore, Windows Store apps are designed to run on the Windows 8 or Windows RT operating system.

All Windows Store apps have a common set of features. Let me explain these features by pointing them out in the context of the Bing News app that's included with Windows 8.

NOTE

It is worth pointing out that the standard Windows 8 Bing News app discussed in this section was written using HTML5 and JavaScript (using the same techniques described in this book). In case you are curious, you can view the HTML and JavaScript source for the News app by opening the hidden folder where Windows apps are installed located at *Program Files\WindowsApps*.

Support for Keyboard, Mouse, Touch, and Stylus

One of the most distinctive characteristics of a Windows Store app is its oversized tiles and buttons and generous use of whitespace. All of this user interface (UI) roominess makes Windows Store apps friendly to fat fingers.

Windows Store apps are designed to work equally well when used on a touch-only tablet and when used on a desktop computer with a keyboard and mouse. Windows Store apps are designed to be gropeable.

The nice thing about how Windows 8 works is that you don't need to put a lot of thought into supporting touch as a developer. As long as you stick with the standard WinJS controls, you get both keyboard and touch support for free.

Using the App Bar and Nav Bar

Figure 1.1 contains a screenshot of the Windows 8 Bing News app with the home page of Fox News open. Notice that the only thing that you see is the content of Fox News. No toolbars, no menus, no status bars.

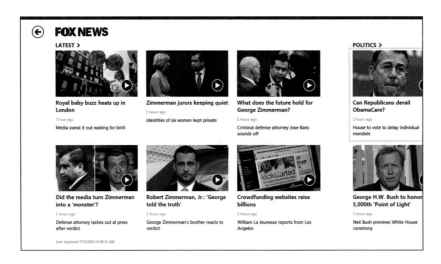

FIGURE 1.1   Windows 8 Bing News app

In a Windows Store app, you hide all of your commands in the app bar. The app bar appears only when you swipe from the bottom or top of the screen or you right-click the screen.

The app bar for the Bing News app includes commands such as Pin to Start, Refresh, and Help. You can see the app bar at the bottom of Figure 1.2.

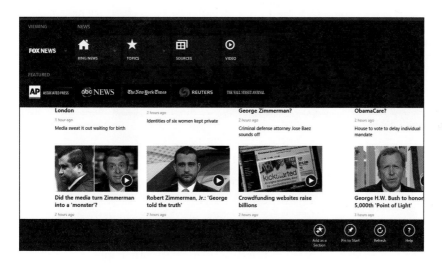

FIGURE 1.2   Using the app bar and nav bar

Notice in Figure 1.2 that there is another bar at the top of the screen. This bar is called the nav bar and you use it to navigate. In the case of the Bing News app, the nav bar enables you to navigate to different news sources such as the *Wall Street Journal*, Fox News, and the *New York Times*.

Using Charms

If you swipe from the right edge of the screen or mouse to either of the right corners or press the keyboard combination Win+C then the charms are revealed (see Figure 1.3).

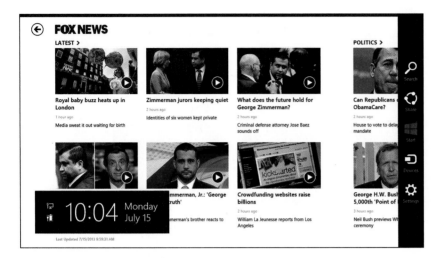

FIGURE 1.3   Viewing charms

Here's a list of the standard charms:

- Search—Enables you to search content in the current app and other apps

- Share—Enables you to share content in the current app with other apps

- Start—Navigates you to the Start screen

- Devices—Enables you to connect to a device

- Settings—Enables you to configure both app settings and system settings

These charms provide you with standard locations to place common application function-ality. For example, all Windows Store app settings should appear in the Settings charm (see Figure 1.4). This makes it much easier for users to find your settings.

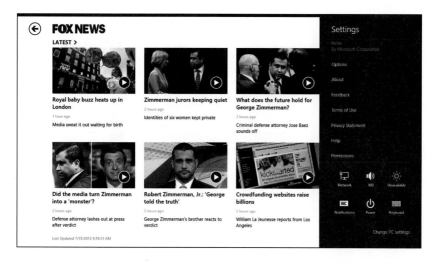

FIGURE 1.4   The Settings charm

When you are building a Windows Store app, you don't build your own Settings menu. Instead, you extend the Settings charm with your custom app settings. I discuss the details of doing this in Chapter 6, "Menus and Flyouts."

Different App Sizes and Orientations

Every Windows 8.1 app supports a minimum width of either 500 pixels or 320 pixels. For example, if a Windows 8.1 app has a minimum horizontal size of 500 pixels then the app can be resized to any size between 500 pixels and the maximum screen size of the device where the app is displayed.

If you are lucky enough to have a sufficiently large screen, then you can display multiple running apps side by side (up to four apps per monitor). For example, Figure 1.5 illustrates three Windows 8.1 apps running side by side (the Calendar, Maps, and News apps).

> **WARNING**
>
> You cannot display more than two 500 pixel apps on a 1,024 pixel by 768 pixel screen because that would violate the laws of mathematics.

FIGURE 1.5   Three Windows 8.1 apps side by side

Windows 8, unlike Windows 8.1, supported running of no more than two apps at once. Furthermore, when using Windows 8, one of the two running apps was required to be snapped to a horizontal resolution of 320 pixels. Windows 8.1 is far more flexible.

A Windows Store app also must work when used with different device orientations. For example, when an app is viewed on a tablet computer, the user always has the option of rotating your app from a landscape to a portrait orientation.

When building Windows Store apps, you need to design the app so it works with different screen resolutions and orientations. At any moment, the horizontal resolution of your app could be dramatically changed. I discuss how to handle switching between different resolutions in Chapter 11, "App Events and States."

People, Not Machines, Use Windows Store Apps

When you buy a Windows Store app, the app is licensed per user and not per machine. When you buy an app, you can use the app on up to five machines—including both tablets and desktops—associated with your user account. You can view and install all of your purchased apps from the Windows Store by right-clicking within the Store app and selecting Your Apps.

Better yet, data from your apps can be shared across multiple machines (roaming application data). So, if you are using an app to read an article on your tablet PC on the bus and then you open the same app on your desktop PC at work, you won't lose your place in the article.

Currently, every Windows Store app gets 100KB of roaming application data. Windows 8.1 handles synchronizing this data between different machines for you automatically.

Closing a Windows Store App

Now close a Windows Store app by moving your cursor over the x at the top-right of the screen. Ha! Tricked you! There is no close button in a Windows Store app because there is no chrome.

> **NOTE**
>
> Even though it is not obvious how to close a Windows Store app, it is possible. You can close a Windows Store app by swiping down from the top of the screen to the very bottom of the screen or pressing the keyboard combination Alt+F4.

When interacting with Windows Store apps, there is no obvious way to close an app. This is intentional. Instead of closing a Windows Store app, you are encouraged to simply switch to another running app (by swiping from the left edge of the screen) or launch a new app (by selecting a new app from the Start screen).

When you design a Windows Store app, you must design the app with the knowledge that a user might switch back and forth to your running app at any time. In Chapter 11 I discuss how you can gracefully resume an app after it has been suspended.

Creating Your First Windows Store App

Let's be fearless. In this section, I guide you through building your first Windows Store app. Doing a *Hello World* app would be predictable and boring. Therefore, I suggest that we do something a little more advanced.

I'll show you how you can create an app which enables you to take pictures. When you click the Take Picture command in the app bar, you can take a picture, and then the picture is displayed in the app (see Figure 1.6, which shows a picture of my dog Rover).

> **NOTE**
>
> The code for the completed app can be found in the Chapter 1 folder with the name App1. All of the code for this book is located in a GitHub repository at https://github.com/ StephenWalther/Windows8.1AppsUnleashed.

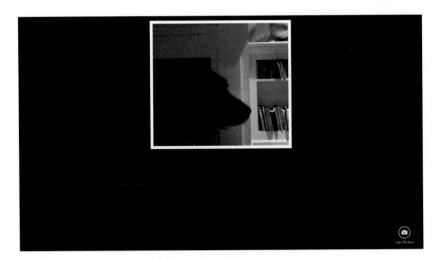

FIGURE 1.6   Your first Windows Store app

Creating the Visual Studio Project

The first step is to create a Microsoft Visual Studio Project. I used Visual Studio 2013 to create almost all of the code samples for this book. In most cases, I used the free version of Visual Studio—Visual Studio Express 2013 for Windows—which you can download from Microsoft.com.

> **NOTE**
>
> You can create Windows Store apps with either Microsoft Visual Studio 2013 or Microsoft Blend. If you need to release to the Windows Store then I recommend using Microsoft Visual Studio 2013.
>
> In order to build Windows Store apps, you must use Visual Studio on Windows 8.1. If you don't have a dedicated Windows 8.1 computer, you can use a virtual machine running Windows 8.1 such as VMware Player.

Go ahead and launch Visual Studio. Next, select the menu option File, New Project. On the left-side of the New Project dialog, select JavaScript and select the *Blank App* project template. Enter the name `App1` for your project and click the OK button (see Figure 1.7).

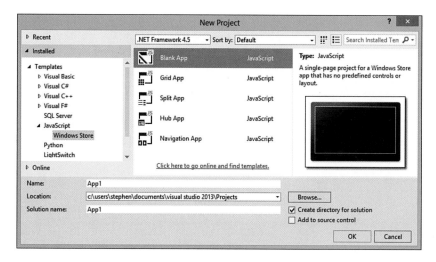

FIGURE 1.7   Using the Visual Studio New Project dialog

After you create your project, you can see all of the files for your project in the Solution Explorer window (Figure 1.8). When you create a new Windows Store app, you get a default.html file (in the root of your project), a default.js file (in the js folder), and a default.css file (in the css folder). These three files are the starting point for your app.

FIGURE 1.8   Windows Store app default files

Declaring App Capabilities

Before we can jump into writing code, there is one other thing that we must do first. We are building an app that takes pictures. That is scary. Potentially, an app could take pictures of you without your knowledge and send the pictures back to an evil hacker lurking on the Internet (or the CEO of Microsoft).

When your app does something scary, you must declare that your app will do this scary thing up front so the user can consent. You declare the capabilities of your app in your application manifest file. You can open the editor for your application manifest by double-clicking the package.appxmanifest file in the Solution Explorer window.

Click the Capabilities tab to view all of the declared capabilities of your application. For example, if you want your app to be able to record from the computer microphone then you need to select the Microphone capability, or if you want your app to be able to save new photos in the user's Pictures library then you need to select the Pictures Library capability. For our app, we need to enable the Webcam capability so we can take pictures (see Figure 1.9).

Application UI	Capabilities

Use this page to specify system features or devices

Capabilities:

- ☐ Enterprise Authentication
- ☑ Internet (Client)
- ☐ Internet (Client & Server)
- ☐ Location
- ☐ Microphone
- ☐ Music Library
- ☐ Pictures Library
- ☐ Private Networks (Client & Server)
- ☐ Proximity
- ☐ Removable Storage
- ☐ Shared User Certificates
- ☐ Videos Library
- ☑ Webcam

FIGURE 1.9   Enabling the capability to take pictures

When a user first runs our app, the user will need to consent to allowing the app to access the webcam (see Figure 1.10). The user only needs to consent once.

FIGURE 1.10   Asking for consent to access your webcam

> **NOTE**
>
> After a user consents, the user can deny an app permission to use a particular capability by using the Permissions setting under the Settings charm.

Creating the HTML Page

When you create a Windows Store app, you get a default.html file in the root of your application. This is the first page that is opened when you run your app. Let's go ahead and customize this page for our picture app (see Listing 1.1).

LISTING 1.1   Modified default.html Page

```html
<!DOCTYPE html>
<html>
<head>
    <meta charset="utf-8" />
    <title>App1</title>

    <!-- WinJS references -->
    <link href="//Microsoft.WinJS.2.0/css/ui-dark.css" rel="stylesheet" />
    <script src="//Microsoft.WinJS.2.0/js/base.js"></script>
    <script src="//Microsoft.WinJS.2.0/js/ui.js"></script>

    <!-- App1 references -->
    <link href="/css/default.css" rel="stylesheet" />
    <script src="/js/default.js"></script>
</head>
<body>

    <img id="imgPhoto" src="/images/placeholder.png" />

    <!-- AppBar Control -->
    <div id="appBar1"
        data-win-control="WinJS.UI.AppBar">
        <button data-win-control="WinJS.UI.AppBarCommand"
            data-win-options="{
                id:'cmdTakePicture',
                label:'Take Picture',
                icon:'camera',
                tooltip:'Take Picture'
            }">
        </button>
    </div>
</body>
</html>
```

The HTML page in Listing 1.1 has been modified so it contains new content in the body of the page. First, notice that the page contains an IMG tag with the ID imgPhoto. We'll display the photo which we take from the camera here.

Notice, furthermore, that the page contains a DIV tag with a data-win-control="WinJS. UI.AppBar" attribute. This is an example of a WinJS control. This control renders an app bar that contains a command for taking a picture (see Figure 1.11).

FIGURE 1.11   The Take Picture command in the app bar

Creating the Style Sheet

When you create a new Windows Store app, you also get a default style sheet named default.css which is located in the css folder. You can modify this file to control the appearance of your app.

For our app, I've modified the default.css to format the appearance of the photo. It appears in the IMG tag like this:

```
#imgPhoto {
    display:block;
    margin: 15px auto;
    border: 10px solid white;
    max-width: 90%;
    max-height: 90%;
}
```

Creating the JavaScript File

The third file that we need to modify is the JavaScript file named default.js which is located in the js folder. This file contains all of the code associated with the default.html page.

We are going to delete all of the default content of this file and start over. The complete contents of the modified version of default.js are contained in Listing 1.2.

LISTING 1.2   The default.js JavaScript file

```javascript
(function () {
    "use strict";

    // Aliases
    var capture = Windows.Media.Capture;

    // Executed immediately after page content is loaded
    function init() {
        // Process all of the controls
        WinJS.UI.processAll().done(function () {
            // References to DOM elements
            var cmdTakePicture = document.getElementById("cmdTakePicture");
            var imgPhoto = document.getElementById("imgPhoto");

            // Handle Take Picture command click
            cmdTakePicture.addEventListener("click", function () {
                var captureUI = new capture.CameraCaptureUI();
                captureUI.photoSettings.format = capture.CameraCaptureUIPhotoFormat.
➥png;
                captureUI.captureFileAsync(capture.CameraCaptureUIMode.photo).
➥done(function (photo) {
                    if (photo) {
                        // Use HTML5 File API to create object URL to refer to the
➥photo file
                        var photoUrl = URL.createObjectURL(photo);

                        // Show photo in IMG element
                        imgPhoto.src = photoUrl;
                    }
                });
            });
        });
    }

    document.addEventListener("DOMContentLoaded", init);
})();
```

NOTE

The JavaScript code contained in the Default.js file, which we deleted, is used to handle app lifecycle events such as app activation and suspension. I discuss these app events in detail in Chapter 11.

There is a lot of interesting stuff happening in the JavaScript code in Listing 1.2. Let's walk through the code.

First, I've created an `init()` function that is executed when the `DOMContentLoaded` event is raised. The `DOMContentLoaded` event is a standard `DOM` event that is raised when a browser finishes parsing an HTML document.

I put all of my code into the `init()` function so the code won't be executed until the `DOM` is ready. Otherwise, if I attempted to access any of the HTML elements in the page then I would get an exception because the elements would not yet exist.

The first thing that I do within the `init()` method is call the `WinJS.UI.processAll()` method. This method processes all of the controls in a page. In particular, it converts the `DIV` tag with the `data-win-control="WinJS.UI.AppBar"` attribute into an actual app bar.

Next, I setup an event handler for the Take Picture command. When you click the Take Picture command in the app bar, an instance of the `Windows.Media.Capture.CameraCaptureUI` class is created. The `CameraCaptureUI` class is an example of a Windows Runtime class.

The `CameraCaptureUI.captureFileAsync()` method displays the screen for taking a picture (see Figure 1.12). When you click the OK button, the `done()` method is called and the picture is displayed in the page.

FIGURE 1.12   The camera capture UI screen

An object URL is created for the photo blob (the actual image data) returned by the `captureFileAsync()` method by calling the `URL.createObjectURL()` method. This `createObjectURL()` method is part of the HTML5 File API.

The photo is displayed in the HTML page with the following line of code:

```
// Show photo in IMG element
imgPhoto.src = photoUrl;
```

And that is all there is to it! We built an app that enables us to take pictures from our computer and display the pictures in an HTML page.

Notice that our JavaScript file contains a combination of standard JavaScript methods, HTML5 methods, Windows Library for JavaScript methods, and Windows Runtime methods. This is normal for all of the JavaScript files that you create when creating a Windows Store app.

Running the App

After you create the app, you can run it by pressing the green Run button in the Visual Studio toolbar (see Figure 1.13) or just press the F5 key.

FIGURE 1.13   Running a Windows Store app

Assuming that your laptop or tablet has a camera, you can start taking pictures.

> **WARNING**
>
> Remember that the Take Picture command is contained in the app bar and the app bar does not appear by default. You need to either right-click the app or swipe from the top or bottom edge of your computer to display the app bar.

Elements of a Windows Store App

As we saw in the previous section, a Windows Store app is built using several technologies. A Windows Store app is built out of a combination of open and familiar web technologies, such as HTML5, JavaScript, and CSS3 and Microsoft technologies such as the Windows Library for JavaScript and the Windows Runtime. Let me say a little more about each of these elements of a Windows Store app.

JavaScript

This book is all about writing Windows Store apps using JavaScript. As an alternative to JavaScript, you also could write Windows Store apps using C#, Visual Basic, or even C++.

When writing Windows Store apps, you can take advantage of the features of ECMAScript 5 which is the latest version of JavaScript. This means that you can use the new JavaScript

Array methods such as `indexOf()` and `forEach()`. You also can use property setters and getters and the `use strict` statement.

HTML5

When writing Windows Store apps, you can take advantage of many of the new features of HTML5 and related standards. Here is a list of some of the most important of these new features:

▶ **Form Validation Attributes**—You can take advantage of the new validation attributes in the HTML5 standard to perform form validation. I discuss these new validation attributes and how you can use them in a Windows Store app in Chapter 5, "Creating Forms."

▶ **data-***—The *data dash star* standard enables you to add custom attributes to existing HTML5 elements. The WinJS library uses data-* for declarative data-binding and declarative control instantiation.

▶ **Indexed Database API (IndexedDB)**—The Indexed Database API exposes a database in the browser. If you need to store a list of products in a database within a Windows Store app, then you can take advantage of IndexedDB. I explain how to use IndexedDB in Chapter 9, "Creating Data Sources."

▶ **File API**—The HTML5 File API enables you work with files in the browser. We used the HTML5 API in the previous section when building our first Windows Store app (the `URL.createObjectURL()` method).

▶ **Canvas**—Enables you to draw graphics using JavaScript. I provide you with an introduction to Canvas in Chapter 15, "Graphics and Games."

▶ **Web Workers**—Enables you to execute background tasks without blocking the user interface thread.

▶ **WebGL**—This is new with Windows 8.1. WebGL enables you to build 3D games with JavaScript.

Cascading Style Sheets 3

When you build Windows Store apps, you can take advantage of several new features of the Cascading Style Sheets 3 standard (and related standards) including the following:

▶ **Media Queries**—Enables you to apply different styles depending on the characteristics of a device, such as the height, width, or orientation of the device. I discuss Media Queries in Chapter 11.

▶ **CSS3 Grid Layout**—Enables you to lay out HTML content in columns and rows without using HTML tables.

▶ **CSS3 Flexible Box Layout (FlexBox)**—Enables you to preserve relative element position and size when displaying HTML content in different devices.

Windows Runtime

The Windows Runtime (WinRT) contains a class library that you can use in your Windows Store apps. These classes are projected directly into JavaScript, so they appear to be built-in JavaScript objects.

For example, when we wrote our first Windows Store app, we took advantage of the WinRT `Windows.Media.Capture.CameraCaptureUI` class. When we called the `CameraCaptureUI.captureFileAsync()` method, we were able to take a picture.

All of the WinRT classes are exposed in JavaScript from the root Windows namespace. For example, you create an instance of the `CameraCaptureUI` class with the following code:

```
var captureUI = new Windows.Media.Capture.CameraCaptureUI ();
```

> **NOTE**
>
> Notice that WinRT class names can get silly long. For this reason, it is a good idea to alias the namespaces like this:
>
> ```
> var capture = Windows.Media.Capture;
> ```

The WinRT classes extend JavaScript with all of the functionality that you need when building a Windows application. These classes enable you to do fun and amazing things such as:

▶ **Geolocation**—Use the WinRT `Windows.Devices.Geolocation.Geolocator` class to get your current latitude and longitude.

▶ **File Access**—Read and write to the file system by taking advantage of the WinRT classes in the `Windows.Storage` namespace.

▶ **Compass**—Always know the direction of True North with the `Windows.Devices.Sensors.Compass` class.

▶ **Print**—Print from your Windows Store app by using the `Windows.Printing.PrintManager` class.

▶ **Compress Files**—Compress and decompress files using the classes in the WinRT `Windows.Storage.Compression` namespace.

Windows Library for JavaScript

The Windows Library for JavaScript (WinJS) is a pure JavaScript library created by Microsoft specifically for building Windows Store apps. Understanding how to use this library is the primary focus of this book.

The WinJS library contains all of the WinJS controls. These are the controls that you use to build the user interface for your Windows Store app. For example, the WinJS library includes a DatePicker control that displays a user interface widget for selecting a date.

What About jQuery?

jQuery is the most popular JavaScript library in the universe. An obvious question, therefore, is can you use jQuery when building Windows store apps?

> **NOTE**
>
> According to BuiltWith, more than 57% of the top 10,000 websites use jQuery. This is (by a wide margin) the most common JavaScript framework used on websites. See http://trends.BuiltWith.com/javascript.

The answer is yes. You can use jQuery when building Windows Store apps. Let me show you.

The easiest way to add jQuery to a Windows Store app project is to use the Library Package Manager in Visual Studio. Select the menu option Tools, Library Package Manager, Package Manager Console. Enter the command `install-package jQuery` into the Package Manager Console window (see Figure 1.14).

```
Package Manager Console
 Package source:  NuGet official package source  ▾  ⚙  | Default project:
PM> Install-Package jQuery
Installing 'jQuery 2.0.2'.
Successfully installed 'jQuery 2.0.2'.
Adding 'jQuery 2.0.2' to jQueryWindows8.
Successfully added 'jQuery 2.0.2' to jQueryWindows8.

PM> |
100 %   ▾  ◂
 Package Manager Console  Output
```

FIGURE 1.14   Adding jQuery with the Library Package Manager Console

Executing the `install-package jQuery` command adds a Scripts folder with four files: the full version of jQuery, the minified version of jQuery, an IntelliSense file, and a source map. The IntelliSense file enables Visual Studio to provide jQuery intellisense when you use jQuery methods and the source map provides debugging support.

Listing 1.3 contains a combined HTML and JavaScript file that uses jQuery.

LISTING 1.3   Using jQuery in a Windows Store App

```html
<!DOCTYPE html>
<html>
<head>
    <meta charset="utf-8" />
    <title>jQueryWindows8</title>

    <!-- WinJS references -->
    <link href="//Microsoft.WinJS.2.0/css/ui-dark.css" rel="stylesheet" />
    <script src="//Microsoft.WinJS.2.0/js/base.js"></script>
    <script src="//Microsoft.WinJS.2.0/js/ui.js"></script>

    <!-- jQueryWindows8 references -->
    <script type="text/javascript" src="Scripts/jquery-2.0.2.js"></script>

    <style type="text/css">
        #divMessage {
            display:none;
            padding:10px;
            border: solid 1px white;
            background-color: #ff6a00;
        }
    </style>
</head>
<body>
    <button id="btnShow">Click Here</button>
    <div id="divMessage">
        Secret Message
    </div>

    <script type="text/javascript">
        $("#btnShow").click(function () {
            $("#divMessage").fadeToggle("slow");
        });
    </script>

</body>
</html>
```

The page in Listing 1.3 contains a Button and a DIV element. The contents of the DIV element are hidden by default (with `display:none`). When you click the button, the contents of the DIV `fade` slowly into view (see Figure 1.15).

FIGURE 1.15   Using jQuery to animate a DIV element

NOTE

The code in Listing 1.3 is contained in the Chapter 1 folder in a folder named jQueryWindows8.

Microsoft worked directly with the jQuery team to ensure that jQuery 2.0 works correctly with Windows Store apps. As long as you are using a version of jQuery more recent than jQuery 2.0 then you should not encounter any issues.

WARNING

The fact that Windows Store apps are compatible with jQuery does not mean that Windows Store apps are compatible with every jQuery plugin or popular JavaScript library.

In a Windows Store app, JavaScript code executed in the local context has extra security restrictions to prevent script injection attacks. In particular, you cannot assign HTML to the `innerHTML` property, which contains potentially dangerous content such as scripts or malformed HTML.

If you are using a JavaScript library that was not written with these security restrictions in mind then you will need to modify the library to work with a Windows Store app. If you trust the content being assigned to the `innerHTML` property then instead of using the `innerHTML` property, you can use the `WinJS.Utilities.setInnerHTMLUnsafe()` method.

Building Windows Store Apps with Visual Studio

This book focuses on building Windows Store apps with Visual Studio. In this section, I want to devote a few pages to describing the features of Visual Studio that matter when building Windows Store apps. You learn how to select a project template for a Windows Store app, how to run a Windows Store app, and how to debug a Windows Store app.

Windows Store App Project Templates

When you select the File, New Project menu option in Visual Studio, you can select from five different project templates as your starting point for your Windows Store app:

1. Blank App—The simplest of the templates. Contains a single default.html, default.css, and default.js file.

2. Navigation App—Use this template for apps that require multiple pages.

3. Grid App—Contains three pages for displaying groups of items.

4. Split App—Contains two pages for displaying groups of items.

5. Hub App—Contains three pages. One page displays a navigation hub and the other two pages display section and item detail. This project template is new with Windows 8.1.

We already used the Blank App project template when creating our first Windows app. Let me discuss the other project templates in more detail.

Navigation App Project Template

The Blank App template is a good template to use when building a simple, single-page app. If you need to support multiple pages, on the other hand, then you should use the Navigation App template.

The Navigation App project template includes a single page named home. You can add additional pages by adding new Page Controls to the pages subfolder (see Figure 1.16). I describe how you can create multi-page applications in detail in Chapter 12, "Page Fragments and Navigation."

FIGURE 1.16   Creating a multi-page app with the Navigation App project template

The next three project templates—the Grid App, the Split App, and the Hub App project templates—are built on top of the Navigation App template. In other words, these project templates are multi-page apps with additional pages.

Grid App Project Template

The Grid App project template contains three pages. The main page displays groups of items in a horizontal scrolling grid. You can click a group to view group details or click an item to view item details.

Imagine, for example, that you are creating a product catalog. In that case, you might create different product categories such as Beverages and Fruit. Each category is a group and each category contains a set of product items.

You can use the Grid App `groupedItems` page to display a horizontal scrolling grid of the product categories and associated products (see Figure 1.17). If you click a product category then you can view details for that category (see Figure 1.18). If you click a product then you can view details for that product (see Figure 1.19).

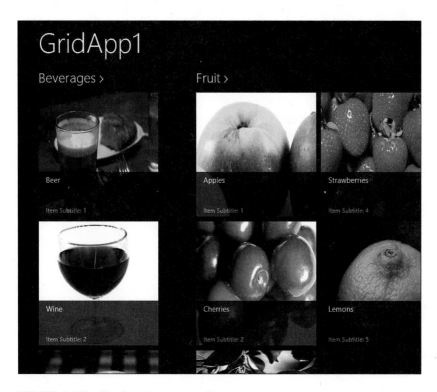

FIGURE 1.17   The Grid App groupedItems page

FIGURE 1.18   The Grid App groupDetail page

FIGURE 1.19   The Grid App itemDetail page

Split App Project Template

The Split App project template also can be used to display groups of items such as products grouped into product categories. The Split App project template has two pages: items and split.

The items page displays the list of groups. For example, in Figure 1.20, the items page displays the product categories.

FIGURE 1.20   The Split App items page

If you click a group then you navigate to the split page. This page displays a list of items in the group—the products in the category—and enables you to select an item to see item details (see Figure 1.21).

FIGURE 1.21   The Split App split page

Hub App Project Template

The Hub App project template is new with Windows 8.1. The Hub App template consists of three pages. The main page contains a Hub control and displays a horizontal list of sections (see Figure 1.22). If you click a section title then you navigate to the section page. If you click an item then you navigate to the item page.

> **NOTE**
>
> The Hub control is covered in Chapter 4, "Using WinJS Controls."

The special thing about the Hub App template is that you can display anything you want within the Hub sections. You can display a list of items, you can display a paragraph of text, or you can display anything else which you heart desires.

For example, in Figure 1.22, Section 1 contains a paragraph of text and Section 2 contains a list of items. Each Hub section can contain different types of content.

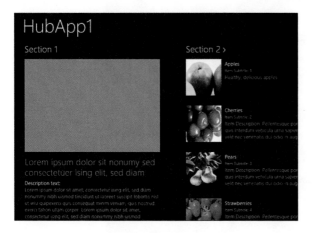

FIGURE 1.22   The Hub App template

Running a Windows Store App

Visual Studio provides you with three different options for running a Windows Store app:

▶ Local Machine

▶ Simulator

▶ Remote Machine

The Local Machine option runs a Windows Store app as if the app was installed on the local machine. The Windows Store app will run using the screen resolution and capabilities of your development machine (the machine running Visual Studio).

The Simulator option runs your app in a separate window (see Figure 1.23). The advantage of using the simulator is that you can simulate different types of devices. For example, you can switch from *mouse mode* to *basic touch mode* to simulate a touch device such as a tablet PC. You also can switch to different screen resolutions to test your app at different resolutions.

The final option is to deploy and run your Windows Store app on a remote machine. Before you can run your app on a remote machine, you must first specify the remote machine name in the Project Property Pages window (see Figure 1.24).

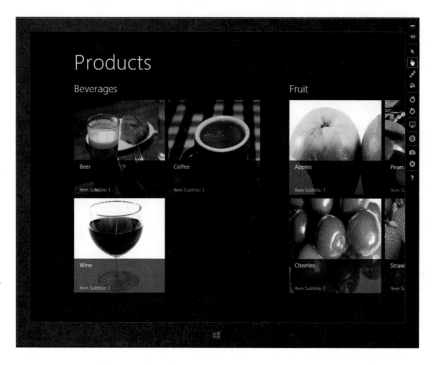

FIGURE 1.23   Using the Visual Studio simulator

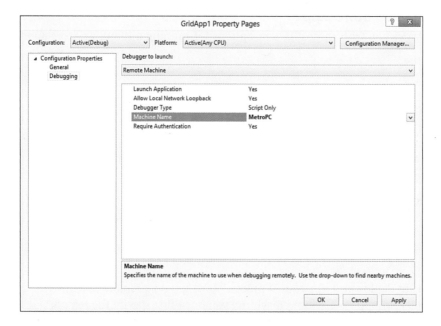

FIGURE 1.24   Specifying the remote machine name

After you specify the name of the remote machine, you can deploy and run your app on the remote machine by picking this option from the Visual Studio toolbar.

> **WARNING**
>
> To deploy and run an app on a remote machine, you need to install the Remote Tools for Visual Studio 2013 on the remote machine. You can download the Remote Tools from the Microsoft.com website.

Debugging a Windows Store App

I'm always optimistic and believe that any code that I write will run without error the first time that I run it. To date, that has never happened. I spend a significant amount of my time debugging code that does not do what I want it to do.

In this section, I discuss the tools in Visual Studio that you can use to debug your code. I discuss how you can use the JavaScript Console window, use breakpoints, and use the DOM Explorer.

Using the Visual Studio JavaScript Console Window

When I write JavaScript code for pages used in websites, I use the JavaScript console window to view JavaScript errors. I also write custom messages to the console window using `console.log()` so I can debug my code. (See Figure 1.25.)

FIGURE 1.25   Debugging with the Google Chrome JavaScript console

When running a Windows Store app, you don't have access to the browser JavaScript console. Instead of using the browser JavaScript console, you need to use the *Visual Studio JavaScript Console* (see Figure 1.26).

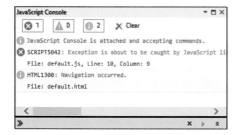

FIGURE 1.26   The Visual Studio JavaScript Console Window

You can view JavaScript errors and write debug messages to the Visual Studio JavaScript console window by using `console.log()` in exactly the same way as you would write to a browser console window.

If you hit an error and you want to display the value of a JavaScript variable then you can enter the variable name in the bottom of the JavaScript Console (see Figure 1.27).

FIGURE 1.27   Dumping a JavaScript variable to the JavaScript Console window

> **NOTE**
>
> The Visual Studio Console window only appears when an app is running. If you can't find the window, use the menu option Debug, Windows, JavaScript Console.

Setting Breakpoints

If you are building a Windows Store app, and the Windows Store app is behaving in ways that you don't understand, then it is useful to set breakpoints and step through your code.

You set a breakpoint by clicking in the left gutter of the Visual Studio code editor next to the line that you want to break on (see Figure 1.28). When you run your app in debug mode, and the breakpoint is hit, you can examine the values of your variables by hovering over them with a mouse.

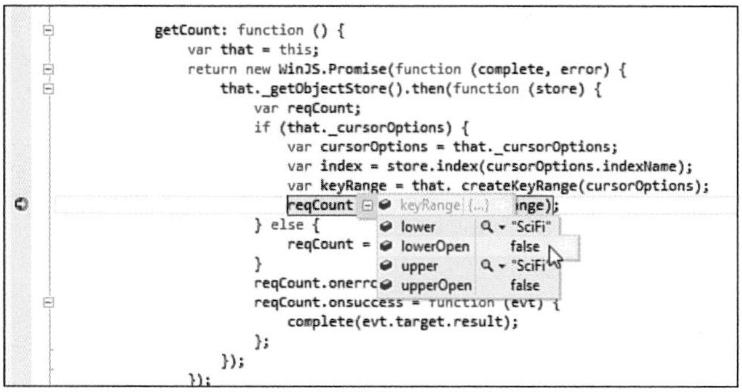

```
getCount: function () {
    var that = this;
    return new WinJS.Promise(function (complete, error) {
        that._getObjectStore().then(function (store) {
            var reqCount;
            if (that._cursorOptions) {
                var cursorOptions = that._cursorOptions;
                var index = store.index(cursorOptions.indexName);
                var keyRange = that.createKeyRange(cursorOptions);
                reqCount      keyRange (...)    inge);
            } else {             lower      "SciFi"
                reqCount =       lowerOpen  false
            }                    upper      "SciFi"
            reqCount.onerrc      upperOpen  false
            reqCount.onsuccess = function (evt) {
                complete(evt.target.result);
            };
        });
    });
};
```

FIGURE 1.28   Setting a breakpoint

You can step through your code, line by line, by using the Step Into toolbar button or by pressing F11.

NOTE

As an alternative to setting a breakpoint with Visual Studio, you can create a breakpoint in code by using the JavaScript `debugger` statement.

Using the DOM Explorer

Another of my favorite browser developer tools is the HTML inspector (this is a feature, for example, of Firebug). You can use this tool to view the live HTML and CSS in a document.

Visual Studio supports a similar tool named the DOM Explorer. You can use the DOM Explorer to inspect the property of any HTML element in a running Windows Store app.

After running a Windows store app in Visual Studio, you can view the DOM Explorer window by selecting the menu option Debug, Windows, DOM Explorer. Within the DOM Explorer window, you can click any element and view all of the properties of the element including information about all of the styles associated with the element (see Figure 1.29).

FIGURE 1.29   Using the DOM Explorer Window

If you click an element associated with a WinJS control then you can see all of the HTML attributes and elements rendered by the control. Adding a `ListView` control to a page, for example, adds a lot of new DIV elements to the page.

Publishing to the Windows Store

One of the main motivations for building a Windows Store app is to sell your app in the Windows Store for either fame or profit. In this section, I discuss the steps you need to follow to publish your Windows Store app to the Windows Store.

> **NOTE**
>
> You can distribute your app without publishing to the Windows Store by taking advantage of a feature called *sideloading*. In order to take advantage of sideloading, you must sign your app and configure the right group policy settings on the target computers. You can learn about sideloading by visiting http://technet.microsoft.com/en-us/library/hh852635.aspx.

Register as a Windows Developer

Before you can publish an app to the Windows Store, you must first register as a Windows Store developer. You can sign up at the Windows Store Dashboard on the Windows Dev Center by selecting the menu option Project, Store, Open Developer Account within Visual Studio (see Figure 1.30).

The sign-up procedure is painless. Currently, it costs either $49 (for an individual account) or $99 (for a company account) a year to become a registered Windows Store developer, or it is free with a MSDN subscription.

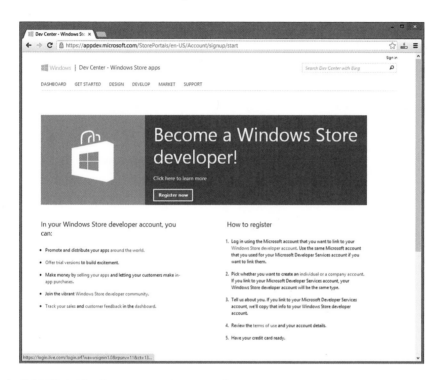

FIGURE 1.30   Register as a Windows Store developer

Submitting Your App

After you register, you can access the Windows Store dashboard and submit a new app. The process of submitting an app is broken down into 8 steps (see Figure 1.31).

One of the most important steps is selecting the name for your app. You can reserve an app name in the Windows Store even before you have finished creating the app. Picking an app name is similar to picking a domain name—so I recommend that you acquire the name that you want as soon as possible.

You also need to decide on how much you want to charge for your app. Currently, you can charge anywhere from $1.49 to $999.99. Or, you have the option of providing your app for free. You also have the option of providing your app with a limited free trial or making your app free with advertising.

FIGURE 1.31   Submitting an app to the Windows Store

When you reach the sixth step, the Packages step, you can upload your finished Windows Store app to the Windows Store. Within Visual Studio, use the menu option Project, Store, Create App Package to package up your Windows Store app (see Figure 1.32). Next, you can click the Packages step to upload the package.

FIGURE 1.32   Creating your app package

Passing App Certification

Microsoft must review your app before it gets published to the Windows Store. In other words, your app must go through a certification process. Part of this certification process is automated and part of the certification process must be done by a human.

There are many requirements for certification. Some of these requirements are obvious. For example, your app can't contain programming errors that cause it to immediately crash and your app cannot simply be a big ad for your business.

Some of the certification requirements are not so obvious. For example, to be certified, your app cannot unexpectedly transport large amounts of data over a metered network connection, your app must start up quickly, and your app must be complete (no "coming soon" features). Also, if your app links to the Internet, you must provide a privacy policy.

NOTE

The Windows Store certification requirements are detailed at http://msdn.microsoft.com/en-us/library/windows/apps/hh694083.aspx.

You can use the Windows App Certification Kit to run the automated certification tests on your app before you upload your package to the Windows Store. The easiest way to run the Windows Certification Kit is to package your app within Visual Studio by selecting the menu option Package, Store, Create App Package. The last step in the Create App Package Wizard enables you to launch the Windows App Certification Kit (Figure 1.33).

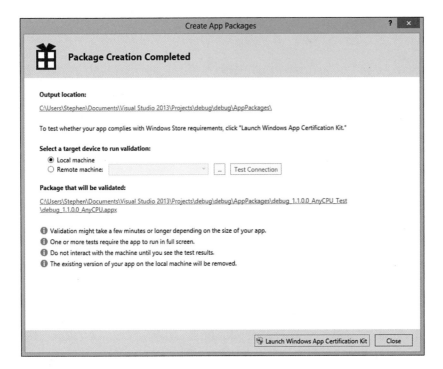

FIGURE 1.33   Launching the Windows App Certification Kit

NOTE

The Windows App Certification Kit is installed at the same time as you install Visual Studio. You can run it independently of Visual Studio by launching the Windows App Cert Kit from the Start screen.

When you run the Windows App Certification Kit, the App Certification Kit launches and runs your app and then, after your computer does crazy stuff for a while, a report is generated that details whether your app passes or fails (see Figure 1.34).

NOTE

If you are using Team Foundation Server, you can even integrate the Windows App Certification Kit into your build process. Every time you do a new build of your app, you can run the technical certification tests automatically.

FIGURE 1.34   A (successful) certification report generated by the Windows App Certification Kit

After your app passes all the certification requirements—after it has been approved by Microsoft—your app appears in the Windows Store and you can start collecting money. When anyone buys your app, money is added to a payout account, which you set up on the Windows Store dashboard.

Migrating from Windows 8 to Windows 8.1

Windows 8.1 is the second release of Windows 8. There are already tens of thousands of apps written for Windows 8.

If you already created a Windows Store app for Windows 8 and you want to migrate the app to Windows 8.1 then the process is dead easy. When you open your Windows 8 app in Visual Studio 2013, Visual Studio recommends retargeting your app to Windows 8.1 (see Figure 1.35).

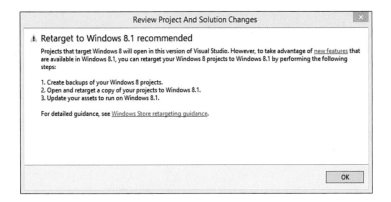

FIGURE 1.35   Retargeting to Windows 8.1

You can right-click your project in the Solution Explorer window and select the menu option Retarget to Windows 8.1 to migrate your app to Windows 8.1.

Retargeting your app updates all of your script references to point to the Windows Library for JavaScript 2.0 instead of the Windows Library for JavaScript 1.0. If you prefer, you could do this by hand by adding a reference to the Windows Library for JavaScript 2.0 to your project and updating the `<script>` tags in all of your HTML pages.

After you retarget your app, you might need to make code changes. For example, as I mentioned earlier in this chapter, Windows 8.1, unlike Windows 8, no longer supports a snapped view state. A list of all of the deprecated Windows 8 application programming interface (APIs) is displayed after you retarget your app.

> **NOTE**
>
> You need Visual Studio 2013 Professional, Premium, or Ultimate to edit an existing Windows 8 app. Visual Studio 2013 Express requires you to retarget a Windows 8 app to Windows 8.1 before you can modify it.

This might be obvious, but I am going to say it anyway. Apps written for Windows 8.1 won't run on Windows 8. The Windows Runtime in Windows 8.1 has changed so you won't see Windows 8.1 apps in the Windows Store on a computer running Windows 8. You still can use Windows 8 apps, on the other hand, with Windows 8.1—you can install both Windows 8 and Windows 8.1 apps from the Windows Store on a computer running Windows 8.1.

Summary

The goal of this chapter was to introduce you to Windows Store apps. I started this chapter by providing you with an overview of the Microsoft design style principles. You also learned about the standard features of Windows Store apps such as the app bar and charms.

I then led you, step by step, through the process of building your first Windows Store app. We created a really cool camera app that you could never create as a standard web application.

You also learned about the standard elements of a Windows Store app. You learned how a Windows Store app is composed of standard HTML5, JavaScript, and CSS3. You also learned how Windows Store apps take advantage of Microsoft technologies such as the Windows Runtime and the Windows Library for JavaScript.

I also explained how you can take advantage of the features of Visual Studio when building a Windows Store app. You learned how to run a Windows Store app using the simulator. You also learned how to debug a Windows Store app by using breakpoints and the Visual Studio JavaScript Console window.

Finally, you learned how you can make money from your Windows Store app by publishing your app to the Windows Store. You learned how to register your app, submit your app, and pass certification.

CHAPTER 2
WinJS Fundamentals

The goal of this chapter is to explain the features included in the base WinJS library. These are the features that you will use in just about any application that you build.

The first part of this chapter is devoted to the topic of namespaces, modules, and classes. You learn the recommended patterns for organizing your JavaScript code.

Next, you learn how to take advantage of another feature of the base WinJS library called *promises*. Promises provide you with an elegant way to perform asynchronous programming in your JavaScript code.

In this chapter, you also learn how to use *Query Selectors* when working with the WinJS library. Query Selectors enable you to efficiently retrieve DOM elements from an HTML document (think jQuery selectors).

You also learn how to work with a function included in the base WinJS library named the xhr() function. The xhr() function enables you to perform Ajax calls—including cross-domain calls.

Finally, you are provided with an introduction to the WinJS Scheduler. The Scheduler is a new feature of Windows 8.1 that enables you to improve the performance of your app by executing JavaScript code with different priorities.

Namespaces, Modules, and Classes

When you build Windows Store apps with the WinJS library, Microsoft recommends that you follow particular patterns when organizing your JavaScript code. In particular, Microsoft recommends that you organize your code into namespaces, modules, and classes.

By following these patterns, you can build JavaScript code that is less buggy and easier to maintain over time.

Using Namespaces

Let me start by explaining the methods in the WinJS library for defining namespaces.

Before we do anything else, we should start by answering the question: Why do we need namespaces? What function do they serve? Do they just add needless complexity to our Windows Store apps?

After all, plenty of JavaScript libraries do just fine without introducing support for namespaces. For example, jQuery has no support for namespaces and jQuery is the most popular JavaScript library in the universe. If jQuery can do without namespaces, why do we need to worry about namespaces at all?

Namespaces perform two functions in a programming language. First, namespaces prevent naming collisions. In other words, namespaces enable you to create more than one object with the same name without conflict.

For example, imagine that two companies—company A and company B—both want to make a JavaScript shopping cart control and both companies want to name the control `ShoppingCart`. By creating a `CompanyA` namespace and `CompanyB` namespace, both companies can create a `ShoppingCart` control: a `CompanyA.ShoppingCart` and a `CompanyB.ShoppingCart` control.

The second function of a namespace is organization. Namespaces are used to group related functionality even when the functionality is defined in different physical files. For example, I know that all of the methods in the WinJS library related to working with classes can be found in the `WinJS.Class` namespace. Namespaces make it easier to understand the functionality available in a library.

If you are building a simple JavaScript application then you won't have much reason to care about namespaces. If you need to use multiple libraries written by different people then namespaces become very important.

Using `WinJS.Namespace.define()`

In the WinJS library, the most basic method of creating a namespace is to use the `WinJS.Namespace.define()` method. This method enables you to declare a namespace (of arbitrary depth).

The `WinJS.Namespace.define()` method has the following parameters:

- ▶ `name`—A string representing the name of the new namespace. You can add nested namespace by using dot notation.

- ▶ `members`—An optional collection of objects to add to the new namespace.

For example, the code sample in Listing 2.1 declares two new namespaces named CompanyA and CompanyB.Controls. Both namespaces contain a ShoppingCart object which has a checkout() method:

LISTING 2.1   Creating Namespaces (namespaces\namespaces.html)

```
// Create CompanyA namespace with ShoppingCart
WinJS.Namespace.define("CompanyA");
CompanyA.ShoppingCart = {
    checkout: function () { return "Checking out from A"; }
};


// Create CompanyB.Controls namespace with ShoppingCart
WinJS.Namespace.define(
    "CompanyB.Controls",
    {
        ShoppingCart: {
            checkout: function () { return "Checking out from B"; }
        }
    }
);


// Call CompanyA ShoppingCart checkout method
console.log(CompanyA.ShoppingCart.checkout());   // Writes "Checking out from A"

// Call CompanyB.Controls checkout method
console.log(CompanyB.Controls.ShoppingCart.checkout());   // Writes "Checking out
➥from B"
```

In Listing 2.1, the CompanyA namespace is created by calling WinJS.Namespace. define("CompanyA"). Next, the ShoppingCart is added to this namespace. The namespace is defined and an object is added to the namespace in separate lines of code.

A different approach is taken in the case of the CompanyB.Controls namespace. The namespace is created and the ShoppingCart object is added to the namespace with the following single statement:

```
WinJS.Namespace.define(
    "CompanyB.Controls",
    {
        ShoppingCart: {
            checkout: function () { return "Checking out from B"; }
        }
    }
);
```

Notice that CompanyB.Controls is a nested namespace. The top level namespace CompanyB contains the namespace Controls. You can declare a nested namespace using dot notation and the WinJS library handles the details of creating one namespace within the other.

After the namespaces have been defined, you can use either of the two shopping cart controls in the same JavaScript file without conflict. You call CompanyA.ShoppingCart.checkout() or you can call CompanyB.Controls.ShoppingCart.checkout().

Using WinJS.Namespace.defineWithParent()

The WinJS.Namespace.defineWithParent() method is similar to the WinJS.Namespace.define() method. Both methods enable you to define a new namespace. The difference is that the defineWithParent() method enables you to add a new namespace to an existing namespace.

The WinJS.Namespace.defineWithParent() method has the following parameters:

▶ **parentNamespace**—An object which represents a parent namespace

▶ **name**—A string representing the new namespace to add to the parent namespace

▶ **members**—An optional collection of objects to add to the new namespace

The following code sample demonstrates how you can create a root namespace named CompanyA and add a Controls child namespace to the CompanyA parent namespace:

```
WinJS.Namespace.define("CompanyA");
WinJS.Namespace.defineWithParent(CompanyA, "Controls",
    {
        ShoppingCart: {
            checkout: function () { return "Checking out"; }
        }
    }
);
console.log(CompanyA.Controls.ShoppingCart.checkout()); // Writes "Checking out"
```

One significant advantage of using the defineWithParent() method over the define() method is the defineWithParent() method is strongly-typed. In other words, you use an object to represent the base namespace instead of a string. If you misspell the name of the object (CompnyA) then you get a runtime error.

Using the Module Pattern

When you are building a JavaScript library, you want to be able to create both public and private methods. Some methods, the public methods, are intended to be used by consumers of your JavaScript library. The public methods act as your library's public API.

Other methods, the private methods, are *not* intended for public consumption. Instead, these methods are internal methods required to get the library to function. You don't want people calling these internal methods because you might need to change them in the future.

JavaScript does not support access modifiers. You can't mark an object or method as public or private. Anyone gets to call any method and anyone gets to interact with any object.

The only mechanism for encapsulating (hiding) methods and objects in JavaScript is to take advantage of functions. In JavaScript, a function determines variable scope. A JavaScript variable either has global scope—it is available everywhere—or it has function scope—it is available only within a function. If you want to hide an object or method then you need to place it within a function.

For example, the following code contains a function named doSomething() that contains a nested function named doSomethingElse():

```
function doSomething() {
    console.log("doSomething");

    function doSomethingElse() {
        console.log("doSomethingElse");
    }
}


doSomething(); // Writes "doSomething"
doSomethingElse(); // Throws ReferenceError
```

You can call doSomethingElse() only within the doSomething() function. The doSomethingElse() function is encapsulated in the doSomething() function.

The WinJS library takes advantage of function encapsulation to hide all of its internal methods. All of the WinJS methods are defined within self-executing anonymous functions. Everything is hidden by default. Public methods are exposed by explicitly adding the public methods to namespaces defined in the global scope.

Imagine, for example, that I want a small library of utility methods. I want to create a method for calculating sales tax and a method for calculating the expected ship date of a product. The library in Listing 2.2 encapsulates the implementation of my library in a self-executing anonymous function.

LISTING 2.2   Encapsulating Functions with a Module (modules\modules.html)

```
(function (global) {

    // Public method which calculates tax
    function calculateTax(price) {
        return calculateFederalTax(price) + calculateStateTax(price);
    }
```

```
    // Private method for calculating state tax
    function calculateStateTax(price) {
        return price * 0.08;
    }

    // Private method for calculating federal tax
    function calculateFederalTax(price) {
        return price * 0.02;
    }

    // Public method which returns the expected ship date
    function calculateShipDate(currentDate) {
        currentDate.setDate(currentDate.getDate() + 4);
        return currentDate;
    }

    // Export public methods
    WinJS.Namespace.define("CompanyA.Utilities",
        {
            calculateTax: calculateTax,
            calculateShipDate: calculateShipDate
        }
    );

})(this);

// Show expected ship date
var shipDate = CompanyA.Utilities.calculateShipDate(new Date());
console.log(shipDate);

// Show price + tax
var price = 12.33;
var tax = CompanyA.Utilities.calculateTax(price);
console.log(price + tax);
```

In Listing 2.2, the self-executing anonymous function contains four functions: `calculateTax()`, `calculateStateTax()`, `calculateFederalTax()`, and `calculateShipDate()`. The following statement is used to expose only the `calcuateTax()` and the `calculateShipDate()` functions:

```
// Export public methods
WinJS.Namespace.define("CompanyA.Utilities",
    {
        calculateTax: calculateTax,
        calculateShipDate: calculateShipDate
    }
);
```

Because the `calculateTax()` and `calculateShipDate()` functions are added to the `CompanyA.Utilities` namespace, you can call these two methods outside of the self-executing function. These are the public methods of your library that form the public API.

The `calculateStateTax()` and `calculateFederalTax()` methods, on the other hand, are forever hidden within the black hole of the self-executing function. These methods are encapsulated and can never be called outside of the scope of the self-executing function. These are the internal methods of your library.

Using Classes

Unlike other popular computer languages—such as C# or Java—JavaScript does not have any built-in support for classes. In JavaScript, you do not distinguish between a type (a class) and an instance of that type (an object). Everything in JavaScript is an object.

The WinJS library includes extensions to JavaScript for creating classes. These methods are used extensively within the WinJS library itself. For example, all of the WinJS JavaScript controls are created using these methods. In this section, we discuss how you can define new classes by taking advantage of the methods in the WinJS library.

Using `WinJS.Class.define()`

In the WinJS library, new JavaScript classes are created by calling the `WinJS.Class.define()` method. This method accepts three arguments:

- ▶ `constructor`—The constructor function used to initialize the new object. If you pass null then an empty constructor is created

- ▶ `instanceMembers`—A collection of instance properties and methods

- ▶ `staticMembers`—A collection of static properties and methods

The code in Listing 2.3 demonstrates how to create a `Robot` class and then create a `Roomba` robot object from the `Robot` class.

LISTING 2.3   Creating a Class (classes\classes.html)

```
var Robot = WinJS.Class.define(
    function (name, price) {
        this.name = name;
        this.price = price;
    },
    {
        _name: undefined,
        _price: 0,

        price: {
            set: function (value) {
                if (value < 0) {
                    throw new Error("Invalid price!");
```

```
                }
                this._price = value;
            },
            get: function () { return this._price; }
        },
        makeNoise: function () {
            return "Burp, Wow!, oops!";
        }
    }
);

// Create a robot
var roomba = new Robot("Roomba", 200.33);

console.log(roomba.price); // Writes "200.33"
console.log(roomba.makeNoise()); // Writes "Burp, Wow!, oops!"

// Set invalid price
roomba.price = -88; // Throws "Invalid price!"
```

The `Robot` class is defined using the `WinJS.Class.define()` method. The first argument passed to this method is the constructor function for the `Robot` class. This constructor function initializes the `Robot` name and price properties.

The next argument passed to the `WinJS.Class.define()` method is a collection of instance members. This collection is used to define the `_name` and `_price` fields and the `price` property. This collection also contains the definition of the `makeNoise()` method.

> **NOTE**
>
> There is a convention of naming all private members of a class—fields, properties, and methods—with a leading underscore. For example, the private field backing the price property in Listing 2.3 is named `_price` instead of `price`.

Notice that the price property includes a getter and a setter. If you attempt to assign an invalid price to the `Robot` then the setter throws an error as illustrated in Figure 2.1.

FIGURE 2.1   An Invalid price! exception

Using WinJS.Class.derive()

The WinJS.Class.derive() method enables you to use prototype inheritance to derive one class from another class. The WinJS.Class.derive() method accepts the following four arguments:

▶ baseClass—The class to inherit from.

▶ constructor—A constructor function that can be used to initialize the new class

▶ instanceMembers—New instance properties and methods

▶ staticMembers—New static properties and methods

Here is a basic example. In the code in Listing 2.4, three classes are defined: Robot, Roomba, and AIBO. The Robot class is the base class and the Roomba and AIBO classes derive from the Robot class.

LISTING 2.4   Deriving a Class (derive\derive.html)

```javascript
var Robot = WinJS.Class.define(
    function () {
        this.type = "Robot"
    },
    {
        sayHello: function () {
            return "My name is " + this.name
                + " and I am a " + this.type;
        }
    }
);

var Roomba = WinJS.Class.derive(
    Robot,
    function (name) {
        this.name = name;
        this.type = "Roomba";
    }
);

var AIBO = WinJS.Class.derive(
    Robot,
    function (name) {
        this.name = name;
        this.type = "AIBO";
    }
);

// Create a Roomba
```

```
var myRoomba = new Roomba("rover");
console.log(myRoomba.sayHello());

// Create an AIBO
var myAIBO = new AIBO("spot");
console.log(myAIBO.sayHello());
```

When you run the code in Listing 2.4, the messages in Figure 2.2 are written to the Visual Studio JavaScript Console.

FIGURE 2.2   Derived robots

In Listing 2.4, the constructor function for the `Robot` class is never called. The `Roomba` and the `AIBO` constructor functions are called instead. However, both the `Roomba` and `AIBO` classes inherit the `sayHello()` method from the base `Robot` class.

Using `WinJS.Class.mix()`

As an alternative to using the `WinJS.Class.derive()` method, you can use the `WinJS.Class.mix()` method. This method enables you to create mixins. A mixin enables you to combine methods and properties from multiple JavaScript objects into a single object.

Behind the scenes, the `WinJS.Class.derive()` method that we discussed in the previous section uses prototype inheritance, and prototype inheritance has performance drawbacks. Following a prototype chain requires processor time. Therefore, the suggestion is that you avoid prototype inheritance by using mixins instead.

When you use a mixin instead of prototype inheritance, the methods and properties are combined into a single object. You don't get a long prototype chain.

The `WinJS.Class.mix()` method has the following parameters:

▶ `constructor`—A constructor function used to initialize the new class

▶ `mixin`—A parameter array that contains the mixin methods

The code in Listing 2.5 demonstrates how you can use the `WinJS.Class.mix()` method to simulate single inheritance.

LISTING 2.5   Creating a Mixin (mixins\mixins.html)

```
var Robot = {
    makeNoise: function () {
```

```
        return "beep";
    }
};

var Roomba = WinJS.Class.mix(
    function (name) {
        this.name = name;
    },
    Robot
);

var myRoomba = new Roomba("rover");
console.log(myRoomba.makeNoise()); // Writes "beep"
```

In Listing 2.5, the `Roomba` class contains all of the methods of the Robot object.

One of the advantages of mixins is that you can use mixins to support something like multiple inheritance. You can use a mixin to combine as many sets of methods and properties as you need. For example, the code sample in Listing 2.6 demonstrates how you can build a `Roomba` from `Robot` methods, `Product` methods, and `Vacuum` methods.

LISTING 2.6   Combining Multiple Objects (mixinMultiple\mixinMultiple.html)

```
"use strict";

var Robot = {
    makeNoise: function () {
        return "beep";
    }
};

var Product = {
    price: {
        set: function (value) {
            if (value < 0) {
                throw new Error("Invalid price!");
            }
            this._price = value;
        },
        get: function () { return this._price; }
    },
    sayName: function () {
        return this.name;
    }
}
```

```
var Vacuum = {
    vacuum: function () { return "bzzzzzz"; }
}

var Roomba = WinJS.Class.mix(
    function (name) {
        this.name = name;
    },
    Robot, Product, Vacuum
);

var myRoomba = new Roomba("rover");
console.log(myRoomba.makeNoise()); // Writes "beep"
console.log(myRoomba.sayName()); // Writes "rover"
console.log(myRoomba.vacuum()); // Writes "bzzzzz"
myRoomba.price = -88 // Throws Error
```

Notice that a mixin can contain both methods and properties. Furthermore, a mixin property can contain a setter and getter. For example, the `price` property included in the `Product` mixin includes a setter that performs validation.

When you execute the code in Listing 2.5, the results shown in Figure 2.3 are displayed in your Visual Studio JavaScript Console window.

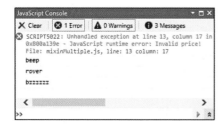

FIGURE 2.3   Robot noises

> **NOTE**
>
> The WinJS library includes several mixins that you can use in your code, including the `WinJS.Utilities.eventMixin`, `WinJS.UI.DOMEventMixin`, and the `WinJS.Binding.dynamicObservableMixin`.

Asynchronous Programming with Promises

Some code executes immediately, some code requires time to complete or might never complete at all. For example, retrieving the value of a local variable is an immediate operation. Retrieving data from a remote website with an Ajax request takes longer or might not complete at all.

When an operation might take a long time to complete, you should write your code so that it executes asynchronously. Instead of waiting for an operation to complete, you should start the operation and then do something else until you receive a signal that the operation is complete.

An analogy: Some telephone customer service lines require you to wait on hold—listening to really bad music—until a customer service representative is available. This is synchronous programming and very wasteful of your time.

Some newer customer service lines enable you to enter your telephone number so a customer service representative can call you back when a customer representative becomes available. This approach is much less wasteful of your time because you can do useful things while waiting for the callback.

There are several patterns that you can use to write code that executes asynchronously. The most popular pattern in JavaScript is the callback pattern. When you call a function which might take a long time to return a result, you pass a callback function to the function.

Using callbacks is a natural way to perform asynchronous programming with JavaScript. Instead of waiting for an operation to complete, sitting there and listening to really bad music, you can get a callback when the operation is complete.

Using Promises

The CommonJS website defines a promise like this (http://wiki.commonjs.org/wiki/Promises):

"Promises provide a well-defined interface for interacting with an object that represents the result of an action that is performed asynchronously, and may or may not be finished at any given point in time. By utilizing a standard interface, different components can return promises for asynchronous actions and consumers can utilize the promises in a predictable manner."

A promise provides a standard pattern for specifying callbacks. In the WinJS library, when you create a promise, you can specify three callbacks: a complete callback, a failure callback, and a progress callback (both the failure and progress callbacks are optional).

Promises are used extensively in the WinJS library. The methods in the animation library, the control library, and the binding library all use promises.

For example, the xhr() method included in the WinJS base library returns a promise. The xhr() method wraps calls to the standard XmlHttpRequest object in a promise. The code in Listing 2.7 illustrates how you can use the xhr() method to perform an Ajax request that retrieves the feed from my blog at StephenWalther.com.

LISTING 2.7   Making a promise (promises\promises.html)

```
var options = {
    url: "http://stephenwalther.com/feed",
    responseType: "document"
};

WinJS.xhr(options).done(
    function (xmlHttpRequest) {
        console.log("success");

        // Display title of first blog entry
        var firstTitle = xmlHttpRequest.response.querySelector("item>title");
        console.log(firstTitle.textContent);
    },
    function (xmlHttpRequest) {
        console.log("fail");
    },
    function (xmlHttpRequest) {
        console.log("progress");
    }
)
```

The WinJS.xhr() method returns a promise. The Promise class includes a done() method that accepts three callback functions: a complete callback, an error callback, and a progress callback:

```
Promise.done(completeCallback, errorCallback, progressCallback)
```

In the code in Listing 2.7, three anonymous functions are passed to the done() method. Unless there is a network error, the error function is never called. The progress function is called repeatedly during the Ajax request. Finally, the complete callback is done when the Ajax call completes. The complete callback displays the title of the first blog entry retrieved (see Figure 2.4).

FIGURE 2.4   Using a promise

Using `then()` Versus `done()`

In the previous section, we used the `Promise` object `done()` method to set up our complete, error, and progress callbacks. The `Promise` object exposes another method that is closely related to `done()`: the `then()` method.

The then() method—just like the done() method—enables you to set up a complete, error, and progress callback function. So why does the `then()` method exist? There are two important differences between `then()` and `done()`.

The `then()` method, unlike the `done()` method, supports chaining. If you need to chain multiple promises together then you are forced to use the `then()` method. For example, the code in Listing 2.8 illustrates how you can make one Ajax call that downloads the URL of the most recent blog entry from my blog and *then* make a second Ajax call that downloads the contents of that blog entry. The second Ajax call is not made until the first Ajax call completes.

LISTING 2.8   Chaining Promises (promiseChain\promiseChain.html)

```
var options = {
    url: "http://stephenwalther.com/feed",
    responseType: "document"
};



WinJS.xhr(options).then(
    function (xmlHttpRequest) {
        // Get link for first blog entry
        var firstLink = xmlHttpRequest.response.querySelector("item>link");

        // Make second Ajax request (returns a promise)
        return WinJS.xhr({
            url: firstLink.textContent,
            responseType: "document"
        });
    }
).done(
    function (xmlHttpRequest) {
        // Get body of blog post
        var postBody = xmlHttpRequest.response.querySelector("div.entry");

        // Write first 200 characters of blog post
        console.log(postBody.textContent.trim().substr(0, 200));
    }
);
```

In Listing 2.8, notice that the complete function passed to the `then()` method returns a second promise. Calling `WinJS.xhr()` returns a new promise.

If the second promise completes successfully then the complete function passed to the `done()` method executes. This method displays the first 200 characters of the blog entry.

You can chain together as many promises as you need by calling `then().then().then()....` The last call in the chain should be a call to `done()`.

The second difference between `then()` and `done()` concerns error handling. You can pass an error function to both the `then()` and `done()` methods as the second parameter to handle errors and, as a best-practice, you should do this. But, if you don't supply an error function then the `done()` method throws an exception but the `then()` method does not. Instead, the `then()` method returns a promise in the error state.

For example, the code in Listing 2.9 performs an Ajax request with a bad URL. The request made with the `then()` method does not raise an error. An error message is written to the JavaScript Console, but execution of the app is not halted.

LISTING 2.9   `done()` Versus `then()` (promiseErrors\promiseErrors.html)

```
var options = {
    url: "http://BadURL"
};

WinJS.xhr(options).then();   // DOES NOT throw an exception

WinJS.xhr(options).done();   // DOES throw an exception
```

If you don't want your code to fail silently, like the `then()` method in Listing 2.9, then you should use `done()` instead of `then()`. If you are chaining promises, always use `done()` as the last link in the chain. In other words, errors raised in the chain of `then()` methods are passed down the chain to the final `done()` where they may be exposed to the error handling function.

Creating Promises

If your app has a function that takes more then a few milliseconds to complete then you should return a promise so that your app can continue to work while the function is completing. You can create your own promises by creating a new instance of the Promise class. The constructor for the Promise class requires a function that accepts three parameters: a complete, error, and progress function parameter.

For example, the code in Listing 2.10 illustrates how you can create a method named `wait10Seconds()` which returns a promise. The progress function is called every second and the complete function is not called until 10 seconds have passed.

LISTING 2.10   Creating a Promise (promiseCreate\promiseCreate.html)

```
function wait10Seconds() {
    return new WinJS.Promise(function (complete, error, progress) {
        var seconds = 0;
        var intervalId = window.setInterval(function () {
            seconds++;
            progress(seconds);
            if (seconds > 9) {
                window.clearInterval(intervalId);
                complete();
            }
        }, 1000);
    });
}

wait10Seconds().done(
        function () { console.log("complete") },
        function () { console.log("error") },
        function (seconds) { console.log("progress:" + seconds) }
);
```

All of the work happens in the constructor function for the promise. The `window.`
`setInterval()` method is used to execute code every second. Every second, the
`progress()` callback method is called. If more than 10 seconds have passed then
the `complete()` callback method is called and the `clearInterval()` method is called.

When you execute the code in Listing 2.10, you can see the output in the Visual Studio
JavaScript Console in Figure 2.5.

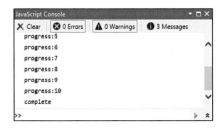

FIGURE 2.5   Output of a custom promise

Creating a Timeout Promise

In the previous section, we created a custom promise that uses the `window.setInterval()`
method to complete the promise after 10 seconds. We really did not need to create a
custom promise because the `Promise` class already includes a static method for returning
promises that complete after a certain interval.

The code in Listing 2.11 illustrates how you can use the `timeout()` method. The `timeout()` method returns a promise that completes after a certain number of milliseconds.

LISTING 2.11   A timeout promise (promiseTimeout\promiseTimeout.html)

```
WinJS.Promise.timeout(3000).then(
    function () { console.log("complete") },
    function () { console.log("error") },
    function () { console.log("progress") }
);
```

In Listing 2.11, the promise completes after 3 seconds (3000 milliseconds). The promise returned by the `timeout()` method does not support progress events. Therefore, the only message written to the console is the message "complete" after 3 seconds.

Canceling Promises

It is useful to have the ability to stop long running functions. For this reason, some promises support cancellation. Some promises, but not all, support cancellation. When you cancel a promise, the promise's error callback is executed.

For example, the code in Listing 2.12 uses the `WinJS.xhr()` method to perform an Ajax request. However, immediately after the Ajax request is made, the request is canceled.

LISTING 2.12   Canceling a Promise (promiseCancel\promiseCancel.html)

```
// Specify Ajax request options
var options = {
    url: "http://StephenWalther.com"
};

// Make the Ajax request
var request = WinJS.xhr(options).then(
    function (xmlHttpRequest) {
        console.log("success");
    },
    function (xmlHttpRequest) {
        console.log("fail: " + xmlHttpRequest.message);
    },
    function (xmlHttpRequest) {
        console.log("progress");
    }
);

// Cancel the Ajax request
request.cancel();
```

When you run the code, the message `fail: Canceled` is written to the Visual Studio JavaScript Console (see Figure 2.6). Because `then()` unlike `done()` returns a promise, canceling is only supported when calling `then()` and not `done()`.

FIGURE 2.6   Canceling a promise (promiseCancel\promiseCancel.html)

Composing Promises

You can build promises out of other promises. In other words, you can compose promises. Composing promises is useful when you need to perform multiple asynchronous operations and wait until all or any of the operations complete.

There are two static methods of the `Promise` class that you can use to compose promises: the `join()` method and the `any()` method. When you join promises, a promise is complete when all of the joined promises are complete. When you use the `any()` method, a promise is complete when any of the promises complete.

The following code illustrates how to use the `join()` method. A new promise is created out of two timeout promises. The new promise does not complete until both of the timeout promises complete:

```
WinJS.Promise.join([WinJS.Promise.timeout(1000), WinJS.Promise.timeout(5000)])
    .done(function () { console.log("join complete"); });
```

The message "complete" will not be written to the JavaScript Console until both promises passed to the `join()` method complete. The message won't be written for 5 seconds (5,000 milliseconds).

The `any()` method completes when any promise passed to the `any()` method completes:

```
WinJS.Promise.any([WinJS.Promise.timeout(1000), WinJS.Promise.timeout(5000)])
    .done(function () { console.log("any complete"); });
```

The code writes the message "any complete" to the JavaScript Console after 1 second (1,000 milliseconds). The message is written to the JavaScript console immediately after the first promise completes and before the second promise completes.

Retrieving DOM Elements with Query Selectors

When you are building a Windows Store app with JavaScript, you need some way of easily retrieving elements from an HTML document. For example, you might want to retrieve all of the input elements that have a certain CSS class. Or, you might want to retrieve the one and only element with an id of favoriteColor.

The standard way of retrieving elements from an HTML document is by using a selector. Anyone who has ever created a Cascading Style Sheet has already used selectors. You use selectors in Cascading Style Sheets to apply formatting rules to elements in a document.

For example, the following Cascading Style Sheet rule changes the background color of every INPUT element with a class of .required in a document to the color red:

```
input.required { background-color: red }
```

The input.required part is the selector which matches all INPUT elements with a class of required.

The W3C standard for selectors (technically, their recommendation) is entitled "Selectors Level 3" and the standard is located here: http://www.w3.org/TR/css3-selectors/

Selectors are not only useful for adding formatting to the elements of a document. Selectors are also useful when you need to apply behavior. For example, you might want to select a particular BUTTON element with a selector and add a click handler to the element so that something happens whenever you click the button.

jQuery is famous for its support for selectors. Using jQuery, you can use a selector to retrieve matching elements from a document and modify the elements. The WinJS library enables you to perform the same types of queries as jQuery using the W3C selector syntax.

> **NOTE**
>
> The W3C selector standard is supported for all modern browsers including recent versions of Google Chrome, Apple Safari, and Mozilla Firefox.

Performing Queries with the WinJS.Utilities.query() Method

When using the WinJS library, you perform a query with a selector by using the WinJS.Utilities.query() method.

Listing 2.13 contains a BUTTON and a DIV element.

LISTING 2.13   A Document with a Secret Message (selectorsQuery\selectorsQuery.html)

```
<!DOCTYPE html>
<html>
<head>
    <meta charset="utf-8">
    <title>Selectors Query</title>

    <!-- WinJS references -->
    <link href="//Microsoft.WinJS.1.0/css/ui-dark.css" rel="stylesheet" />
```

```
    <script src="//Microsoft.WinJS.1.0/js/base.js"></script>
    <script src="//Microsoft.WinJS.1.0/js/ui.js"></script>

    <!-- Chapter02 references -->
    <link href="/css/default.css" rel="stylesheet">
    <script type="text/javascript" src="selectorsQuery.js"></script>
</head>
<body>

    <button>Click Me!</button>

    <div style="display:none">

        <h1>Secret Message</h1>

    </div>

</body>
</html>
```

The document contains a reference to the JavaScript file in Listing 2.14 named
selectorsQuery.js.

LISTING 2.14   Using a Selector (selectorsQuery\selectorsQuery.js)

```
(function () {
    "use strict";

    function initialize() {
        WinJS.Utilities.query("button").listen("click", function () {
            WinJS.Utilities.query("div").clearStyle("display");
        });
    };

    document.addEventListener("DOMContentLoaded", initialize);
})();
```

The selectorsQuery.js script uses the WinJS.Utilities.query() method to retrieve all of
the BUTTON elements in the page. The listen() method is used to wire an event handler
to the BUTTON click event. When you click the BUTTON, the secret message contained
in the hidden DIV element is displayed. The clearStyle() method is used to remove the
display:none style attribute from the DIV element (see Figure 2.7).

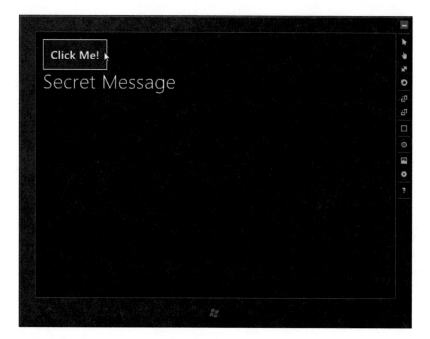

FIGURE 2.7   Displaying the secret message

> **WARNING**
>
> Make sure that you don't try to use the `WinJS.Utilities.query()` method until after the document is loaded. In Listing 2.14, the call to `WinJS.Utilities.query()` is contained within the `initialize()` function, which is triggered by the `DOMContentLoaded` event.

Under the covers, the `WinJS.Utilities.query()` method uses the standard `querySelectorAll()` method. This means that you can use any selector which is compatible with the `querySelectorAll()` method. The `querySelectorAll()` method is defined in the W3C Selectors API Level 1 standard located here: http://www.w3.org/TR/selectors-api/

Unlike the `querySelectorAll()` method, the `WinJS.Utilities.query()` method returns a `QueryCollection`. I talk about the methods of the `QueryCollection` class later in this chapter.

Retrieving a Single Element with the `WinJS.Utilities.id()` Method

If you want to retrieve a single element from a document, instead of matching a set of elements, then you can use the `WinJS.Utilities.id()` method. For example, the following line of code changes the background color of an element to the color red:

```
WinJS.Utilities.id("message").setStyle("background-color", "red");
```

The statement matches the one and only element with an id of `message`. For example, the statement matches the following DIV element:

```
<div id="message">Hello!</div>
```

Notice that you do not use a hash when matching a single element with the `WinJS.Utilities.id()` method. You would need to use a hash when using the `WinJS.Utilities.query()` method to do the same thing like this:

```
WinJS.Utilities.query("#message").setStyle("background-color", "red");
```

Under the covers, the `WinJS.Utilities.id()` method calls the standard `document.getElementById()` method. The `WinJS.Utilities.id()` method returns the result as a `QueryCollection` that contains zero or one matching element.

If no element matches the identifier passed to `WinJS.Utilities.id()` then you do not get an error. Instead, you get a `QueryCollection` with no elements (length=0).

Using the `WinJS.Utilities.children()` method

The `WinJS.Utilities.children()` method enables you to retrieve a `QueryCollection` which contains all of the children of a DOM element. For example, imagine that you have a DIV element which contains children DIV elements like this:

```
<div id="discussContainer">
    <div>Message 1</div>
    <div>Message 2</div>
    <div>Message 3</div>
</div>
```

You can use the following code to add borders around all of the child DIV elements and not the container DIV element (see Figure 2.8):

```
var discussContainer = WinJS.Utilities.id("discussContainer").get(0);
WinJS.Utilities.children(discussContainer).setStyle("border", "2px dashed red");
```

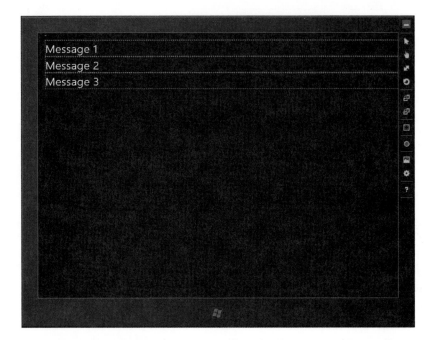

FIGURE 2.8   Retrieving children

It is important to understand that the WinJS.Utilities.children() method only works with a DOM element and not a QueryCollection. Notice that the get() method is used to retrieve the DOM element that represents the discussContainer.

Working with the QueryCollection Class

Both the WinJS.Utilities.query() method and the WinJS.Utilities.id() method return an instance of the QueryCollection class. The QueryCollection class derives from the base JavaScript Array class and adds several useful methods for working with HTML elements:

▶ addClass(name)—Adds a class to every element in the QueryCollection

▶ clearStyle(name)—Removes a style from every element in the QueryCollection

▶ control(ctr, options)—Enables you to transform the items in the query collection into WinJS controls

▶ forEach(callbackFn, thisArg)—Enables you to perform an operation on each item in the QueryCollection

▶ get(index)—Retrieves the element from the QueryCollection at the specified index

▶ getAttribute(name)—Retrieves the value of an attribute for the first element in the QueryCollection

▶ hasClass(name)—Returns true if the first element in the QueryCollection has a certain class

- ▶ **include(items)**—Includes a collection of items in the `QueryCollection`

- ▶ **listen(eventType, listener, capture)**—Adds an event listener to every element in the `QueryCollection`

- ▶ **query(query)**—Performs an additional query on the `QueryCollection` and returns a new `QueryCollection`

- ▶ **removeClass(name)**—Removes a class from the every element in the `QueryCollection`

- ▶ **removeEventListener(eventType, listener, capture)**—Removes an event listener from every element in the `QueryCollection`

- ▶ **setAttribute(name, value)**—Adds an attribute to every element in the `QueryCollection`

- ▶ **setStyle(name, value)**—Adds a style attribute to every element in the `QueryCollection`

- ▶ **template(templateElement, data, renderDonePromiseContract)**—Renders a template using the supplied data for each item in the `QueryCollection`

- ▶ **toggleClass(name)**—Toggles the specified class for every element in the `QueryCollection`

Because the `QueryCollection` class derives from the base Array class, it also contains all of the standard Array methods like `indexOf()` and `slice()`.

Performing Ajax Calls with the `xhr` Function

The WinJS `xhr()` function is a thin wrapper around the browser `XMLHttpRequest` object. Unlike working with the `XMLHttpRequest` object, the `xhr()` function returns a promise. You use the `xhr()` function whenever you want to make an Ajax request.

Listings 2.15 and 2.16 contain the code for making a simple Ajax request. The home page of the Microsoft site is retrieved and the list of all of the links extracted from this page is displayed (see Figure 2.9).

LISTING 2.15   Making a Simple Ajax Request (xhr\xhr.html)

```
<!DOCTYPE html>
<html>
<head>
    <meta charset="utf-8">
    <title>Simple XHR</title>

    <!-- WinJS references -->
    <link href="//Microsoft.WinJS.1.0/css/ui-dark.css" rel="stylesheet" />
    <script src="//Microsoft.WinJS.1.0/js/base.js"></script>
    <script src="//Microsoft.WinJS.1.0/js/ui.js"></script>
```

```
    <!-- Chapter02 references -->
    <link href="/css/default.css" rel="stylesheet">
    <script type="text/javascript" src="xhr.js"></script>
</head>
<body>


    <h1>Here are the Microsoft Site Links:</h1>



    <ul id="ulResults"></ul>


</body>
</html>
```

LISTING 2.16   Making a Simple Ajax Request (xhr\xhr.js)

```
(function () {
    "use strict";

    function initialize() {
        // Create the xhr options
        var options = {
            url: "http://Microsoft.com",
            responseType: "document"
        };

        // Make the Ajax request
        WinJS.xhr(options).done(
            function (xhr) {
                var li;
                var ulResults = document.getElementById("ulResults");
                var links = xhr.response.querySelectorAll("a");
                for (var i = 0; i < links.length; i++) {
                    li = document.createElement("LI");
                    li.innerText = links[i].href;
                    ulResults.appendChild(li);
                }
            },
            function () {
                var messageDialog = new Windows.UI.Popups.MessageDialog("Could not
➥download page!");
                messageDialog.showAsync();
            }
        );
```

```
};

    document.addEventListener("DOMContentLoaded", initialize);
})();
```

FIGURE 2.9   Requesting and displaying links from the Microsoft homepage

The `WinJS.xhr()` function returns a promise. Two anonymous functions are passed to the `WinJS.xhr()` method in Listing 2.16: a promise complete function and a promise error function. The complete function displays the list of links in an HTML UL element and the error page shows a warning message to the user.

Notice that the code in Listing 2.15 makes a request against a remote website. This should be surprising. Normally, the `XMLHttpRequest` object is subject to the same origin policy that prevents you from requesting content from another domain. However, in the context of a Windows Store app, you don't have this restriction.

NOTE

Internet Explorer 10, but not earlier versions, supports the W3C Cross-Origin Resource Sharing (CORS) standard. If the remote server returns the right HTTP header then you can make Ajax requests against the remote server. In the context of a Windows Store app, you can ignore CORS and make cross-origin requests without doing anything special.

Notice that you pass the URL used by the Ajax request to the `WinJS.xhr()` function in an option object. You can pass any of the following options:

▶ **type**—Enables you specify the HTTP method used in the Ajax request. For example, POST, GET, PUT, DELETE, HEAD.

▶ **url**—Enables you to specify the URL used when making the Ajax request.

▶ **user**—Enables you to specify credentials when making the Ajax request.

▶ **Password**—Enables you to specify credentials when making the Ajax request.

▶ **headers**—Enables you to customize the HTTP headers used in the Ajax request.

▶ **data**—Enables you to specify the data passed to the remote server in the Ajax request. You can pass a string, array of unsigned bytes, or even a document. Use `JSON.stringify()` to convert other types of JavaScript objects into a string.

▶ **responseType**—Enables you to specify the type of data returned from the server. Possible values are `arraybuffer`, `blob`, `document`, `ms-stream`, or `text`.

▶ **customRequestInitializer**—Enables you to customize the properties of the underlying `XmlHttpRequest` object.

I'll talk more about both the responseType and customRequestInitializer in the following sections.

Specifying Different Response Types

The `XmlHttpRequest` object—and therefore, the `WinJS.xhr()` function—can be used to return several different types of data including blobs, documents, and text. You can use the `responseType` option to specify how you want the data returned.

The default value of `responseType` is `text`. For example, the following request will return the contents of the XML feed as a string:

```
var options = {
    url: "http://stephenwalther.com/feed"
};


WinJS.xhr(options).done(
    function (xhr) {
        var result = xhr.response;   // xhr.response is a string
    }
);
```

Most likely, you don't want to return an XML document as a string because then you can't use methods like `querySelector()` and `querySelectorAll()` to extract elements from the document. Instead, you want to return an XML document as a document like this:

```
var options = {
    url: "http://stephenwalther.com/blog/feed",
    responseType: "document"
};


WinJS.xhr(options).done(
    function (xhr) {
```

```
        var result = xhr.response;  // xhr.response is a document
    }
);
```

Notice that the options object includes a `responseType` property with the value `document`. When you call the `WinJS.xhr()` method, the data is returned as a document instead of a string. That means that you can query the results using methods like `querySelector()` and `querySelectorAll()`.

> **NOTE**
>
> For backward compatibility, the `XmlHttpRequest` object also has `responseText` and `responseXML` properties. You should favor the new `XmlHttpRequest` response property over these legacy properties.

Customizing the Properties of the `XmlHttpRequest` Object

The `WinJS.xhr()` function is nothing more than a wrapper around the native browser `XmlHttpRequest` object. There are some cases in which you might need to use features of the underlying `XmlHttpRequest` object that are not exposed through the options of the `WinJS.xhr()` function. In these cases, you can take advantage of the `WinJS.xhr()` function's `customRequestInitializer` option to customize the `XmlHttpRequest` object.

Imagine, for example, that you want to request and display the contents of a text file. Furthermore, you want to display download progress during the Ajax request.

The page in Listing 2.17 contains an HTML5 PROGRESS element (for displaying the download progress) and a DIV element (for displaying the contents of the text file).

LISTING 2.17   Customizing the XmlHttpRequest Object (xhrCustom\xhrCustom.html)

```html
<!DOCTYPE html>
<html>
<head>
    <meta charset="utf-8">
    <title>XHR Custom</title>

    <!-- WinJS references -->
    <link href="//Microsoft.WinJS.1.0/css/ui-dark.css" rel="stylesheet" />
    <script src="//Microsoft.WinJS.1.0/js/base.js"></script>
    <script src="//Microsoft.WinJS.1.0/js/ui.js"></script>

    <!-- Chapter02 references -->
    <link href="/css/default.css" rel="stylesheet">
    <script type="text/javascript" src="xhrCustom.js"></script>
</head>
<body>
```

```
<progress id="prgResults" max="100"></progress>

<div id="divResults"></div>

</body>
</html>
```

The code in Listing 2.18 illustrates how you can take advantage of the customRequestInitializer option to hook up a progress event handler to the XmlHttpRequest object used by the WinJS.xhr() function. The progress event handler updates the PROGRESS element so you can watch while a long running Ajax request completes (see Figure 2.10).

LISTING 2.18   Customizing the XmlHttpRequest Object (xhrCustom\xhrCustom.js)

```
(function () {
    "use strict";

    function initialize() {
        // Cache references to DOM elements
        var prgResults = document.getElementById("prgResults");
        var divResults = document.getElementById("divResults");

        // Create xhr options
        var options = {
            url: "products.txt",
            customRequestInitializer: function (xhr) {
                xhr.onprogress = function (evt) {
                    if (evt.lengthComputable) {
                        var percentComplete = (evt.loaded / evt.total) * 100;
                        prgResults.value = percentComplete;
                    }
                };
            }
        };

        // Perform Ajax request
        WinJS.xhr(options).done(
            function (xhr) {
                divResults.innerHTML = xhr.response;
            }
        );
    }

    document.addEventListener("DOMContentLoaded", initialize);
})();
```

Notice that the options object has a `customRequestInitializer` property that represents a function for initializing the `XmlHttpRequest` object. The function adds a `onprogress` handler that displays the amount of progress completed using the HTML5 PROGRESS element.

FIGURE 2.10   Showing Ajax request progress

Using the Scheduler to Prioritize Jobs

You can take advantage of the WinJS Scheduler (introduced in Windows 8.1) to execute a JavaScript function with a specific priority.

Why would you want to do this? A Windows Store app written with JavaScript contains only one user interface thread. That thread must be used to do everything. The thread is used by both your application code and the controls in the WinJS library.

If you want to create an app that responds quickly to user interaction then you need to prioritize the work performed with this one and only user interface thread.

> **NOTE**
>
> A Windows Store app written with JavaScript contains a single user interface thread *unless you use Web Workers*. You can use Web Workers to create additional execution threads. The disadvantage of using Web Workers is that a Web Worker cannot access the DOM. Jobs created with the Scheduler do not have this limitation.

Imagine, for example, that you are creating a RSS Reader app and you are displaying the currently selected blog entry. Quietly, in the background, you want to fetch the next blog entry because you anticipate that the user will want to view the next entry soon.

Using the Scheduler, you can wait to retrieve the next blog entry until the user interface thread is idle. That way, if the user clicks quickly from one entry to another, you won't block the user from interacting with your app.

Let me show you a simple sample of using the Scheduler. You schedule a new job by calling the `WinJS.Utilities.Scheduler.schedule()` method and passing the method a function that represents the job that you want to execute and (optionally) a job priority.

In Listing 2.19, the `WinJS.Utilities.Scheduler.schedule()` method is used to create two jobs named `job1` and `job2`. The first job is given a normal priority and the second job is given a high priority.

LISTING 2.19   Setting job priorities (scheduler\scheduler.js)

```
(function () {
    "use strict";

    function initialize() {
        // Alias the Scheduler
        var Scheduler = WinJS.Utilities.Scheduler;

        // Create the jobs
        var job1 = Scheduler.schedule(
            function () {
                console.log("Hello from job1");
            },
            Scheduler.Priority.normal
        );

        var job2 = Scheduler.schedule(
            function () {
                console.log("Hello from job2");
            },
            Scheduler.Priority.high
        );
    };

    document.addEventListener("DOMContentLoaded", initialize);
})();
```

Calling `WinJS.Utilities.schedule(func)` to execute a function is similar to calling `window.setTimeout(0, func)` or `window.setImmediate(func)`. The function does not execute immediately, but will execute just as soon as the current thread finishes processing.

In Listing 2.19, the code that creates the two jobs executes first and then the Scheduler executes the two jobs in order of priority. The messages `Hello from job2` and `Hello from job1` are written to the JavaScript console window (see Figure 2.11).

FIGURE 2.11   Jobs executed in order of priority

If you need to debug what is happening when using the Scheduler then you can take advantage of the `WinJS.Utilities.Scheduler.retrieveState()` method. This method returns a string that displays the current list of jobs in order of priority. You can dump the value of this string to the JavaScript console window by calling `console.log()` (see Figure 2.12).

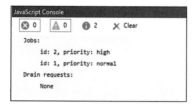

FIGURE 2.12   Displaying the state of the Scheduler

Setting Job Priorities

You can specify a job priority by using the `WinJS.Utilities.Scheduler.Priority` enumeration, or you can specify a number value between -15 and 15. You can use any of the following values:

▶ `min (-15)`

▶ `idle (-13)`

▶ `belowNormal (-9)`

▶ `normal (0)`

▶ `aboveNormal (9)`

▶ `high (13)`

▶ `max (15)`

Keep in mind that priorities are all relative. Scheduling all of your jobs to run at the highest priority won't make your app perform any faster. Instead, you should use the different priorities to schedule the order of execution of your code.

The standard WinJS controls—such as the `ListView` and `Flip`—use the Scheduler with the same priorities. So you can use the Scheduler to prioritize your app code relative to WinJS control code.

Yielding to a Higher Priority Job

Imagine that your app performs a long-running but low-priority job. Imagine, for example, that your app displays a constantly updated inspirational quotation.

If a higher priority job comes along, you might want to yield the low-priority job to the higher priority job. For example, if a user clicks a button then you want to respond to the user interaction immediately. You don't want to get blocked by the lower priority job.

The code in Listing 2.20 illustrates how you can yield a low-priority job by taking advantage of the `shouldYield` property.

LISTING 2.20   Setting Job Priorities (scheduler\scheduler.js)

```javascript
(function () {
    "use strict";

    function initialize() {
        // Alias the Scheduler
        var Scheduler = WinJS.Utilities.Scheduler;

        // Create low priority job
        Scheduler.schedule(showQuote, Scheduler.Priority.idle);

        // Handle click event
        document.getElementById("btn").addEventListener("click", function () {
            writeMessage("Do Something");
        });
    };

    function showQuote(jobInfo) {
        var allQuotes = [
            "Obstacles are those frightful things you see when you take your eyes
off your goal - Ford",
            "I have not failed. I've just found 10,000 ways that won't work -
Edison",
            "You can't build a reputation on what you are going to do - Ford"
        ];

        // Busy loop -- don't ever do this!
        while (true) {
            // Yield to higher priority job
            if (jobInfo.shouldYield) {
                writeMessage("Yielding");
                jobInfo.setWork(showQuote);
                break;
            }

            // Display random quote
            var quote = allQuotes[random(allQuotes.length)];
            writeMessage(quote);
        }
    }

    function writeMessage(message) {
```

```
        var messages = document.getElementById("messages");
        messages.innerHTML = "<li>" + message + "</li>" + messages.innerHTML;
    }

    function random(upperBound) {
        return Math.floor(Math.random() * upperBound);
    }

    document.addEventListener("DOMContentLoaded", initialize);
})();
```

The showQuote() method in Listing 2.20 displays an inspirational quote in a never-ending busy loop. Normally, including a busy loop in your JavaScript code would block the JavaScript user interface thread and prevent anything from happening. Normally, nothing would even get rendered to the screen.

However, the code in Listing 2.20 does not block the user interface thread. The inspirational quotes appear on the screen and clicking the Do Something button displays a message (see Figure 2.13).

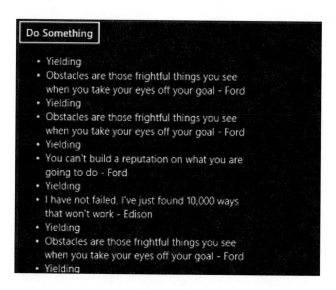

FIGURE 2.13   Displaying the state of the Scheduler

The showQuote() method includes a jobInfo parameter. Within the showQuote() method, the jobInfo.shouldYield property is checked to determine if the showQuote() method should yield to a higher priority job.

If shouldYield returns true then the showQuote() method uses the jobInfo.setWork() method to indicate the method that should be called to resume the current job after the higher priority job is completed. In this case, the showQuote() method is called again.

A high-priority job yields only when a higher priority job is scheduled. So, if you schedule a job with a high priority, and you call `shouldYield`, then the job will yield only when there is a higher priority job in the queue.

A job scheduled with a lower priority than high—for example, `Priority.normal` or `Priority.idle`—will yield in two situations. First, a lower priority job will always yield to a higher priority job. Also, a job scheduled with a lower priority will yield automatically after a time slice.

Because the `showQuote()` method was scheduled with `Priority.idle`, the `showQuote()` method will yield after a time slice automatically. Even though the `showQuote()` method creates a busy loop, it won't completely block the user interface thread. Checking `shouldYield` breaks the busy loop automatically after every so many milliseconds.

> **WARNING**
>
> Never ever, ever create busy loops in your JavaScript code. I only included a busy loop in Listing 2.20 to dramatize how yielding with the Scheduler works.

Summary

The goal of this chapter was to introduce you to the features of the base WinJS library. In the first section, you learned how to organize your JavaScript code into modules, namespaces, and classes. By taking advantage of modules and namespaces, you can avoid polluting the global namespace and make your app easier to maintain over time.

Next, I discussed how you can take advantage of promises whenever you need to write asynchronous code. I discussed, for example, how you can use promises when performing Ajax requests. You learned how to create promises, cancel promises, chain promises, and compose new promises from existing promises.

I also discussed how you can use WinJS query selectors to retrieve DOM elements. You learned how to use `WinJS.Utilities.query()` to perform a query using a selector and return a query set. You also learned how to retrieve individual elements with `WinJS.Utilities.id()`.

I also explained how you can use the `WinJS.xhr()` function to perform Ajax queries in a Windows Store app. You learned how to control the type of data returned by the `WinJS.xhr()` function by setting the `responseType` option. For example, you learned how to return the results of an Ajax query as a string or a document.

Finally, I showed you how to take advantage of the Scheduler introduced in Windows 8.1 to execute JavaScript code with different priorities. I demonstrated how you can yield a low priority job to a high priority job.

CHAPTER 3

Observables, Bindings, and Templates

In this chapter, I explain how you can display JavaScript objects, such as a single product or array of products, in the pages of your Windows Store apps.

I start by explaining observables. An observable enables you to detect automatically when a JavaScript property has been changed. I also explain how you can take advantage of the `WinJS.Binding.List` object to detect when elements of an array are changed.

Next, I focus on the topic of declarative data binding. You learn how to use both ordinary JavaScript objects and observable JavaScript objects with declarative data binding.

Finally, I discuss how you can display an array of objects using a WinJS template. A template enables you to format and display multiple JavaScript objects at a time.

Understanding Observables

An *observable* is an object that can notify one or more listeners when the value of a property is changed.

Observables enable you to keep your user interface and your application data in sync. For example, by taking advantage of observables, you can update your user interface automatically whenever the properties of a product change. Observables are the foundation of declarative binding in the WinJS library.

NOTE

The WinJS library is not the first JavaScript library to include support for observables. For example, Backbone, Knockout, Ember, and the Microsoft Ajax Library (now part of the Ajax Control Toolkit) all support observables.

Creating an Observable

Imagine that I have created a product object like this:

```
var product = {
    name: "Milk",
    description: "Something to drink",
    price: 12.33
};
```

There's nothing very exciting about this product. It has three properties named name, description, and price.

Now, imagine that I want to be notified automatically whenever any of these properties are changed. In that case, I can create an observable product from my product object like this:

```
var observableProduct = WinJS.Binding.as(product);
```

This line of code creates a new JavaScript object named observableProduct from the existing JavaScript object named product. This new object also has a name, description, and price property. However, unlike the properties of the original product object, the properties of the observable product object trigger notifications when the properties are changed.

Each of the properties of the new observable product object has been changed into accessor properties that have both a getter and a setter. For example, the observable product price property looks something like this:

```
price: {
        get: function () { return this.getProperty("price"); }
        set: function (value) { this.setProperty("price", value); }
}
```

When you read the price property then the getProperty() method is called and when you set the price property then the setProperty() method is called. The getProperty() and setProperty() methods are methods of the observable product object.

The observable product object supports the following methods and properties:

▶ **addProperty(name, value)**—Adds a new property to an observable and notifies any listeners

▶ **backingData**—An object that represents the value of each property

▶ **bind(name, action)**—Enables you to execute a function when a property changes

▶ **getProperty(name)**—Returns the value of a property using the string name of the property

▶ `notify(name, newValue, oldValue)`—A private method that executes each function in the `_listeners` array

▶ `removeProperty(name)`—Removes a property and notifies any listeners

▶ `setProperty(name, value)`—Updates a property and notifies any listeners

▶ `unbind(name, action)`—Enables you to stop executing a function in response to a property change

▶ `updateProperty(name, value)`—Updates a property and notifies any listeners

So when you create an observable, you get a new object with the same properties as an existing object. However, when you modify the properties of an observable object, then you can notify any listeners of the observable that the value of a particular property has changed automatically.

Imagine that you change the value of the price property like this:

```
observableProduct.price = 2.99;
```

In that case, the following sequence of events is triggered:

1. The price setter calls the `setProperty("price", 2.99)` method.

2. The `setProperty()` method updates the value of the `backingData.price` property and calls the `notify()` method.

3. The `notify()` method executes each function in the collection of listeners associated with the price property.

When an observable property is updated, you can execute one or more functions (listeners) automatically.

WARNING

If you call the `WinJS.Binding.as()` method on a WinRT object then you will get an exception. The problem is that WinRT objects are immutable and the `WinJS.Binding.as()` method attempts to add a new method named `_getObservable()` to the immutable object. You can make JavaScript objects observable, but not WinRT objects.

Creating Observable Listeners

If you want to be notified when a property of an observable object is changed, then you need to register a listener. You register a listener by using the `bind()` method as in Listing 3.1.

LISTING 3.1   Binding an Object Property to a Listener (observables\observables.html)

```
// Simple product object
var product = {
    name: "Milk",
    description: "Something to drink",
    price: 12.33
};

// Create observable product
var observableProduct = WinJS.Binding.as(product);

// Execute a function when price is changed
observableProduct.bind("price", function (newValue, oldValue) {
    console.log(newValue + " was " + oldValue);
});

// Change the price
observableProduct.price = 2.99;
```

In Listing 3.1, the bind() method is used to associate the price property with a function. When the price property is changed, the function logs the new value and old value of the price property to the Visual Studio JavaScript console (see Figure 3.1).

FIGURE 3.1   Binding to a property

The price property is associated with the function using the following code:

```
// Execute a function when price is changed
observableProduct.bind("price", function (newValue, oldValue) {
    console.log(newValue + " was " + oldValue);
});
```

Notice that the function bound to the price property is called twice. It is called for the initial value of the property, and it is called when the property is changed.

NOTE

You can bind a listener to a complex property by supplying an object to the second parameter of the `WinJS.Binding.bind()` method like this:

```
// Create object with complex property
var customer = {
    shippingAddress: {
        street: "312 Main Street"
    }
};

// Create observable
var observableCustomer = WinJS.Binding.as(customer);

// Bind to complex property
WinJS.Binding.bind(observableCustomer, {
    shippingAddress: {
        street: function (newValue) {
            console.log("Modified shipping address to "
                + newValue);
        }
    }
});

// Change value of complex property
observableCustomer.shippingAddress.street = "100 Grant Street";
```

The second parameter passed to the `WinJS.Binding.bind()` method makes the `street` property observable even though the `street` property is a nested property of the complex `customer` object.

Coalescing Notifications

If you make multiple changes to a property—one change immediately following another—then separate notifications won't be sent. Instead, any listeners are notified only once. The notifications are coalesced into a single notification (see Figure 3.2).

For example, in the code in Listing 3.2, the product `price` property is updated three times. However, only two messages are written to the JavaScript console. Only the initial value and the last value assigned to the price property are written to the JavaScript Console window.

LISTING 3.2   Coalescing Notifications (observablesCoalesce\observablesCoalesce.html)

```
// Simple product object
var product = {
    name: "Milk",
    description: "Something to drink",
    price: 12.33
};

// Create observable product
var observableProduct = WinJS.Binding.as(product);

// Execute a function when price is changed
observableProduct.bind("price", function (newValue, oldValue) {
    console.log(newValue + " was " + oldValue);
});

// Change the price
observableProduct.price = 3.99;
observableProduct.price = 2.99;
observableProduct.price = 1.99;
```

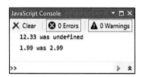

FIGURE 3.2   Coalescing notifications

If there is a time delay between changes to a property then the changes result in different notifications.

If you need to prevent multiple notifications from being coalesced into one—and you don't want to create an artificial time delay—then you can take advantage of promises. Because the updateProperty() method returns a promise, you can create different notifications for each change in a property by using the following code:

```
// Change the price
observableProduct.updateProperty("price", 3.99)
    .then(function () {
        observableProduct.updateProperty("price", 2.99)
            .then(function () {
                observableProduct.updateProperty("price", 1.99);
            });
    });
```

In this case, even though the price is immediately changed from 3.99 to 2.99 to 1.99, separate notifications for each new value of the `price` property are sent (see Figure 3.3).

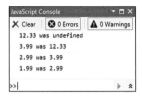

FIGURE 3.3   Using promises with observables

Bypassing Notifications

Normally, if a property of an observable object has listeners and you change the property then the listeners are notified. However, there are certain situations in which you might want to bypass notification. In other words, you might need to change a property value silently without triggering any functions registered for notification.

If you want to change a property without triggering notifications then you should change the property by using the `backingData` property. The code in Listing 3.3 illustrates how you can change the `price` property silently.

LISTING 3.3   Bypassing Notifications (observablesBypass\observablesBypass.html)

```
// Simple product object
var product = {
    name: "Milk",
    description: "Something to drink",
    price: 12.33
};

// Create observable product
var observableProduct = WinJS.Binding.as(product);

// Execute a function when price is changed
observableProduct.bind("price", function (newValue) {
    console.log(newValue);
});

// Change the price silently
observableProduct.backingData.price = 5.99;
console.log(observableProduct.price); // Writes 5.99
```

The price is changed to the value 5.99 by changing the value of `backingData.price`. Because the `observableProduct.price` property is not set directly, any listeners associated with the price property are not notified.

When you change the value of a property by using the `backingData` property, the change in the property happens synchronously. However, when you change the value of an observable property directly, the change is always made asynchronously.

Working with the `WinJS.Binding.List` Object

If you want to be notified whenever a change is made to an array of items—in other words, you want to work with an observable collection—then you should use the `WinJS.Binding.List` object.

The `WinJS.Binding.List` object wraps a standard JavaScript array in a new object and adds additional methods and events to support change notifications. The `WinJS.Binding.List` object supports the following events:

- ▶ **iteminserted**—Triggered when a new item is added to the list.

- ▶ **itemchanged**—Triggered when an item in the list is replaced with the `setAt()` method.

- ▶ **itemmoved**—Triggered when an item in the list is moved with the `move()` method.

- ▶ **itemmutated**—Triggered by calling the `notifyMutated()` method.

- ▶ **itemremoved**—Triggered by removing an item from the list.

- ▶ **reload**—Triggered by reordering the items in a list by calling `sort()` or `reverse()`. Also triggered by calling the `notifyReload()` method.

The code in Listing 3.4 demonstrates how you can trigger each of these events and the information passed to each event handler.

LISTING 3.4   Using a WinJS.Binding.List (observablesList\observablesList.html)

```
var products = [
    { name: "Milk", price: 2.99 },
    { name: "Oranges", price: 2.50 },
    { name: "Apples", price: 1.99 }
];

// Create List
var productsList = new WinJS.Binding.List(products);

// Setup event handlers
productsList.oniteminserted = function (evt) {
    var message = "Item Inserted: " + evt.detail.value.name
        + " at index " + evt.detail.index
        + " with key " + evt.detail.key;
    console.log(message);
};
```

```
productsList.onitemchanged = function (evt) {
    var message = "Item Changed: " + evt.detail.oldValue.name
        + " to " + evt.detail.newValue.name
        + " at index " + evt.detail.index
        + " with key " + evt.detail.key;
    console.log(message);
};

productsList.onitemmutated = function (evt) {
    var message = "Item Mutated: " + evt.detail.value.name
        + " with key " + evt.detail.key;
    console.log(message);
};

productsList.onitemremoved = function (evt) {
    var message = "Item Removed: " + evt.detail.value.name
        + " at index " + evt.detail.index
        + " with key " + evt.detail.key;
    console.log(message);
};

productsList.onitemmoved = function (evt) {
    var message = "Item Moved: " + evt.detail.value.name
        + " from index " + evt.detail.oldIndex
        + " to index " + evt.detail.newIndex;
    console.log(message);
};

productsList.onreload = function (evt) {
    var message = "List Reloaded";
    console.log(message);
};

// Insert an item
productsList.push({ name: "Carrots", price: 2.33 }); // triggers iteminserted

// Replace an entire item
productsList.setAt(1, { name: "Navel Oranges", price: 2.50 }); // triggers
➥itemchanged

// Update an item property
productsList.getAt(1).price = 500.00;
productsList.notifyMutated(1); // triggers itemmutated
```

```
// Delete an item
productsList.splice(0, 1); // triggers itemremoved

// Move second item to top
productsList.move(1, 0); // triggers itemmoved

// Sort the list
productsList.sort(); // triggers reload
```

In Listing 3.4, a JavaScript array named products is created that represents a list of products with name and price properties. Next, a WinJS.Binding.List is created with the following line of code:

```
var productsList = new WinJS.Binding.List(products);
```

Event handlers for all of the WinJS.Binding.List events are created. Each event handler writes a message to the Visual Studio JavaScript Console (see Figure 3.4).

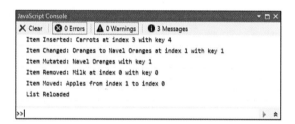

FIGURE 3.4   WinJS.Binding.List events

Creating an Observable Collection of Observables

By default, when you create a WinJS.Binding.List from a JavaScript array, the list is observable but not the items in the list. The WinJS.Binding.List simply contains the items from the array and the items are plain old JavaScript objects.

If you want to convert each of the items from the JavaScript array into an observable item, then you need to use the binding option when creating the WinJS.Binding.List like this:

```
var products = [
    { name: "Milk", price: 2.99 },
    { name: "Oranges", price: 2.50 },
    { name: "Apples", price: 1.99 }
];
```

```
// Create List
var productsList = new WinJS.Binding.List(products, { binding: true });

// Listen for changes in price
productsList.getAt(1).bind("price", function () {
    console.log("price changed");
});
```

The `productsList` in the code above contains a list of observable objects. Because each object in the list is observable, you can hook up a listener function that gets triggered when a change is made to a property. In the preceding code, a message is written to the Visual Studio JavaScript console whenever the `price` property is modified.

Understanding Declarative Data Binding

Declarative data binding enables you to bind the attributes of an HTML element to the properties of a JavaScript object. You can take advantage of declarative data binding whenever you want to display data in an HTML page.

Let me start with a simple example. The page in Listing 3.5 displays product details (see Figure 3.5).

LISTING 3.5   Simple Declarative Data Binding (dataBinding\dataBinding.html)

```
<!DOCTYPE html>
<html>
<head>
    <meta charset="utf-8" />
    <title>Chapter03</title>

    <!-- WinJS references -->
    <link href="//Microsoft.WinJS.2.0/css/ui-dark.css" rel="stylesheet" />
    <script src="//Microsoft.WinJS.2.0/js/base.js"></script>
    <script src="//Microsoft.WinJS.2.0/js/ui.js"></script>

    <!-- Chapter03 references -->
    <link href="/css/default.css" rel="stylesheet" />
    <script src="/dataBinding/dataBinding.js"></script>
</head>
<body>

    <h1>Product Details</h1>
```

```
<div>
    Product Name:
    <span data-win-bind="innerText:name"></span>
</div>
<div>
    Product Price:
    <span data-win-bind="innerText:price"></span>
</div>
<div>
    Product Picture:
    <br />
    <img data-win-bind="src:photo;alt:name" />
</div>
</body>
</html>
```

The product name and price are displayed with HTML SPAN elements. Notice that each SPAN element includes a `data-win-bind` attribute. For example, the product name is displayed with the following SPAN element:

```
<span data-win-bind="innerText:name"></span>
```

This `data-win-bind` attribute binds the value of the name property to the `innerText` property of the SPAN element.

You can use the `data-win-bind` attribute to bind (almost) any attribute of an HTML element to the value of a JavaScript property. For example, the picture of the Tesla is displayed by binding values to the IMG element's `src` and `alt` attributes:

```
<img data-win-bind="src:photo;alt:name" />
```

Notice that the `data-win-bind` attribute accepts a semicolon-delimited list of HTML element attribute names and JavaScript object property names.

> **NOTE**
>
> The one attribute which you cannot use with declarative binding is the ID attribute. By default, the WinJS library generates a unique ID for each element automatically. You can disable this behavior by setting the `optimizeBindingReferences` property to false.

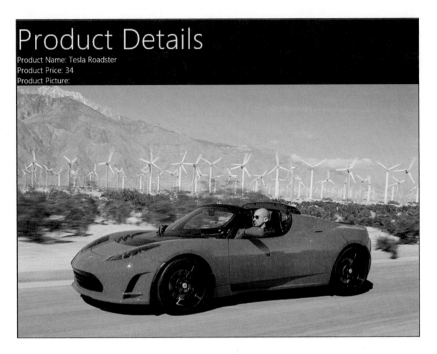

FIGURE 3.5   Showing product details with declarative data binding

The code in Listing 3.6 contains the product that is displayed by the HTML page in Listing 3.5.

LISTING 3.6   Simple Declarative Data Binding (databinding\databinding.js)

```
(function () {
    "use strict";

    function initialize() {
        var product = {
            name: "Tesla Roadster",
            price: 34,
            photo: "tesla.jpg"
        };

        WinJS.Binding.processAll(null, product);
    }

    document.addEventListener("DOMContentLoaded", initialize);

})();
```

There is nothing special about the `product` object in Listing 3.6—it is just a plain old JavaScript object.

Notice the call to `WinJS.Binding.processAll()` in Listing 3.6. The declarative data binding attributes in a page are not processed until you call this method. When you call the `WinJS.Binding.procesAll()` method, you must specify two parameters: the root element and the data context.

The root element determines which elements in a page get processed. If you pass the value null, then the entire document is parsed.

The data context contains the data that you want to bind to the HTML attributes. In Listing 3.6, the product object is passed to the `WinJS.Binding.processAll()` method as the data context.

WARNING

Don't call `WinJS.Binding.processAll()` until the document containing the HTML elements has been loaded. Otherwise, there is nothing to process. In Listing 3.6, the `WinJS.Binding.processAll()` method is called within a function triggered by the `DOMContentLoaded` event.

Declarative Data Binding and Observables

Declarative data binding and observables are a powerful combination. If you use observables with data binding then you can update the contents of an HTML document automatically whenever you change the underlying JavaScript objects.

For example, the HTML page in Listing 3.7 contains a SPAN and a BUTTON element. The page displays the number of times the button has been clicked (see Figure 3.6).

FIGURE 3.6   Displaying a click count

LISTING 3.7   Using Data Binding with an Observable (dataBindingObservables\dataBindingObservables.html)

```
<!DOCTYPE html>
<html>
<head>
    <meta charset="utf-8" />
    <title>Chapter03</title>
```

```
<!-- WinJS references -->
<link href="//Microsoft.WinJS.2.0/css/ui-dark.css" rel="stylesheet" />
<script src="//Microsoft.WinJS.2.0/js/base.js"></script>
<script src="//Microsoft.WinJS.2.0/js/ui.js"></script>

<!-- Chapter03 references -->
<link href="/css/default.css" rel="stylesheet" />
<script src="dataBindingObservables.js"></script>
</head>
<body>

    <div>
        You have clicked the button
        <span data-win-bind="innerText:timesClicked"></span> times.
        <br />
        <button data-win-bind="onclick:click">Click Here!</button>
    </div>


</body>
</html>
```

Notice that the page in Listing 3.7 includes two `data-win-bind` attributes. The first `data-win-bind` attribute is used with a SPAN element to display the click count and the second `data-win-bind` attribute is used with a BUTTON element to handle the `click` event.

The JavaScript code in Listing 3.8 contains an observable object, named `viewModel`, which tracks the click count.

LISTING 3.8   Using Data Binding with an Observable (dataBindingObservables\dataBindingObservables.html)

```
(function () {
    "use strict";

    function initialize() {

        // Create a view model
        var viewModel = {
            timesClicked: 0,
            click: WinJS.UI.eventHandler(function (evt) {
                evt.preventDefault();
                viewModel.timesClicked ++;
            })
        };
```

```
        // Make the view model observable
        viewModel = WinJS.Binding.as(viewModel);


        // Bind the view model to the document
        WinJS.Binding.processAll(null, viewModel);
    }

    document.addEventListener("DOMContentLoaded", initialize);

})();
```

The `viewModel` object in Listing 3.8 has a property, named `timesClicked`, which is used to track the number of times the button has been clicked. The `viewModel` object also has a method named `click()` that is used to update the `timesClicked` property.

> **NOTE**
>
> Notice that the click handler is wrapped in a call to `WinJS.UI.eventHandler()`. For security reasons, the WinJS library requires you to call this method for any event handler which can be invoked from a declarative context such as `data-win-bind`. If you neglect to call this method then nothing happens when you click the button.

The `viewModel` is converted into an observable with the help of the `WinJS.Binding.as()` method. Finally, the `viewModel` is bound to the page and the `data-win-bind` attributes are processed by calling `WinJS.Binding.processAll()`.

Capturing the Contents of an HTML Form

The WinJS library does not support two-way data binding. Change notification is one-way. If you want to capture the contents of an HTML form then you need to do the work of retrieving the values of the form elements yourself.

The page in Listing 3.9 contains an HTML form for creating a new product. It has two INPUT elements for the product name and price (see Figure 3.7). The form uses a single `data-win-bind` attribute. The FORM element has a `data-win-bind` attribute that wires up a form submit handler.

FIGURE 3.7   Creating a new product

LISTING 3.9   Two-Way Data Binding (dataBindingTwoWay\dataBindingTwoWay.html)

```html
<!DOCTYPE html>
<html>
<head>
    <meta charset="utf-8" />
    <title>Chapter03</title>

    <!-- WinJS references -->
    <link href="//Microsoft.WinJS.2.0/css/ui-dark.css" rel="stylesheet" />
    <script src="//Microsoft.WinJS.2.0/js/base.js"></script>
    <script src="//Microsoft.WinJS.2.0/js/ui.js"></script>

    <!-- Chapter03 references -->
    <link href="/css/default.css" rel="stylesheet" />
    <script src="dataBindingTwoWay.js"></script>
</head>
<body>
    <form data-win-bind="onsubmit:submit">
        <div class="field">
            <label>Name:</label>
            <input id="productName" required />
        </div>
        <div class="field">
            <label>Price:</label>
            <input id="productPrice" required />
        </div>
        <div class="field">
            <button>Add Product</button>
        </div>

    </form>

</body>
</html>
```

When you submit the HTML form, the `viewData.submit()` method in Listing 3.10 is invoked. This method grabs the HTML form fields and creates a new product object named `productToAdd`.

LISTING 3.10   Two-Way Data Binding (dataBindingTwoWay\dataBindingTwoWay.js)

```javascript
(function () {
    "use strict";
```

```
function initialize() {

    var viewModel = {
        submit: WinJS.UI.eventHandler(function (evt) {
            // Prevent page from being posted
            evt.preventDefault();

            // Grab form field values
            var productToAdd = {
                name: document.getElementById("productName").value,
                price: document.getElementById("productPrice").value
            };

            // TODO: Add new product to database
            console.log("adding " + productToAdd.name + " to database.")
        })
    };


    WinJS.Binding.processAll(null, viewModel);
}

document.addEventListener("DOMContentLoaded", initialize);
```

```
})();
```

The page in Listing 3.9 uses a `data-win-bind` attribute to wire up the form submit event handler. You might be wondering whether it would be easier to do without the data binding and directly wire up an event handler like this:

```
<form onsubmit="submit">
```

Why use declarative data binding at all? The advantage of using declarative data binding to wire up the event handler is that you do not need to expose the handler through a namespace. When using declarative data binding, a handler does not need to be a public method—the only requirement is that it be part of the data context used with the `WinJS.Binding.processAll()` method.

NOTE

The HTML form in Listing 3.9 uses the HTML5 required attribute to ensure that values are entered in the name and price INPUT elements.

Declarative Data Binding and WinJS Controls

We discuss WinJS controls in detail in the next chapter; however, I want to make sure that you understand that you can use declarative data binding with WinJS controls properties in the same way as you can use declarative data binding with element attributes.

The trick is to use the `winControl` property, which is exposed by every HTML element that is associated with a control. You can use the `winControl` property with the `data-win-bind` attribute.

For example, the page in Listing 3.11 contains a WinJS Rating control (see Figure 3.8).

FIGURE 3.8   Displaying an average rating with declarative data binding

LISTING 3.11   Using Declarative Data Binding with WinJS Controls (dataBindingControls\dataBindingControls.html)

```
<!DOCTYPE html>
<html>
<head>
    <meta charset="utf-8" />
    <title>Chapter03</title>

    <!-- WinJS references -->
    <link href="//Microsoft.WinJS.2.0/css/ui-dark.css" rel="stylesheet" />
    <script src="//Microsoft.WinJS.2.0/js/base.js"></script>
    <script src="//Microsoft.WinJS.2.0/js/ui.js"></script>

    <!-- Chapter03 references -->
    <link href="/css/default.css" rel="stylesheet" />
    <script src="dataBindingControls.js"></script>
</head>
<body>

    <div>
        data-win-control="WinJS.UI.Rating"
        data-win-bind="winControl.averageRating:averageRating">
    </div>

    <div>
        The average rating for this product is:
```

```
        <span data-win-bind="innerText:averageRating"></span>
    </div>

</body>
</html>
```

Listing 3.11 contains a WinJS Rating control. The `averageRating` property of the WinJS Rating control is set with the following `data-win-bind` attribute:

```
data-win-bind="winControl.averageRating:averageRating"
```

The winControl property gets you from the HTML element to its associated control.

The JavaScript file in Listing 3.12 illustrates how you can bind the average rating to the Rating control.

LISTING 3.12   Using Declarative Data Binding with WinJS Controls (dataBindingControls\dataBindingControls.js)

```
(function () {
    "use strict";

    function initialize() {

        // Create a view model
        var viewModel = {
            averageRating: 3
        };

        // Bind the view model to the document
        WinJS.UI.processAll()
            .done(function () {
                WinJS.Binding.processAll(null, viewModel);
            });
    }

    document.addEventListener("DOMContentLoaded", initialize);

})();
```

The code in Listing 3.12 contains two calls to the `processAll()` method. First, the `WinJS.UI.processAll()` method is called to process all of the WinJS controls in the page. Next, the `WinJS.Binding.processAll()` method is called to process all of the data binding attributes in the page. You must call the two `processAll()` methods in that order or there won't be controls with properties to bind to.

Declarative Data Binding and Binding Converters

Binding converters enable you to transform the value of a property when using the property in a `data-win-bind` attribute.

There are all sorts of situations in which a binding converter is useful. For example, formatting dates and times or hiding or displaying content depending on a property value. Whenever you need to alter a JavaScript property value before displaying it, use a binding converter.

Imagine, for example, that you want to display the text `On Sale!` only when a product is on sale. The page in Listing 3.13 displays two products (see Figure 3.9). It uses a binding converter to hide or display the contents of a DIV element that contains the text `On Sale!`

FIGURE 3.9   Using a binding converter

LISTING 3.13   Using a Binding Converter (dataBindingConverters/dataBindingConverters.html)

```
<!DOCTYPE html>
<html>
<head>
    <meta charset="utf-8" />
    <title>Chapter03</title>

    <!-- WinJS references -->
    <link href="//Microsoft.WinJS.2.0/css/ui-dark.css" rel="stylesheet" />
    <script src="//Microsoft.WinJS.2.0/js/base.js"></script>
    <script src="//Microsoft.WinJS.2.0/js/ui.js"></script>

    <!-- Chapter03 references -->
    <link href="/css/default.css" rel="stylesheet" />
    <script src="dataBindingConverters.js"></script>
    <script type="text/javascript" src="myBindingConverters.js"></script>
</head>
<body>
```

```
<div>
    <h1 data-win-bind="innerText:product1.name"></h1>
    <div>
        Price: <span data-win-bind="innerText:product1.price"></span>
    </div>
    <div data-win-bind="style.display:product1.onSale MyBindingConverters.
➥onSaleToDisplay">
        <b>On Sale!</b>
    </div>
</div>
<div>
    <h1 data-win-bind="innerText:product2.name"></h1>
    <div>
        Price: <span data-win-bind="innerText:product2.price"></span>
    </div>
    <div data-win-bind="style.display:product2.onSale MyBindingConverters.
➥onSaleToDisplay">
        <b>On Sale!</b>
    </div>
</div>

</body>
</html>
```

The text On Sale! does not appear after the first product, but it does appear after the second product. The text is displayed with the following DIV element:

```
<div data-win-bind="style.display:product2.onSale MyBindingConverters.
➥onSaleToDisplay">
    <b>On Sale!</b>
</div>
```

The binding converter is applied to the DIV element's `style` attribute. When the binding converter returns the value "none" then the contents of the DIV element are hidden with `display:none`. Otherwise, the binding converter returns the value "block" and the contents of the DIV element are displayed with `display:block`.

The binding converter appears in the value of the `data-win-bind` expression after the name of the JavaScript property being bound. In this case, the binding converter is a function named `MyBindingConverters.onSaleToDisplay`. This binding converter converts a Boolean value into either the value "none" or "block".

The binding converter is contained in a separate file—referenced by the HTML page—named `myBindingConverters.js` (see Listing 3.14). You don't need to create the binding converter in a separate file, but it makes it easier to reuse the binding converter with multiple pages.

LISTING 3.14   A Binding Converter (dataBindingConverters\myBindingConverters.js)

```
(function () {
    "use strict";

    var onSaleToDisplay = WinJS.Binding.converter(function (onSale) {
        return onSale ? "block" : "none";
    });

    WinJS.Namespace.define("MyBindingConverters",
        {
            onSaleToDisplay: onSaleToDisplay
        });

})();
```

You create a binding converter by passing a function to the `WinJS.Binding.converter()`
method. The function converts the value passed to the function to some other value.
In Listing 3.14, the function converts the product `onSale` property (a Boolean property)
into either the value "block" or "none" (a value that can be used with the style display
property).

The two products are created in Listing 3.15. Listing 3.15 contains an object named
`viewModel` which has a `product1` and `product2` property.

LISTING 3.15   Using a Binding Converter (dataBindingConverters/dataBindingConverters.js)

```
(function () {
    "use strict";

    function initialize() {

        var viewModel = {
            product1: {
                name: "Tesla",
                price: 300000.00,
                onSale: false
            },
            product2: {
                name: "BMW",
                price: 80000.00,
                onSale: true
            }
        };
```

```
        WinJS.Binding.processAll(null, viewModel);
    }

    document.addEventListener("DOMContentLoaded", initialize);

})();
```

Creating Date and Price Binding Converters

I can't let you stop reading this section until I mention how to create two other types of converters: date and price converters. I find that I need to use date and price converters in most Windows Store apps which I build in order to format dates and prices.

The JavaScript file in Listing 3.16 contains the two converters.

LISTING 3.16   The Date and Price Converters

```
(function () {
    "use strict";

    // Converts 77.8900 to $77.89
    var price = WinJS.Binding.converter(function (priceToConvert) {
        return "$" + priceToConvert.toFixed(2);
    });

    // Converts full date to 12/25/2013
    var shortDate = WinJS.Binding.converter(function (dateToConvert) {
        return dateToConvert.getMonth() + 1 +
            "/" + dateToConvert.getDate() +
            "/" + dateToConvert.getFullYear();
    });

    WinJS.Namespace.define("MyBindingConverters",
        {
            price: price,
            shortDate: shortDate
        });

})();
```

After you add a reference to the converters to an HTML page, you can use the date and price converters in your binding expressions as demonstrated in Listing 3.17.

LISTING 3.17   Using the Date and Price Converters

```
<div>
    <h1 data-win-bind="innerText:product1.name"></h1>
    <div>
        Price:
        <span data-win-bind="innerText:product1.price MyBindingConverters.
➥price"></span>
    </div>
    <div>
        Date Available:
        <span data-win-bind="innerText:product1.dateAvailable MyBindingConverters.
➥shortDate"></span>
    </div>
</div>
```

The price converter causes the product price to be displayed as $100.00 instead of 99.999999. The shortDate converter causes the product dateAvailable property to be displayed as 12/25/2012 instead of Tue Dec 25 00:00:00 PST 2012.

NOTE

Sadly, you cannot pass additional parameters when using a binding converter. It would be nice if you could pass an additional parameter, for example, that represented the date format. However, you can't do this. Instead, you must create separate dateShort and dateLong binding converters.

Understanding Templates

If you need to display the same fragment of HTML more than one time in a page then you should create a template. A template is a fragment of HTML that can include declarative data binding expressions. There are two ways to create a template: imperatively and declaratively.

Creating an Imperative Template

Imagine that you want to display an array of products in an HTML page (see Figure 3.10). In that case, you can use a template to format each of the products in the array.

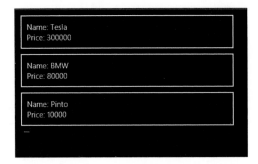

FIGURE 3.10   Displaying a list of products with a template

The HTML page in Listing 3.18 contains a DIV element named `tmplProduct`. This DIV element is not displayed when the page is rendered. Instead, it contains the contents of the template.

The page also contains a second DIV element named `conProducts`. This DIV element acts as the target of the template. When each product is rendered, it is rendered into the `conProducts` DIV element.

LISTING 3.18   Creating an Imperative Template (templatesImperative\templatesImperative.html)

```
<!DOCTYPE html>
<html>
<head>
    <meta charset="utf-8" />
    <title>Chapter03</title>

    <!-- WinJS references -->
    <link href="//Microsoft.WinJS.2.0/css/ui-dark.css" rel="stylesheet" />
    <script src="//Microsoft.WinJS.2.0/js/base.js"></script>
    <script src="//Microsoft.WinJS.2.0/js/ui.js"></script>

    <!-- Chapter03 references -->
    <link href="templatesImperative.css" rel="stylesheet" />
    <script src="templatesImperative.js"></script>
</head>
<body>

    <!-- Template -->
    <div id="tmplProduct">
        <div class="product">
            Name: <span data-win-bind="innerText:name"></span>
            <br />
            Price: <span data-win-bind="innerText:price"></span>
```

```
        </div>
    </div>

    <!-- Place Where Template is Rendered -->
    <div id="conProducts"></div>

</body>
</html>
```

The JavaScript code in Listing 3.19 illustrates how you can create a new template and render the template for each item in an array.

LISTING 3.19   Creating an Imperative Template (templatesImperative\templatesImperative.js)

```
(function () {
    "use strict";

    function initialize() {

        var products = [
            { name: "Tesla", price: 300000 },
            { name: "BMW", price: 80000 },
            { name: "Pinto", price: 10000 }
        ];

        // Get the template and template container
        var tmplProduct = document.getElementById("tmplProduct");
        var conProducts = document.getElementById("conProducts");

        // Create the template
        var template = new WinJS.Binding.Template(tmplProduct)

        // Render each array item using the template
        products.forEach(function (product) {
            template.render(product, conProducts);
        });
    }

    document.addEventListener("DOMContentLoaded", initialize);

})();
```

The template is created by creating a new instance of the WinJS `Template` control:

```
var template = new WinJS.Binding.Template(tmplProduct)
```

Next, the template is rendered for each item in the array within a `forEach()` method:

```
products.forEach(function (product) {
    template.render(product, conProducts);
});
```

When the template is rendered, only the inner contents of the template are rendered for each data item. The containing DIV element—named `tmplProduct` in the code—is not rendered.

Creating a Declarative Template

If you prefer, you can create the template declaratively instead of imperatively. The page in Listing 3.20 contains a WinJS Template control associated with a DIV element named tmplProduct.

LISTING 3.20   Creating a Template Declaratively (templatesDeclare\templatesDeclare.html)

```html
<!DOCTYPE html>
<html>
<head>
    <meta charset="utf-8" />
    <title>Chapter03</title>

    <!-- WinJS references -->
    <link href="//Microsoft.WinJS.2.0/css/ui-dark.css" rel="stylesheet" />
    <script src="//Microsoft.WinJS.2.0/js/base.js"></script>
    <script src="//Microsoft.WinJS.2.0/js/ui.js"></script>

    <!-- Chapter03 references -->
    <link href="templatesDeclare.css" rel="stylesheet" />
    <script src="templatesDeclare.js"></script>
</head>
<body>

    <!-- Template -->
    <div id="tmplProduct" data-win-control="WinJS.Binding.Template">
        <div class="product">
            Name: <span data-win-bind="innerText:name"></span>
            <br />
            Price: <span data-win-bind="innerText:price"></span>
        </div>
    </div>

    <!-- Place Where Template is Rendered -->
    <div id="conProducts"></div>
```

```
</body>
</html>
```

In Listing 3.20, the `Template` control is declared with a `data-win-control="WinJS. Binding.Template"` attribute.

And Listing 3.21 contains the JavaScript code used to render the array of products using the template.

LISTING 3.21   Creating a Template Declaratively (templatesDeclare\templatesDeclare.js)

```
(function () {
    "use strict";

    function initialize() {

        var products = [
            { name: "Tesla", price: 300000 },
            { name: "BMW", price: 80000 },
            { name: "Pinto", price: 10000 }
        ];

        // Get the template and template container
        var tmplProduct = document.getElementById("tmplProduct");
        var conProducts = document.getElementById("conProducts");

        // Render each array item using the template
        WinJS.UI.processAll().done(function () {
            products.forEach(function (product) {
                tmplProduct.winControl.render(product, conProducts);
            });
        });
    }

    document.addEventListener("DOMContentLoaded", initialize);

})();
```

When using a declarative `Template` control, you must call the `WinJS.UI.processAll()` method. Otherwise, the DIV element won't be converted into a template.

Applying a Template with a Query Selector

A query collection includes a `template()` method that you can use to quickly apply a template to either a single DOM element or set of DOM elements. For example, the page in Listing 3.22 displays a list of products.

LISTING 3.22   Using WinJS.Utilities.id() with a Template (templatesQuery\templatesQuery.
html).

```html
<!DOCTYPE html>
<html>
<head>
    <meta charset="utf-8" />
    <title>Chapter03</title>

    <!-- WinJS references -->
    <link href="//Microsoft.WinJS.2.0/css/ui-dark.css" rel="stylesheet" />
    <script src="//Microsoft.WinJS.2.0/js/base.js"></script>
    <script src="//Microsoft.WinJS.2.0/js/ui.js"></script>

    <!-- Chapter03 references -->
    <link href="templatesQuery.css" rel="stylesheet" />
    <script src="templatesQuery.js"></script>
</head>
<body>

    <!-- Template -->
    <div id="tmplProduct" data-win-control="WinJS.Binding.Template">
        <div class="product">
            Name: <span data-win-bind="innerText:name"></span>
            <br />
            Price: <span data-win-bind="innerText:price"></span>
        </div>
    </div>

    <!-- Place Where Template is Rendered -->
    <div id="conProducts"></div>

</body>
</html>
```

The page in Listing 3.22 contains a declarative template named tmplProduct. The page also contains a DIV element named conProducts, which is the place in the page where the template is rendered.

The JavaScript code in Listing 3.23 demonstrates how you can use the WinJS.Utilities. id() method to apply a template to the conProducts DIV element.

LISTING 3.23   Using WinJS.Utilities.id() with a Template (templatesQuery\templatesQuery.js).

```javascript
(function () {
    "use strict";

    function initialize() {
```

```
        var products = [
            { name: "Tesla", price: 300000 },
            { name: "BMW", price: 80000 },
            { name: "Pinto", price: 10000 }
        ];

        WinJS.UI.processAll().done(function () {
            var tmplProduct = document.getElementById("tmplProduct");
            WinJS.Utilities.id("conProducts").template(tmplProduct, products);
        });
    }

    document.addEventListener("DOMContentLoaded", initialize);

})();
```

Notice that you do not need to call `forEach()` when you use the query collection `template()` method. This method performs the `forEach()` internally.

Creating External Templates

If you want to use the same template in multiple pages then it makes sense to create an external template. In other words, you can place a template in a separate file than the page that contains the template.

Here's how you can declare a `Template` control so that it references an external template file. Notice that the following template includes a `href` option that points to a file named `productTemplate.html`.

```
<!-- Template -->
<div id="tmplProduct"
    data-win-control="WinJS.Binding.Template"
    data-win-options="{
        href: 'productTemplate.html'
    }">
</div>
```

The productTemplate.html contains the product template and it looks like this:

```
<div class="product">
    Name: <span data-win-bind="innerText:name"></span>
    <br />
    Price: <span data-win-bind="innerText:price"></span>
</div>
```

Finally, Listing 3.24 contains the JavaScript code for rendering the external template.

LISTING 3.24   Rendering an External Template

```
(function () {
    "use strict";

    function initialize() {

        var products = [
            { name: "Tesla", price: 300000 },
            { name: "BMW", price: 80000 },
            { name: "Pinto", price: 10000 }
        ];

        // Get the template and template container
        var tmplProduct = document.getElementById("tmplProduct");
        var conProducts = document.getElementById("conProducts");

        // Render each array item using the template
        WinJS.UI.processAll().done(function () {
            products.forEach(function (product) {
                tmplProduct.winControl.render(product, conProducts);
            });
        });
    }

    document.addEventListener("DOMContentLoaded", initialize);

})();
```

You can refer to the very same `productTemplate.html` from several `Template` controls located in different pages.

Summary

This chapter was all about displaying JavaScript objects in a page. In the first section, you learned about observables. In particular, you learned how observables enable you to detect automatically when a property of a JavaScript object changes. We also discussed how you can use the `WinJS.Binding.List` object to detect different types of changes in an array of items.

Next, you learned how to take advantage of declarative data binding with both normal JavaScript objects and observable JavaScript objects to display the values of JavaScript properties in a page.

Finally, I discussed how you can use WinJS templates to format and display an array of objects. You learned how to create templates both imperatively and declaratively.

CHAPTER 4

Using WinJS Controls

My goal in this chapter is to provide you with an over-view of the controls included in the WinJS library. I start by explaining how you can add controls to your pages. You learn how to create WinJS controls both declaratively and imperatively and set control options.

The bulk of this chapter is devoted to descriptions and samples of how you can use the basic controls included in the WinJS library. In this chapter, I focus on describing how you can use the following controls:

▶ **Tooltip**—Used to display a pop-up tooltip

▶ **ToggleSwitch**—Used to display a toggle switch that can be used in the same scenarios as a checkbox

▶ **Rating**—Used to display and enter a user rating

▶ **DatePicker**—Used to enter a date

▶ **TimePicker**—Used to enter a time

▶ **Hub**—Used to display multiple sections of content

▶ **WebView**—Used to display an external web page in your app

Introduction to WinJS Controls

You declare a WinJS control in a page by using the `data-win-control` attribute. For example, you can declare the WinJS `DatePicker` control by adding the following DIV element to a page:

```
<div id="dateBirthday"
    data-win-control="WinJS.UI.DatePicker"></div>
```

The DIV element isn't really doing anything. It is just acting as a placeholder for the control. It is a "host" for the `DatePicker` control. The `data-win-control` attribute is used to indicate the type of control that will be associated with the element.

A WinJS control does not actually become a control until you call the `WinJS.UI.processAll()` method. This method parses an HTML document, identifies any and all elements that include a `data-win-control` attribute, and generates a control for those elements.

There is one other important requirement for using WinJS controls: You must include references to the right JavaScript and Cascading Style Sheet files. In order to use any of the controls, you must add the following three references to the top of your HTML page:

```
<link href="//Microsoft.WinJS.2.0/css/ui-dark.css" rel="stylesheet" />
<script src="//Microsoft.WinJS.2.0/js/base.js"></script>
<script src="//Microsoft.WinJS.2.0/js/ui.js"></script>
```

The first reference is a reference to a Cascading Style Sheet file named ui-dark.css. The WinJS library includes two style sheets: ui-dark.css and ui-light.css. If you substitute the ui-light.css reference for the ui-dark.css reference, then you can use a light theme for all of your controls.

Figure 4.1 illustrates the appearance of the `DatePicker` control when the dark theme is used, and Figure 4.2 illustrates the appearance of the `DatePicker` control when the light theme is used.

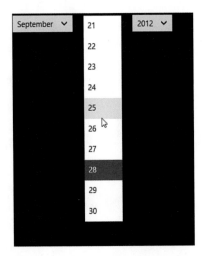

FIGURE 4.1   Using the dark theme

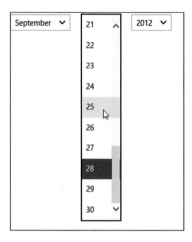

FIGURE 4.2   Using the light theme

The next two references are for the base.js and ui.js JavaScript files. You need references to both of these JavaScript libraries to use the WinJS controls.

All of the JavaScript source code for the WinJS controls is included in the ui.js file. For example, this file contains the source code for the `DatePicker` and `Hub` controls.

You can view the source of all three of these files by expanding the References folder in the Visual Studio Solution Explorer window (see Figure 4.3). If you double-click any of the files then you can view the contents of the files.

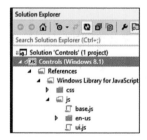

FIGURE 4.3   Viewing the WinJS files in the Solution Explorer window

Creating a WinJS Control Declaratively

There are two ways that you can create a WinJS control: declaratively and imperatively. The HTML page in Listing 4.1 illustrates how you can create a WinJS control declaratively.

LISTING 4.1   Declaring a WinJS Control (declarative\declarative.html)

```
<!DOCTYPE html>
<html>
<head>
    <meta charset="utf-8" />
    <title>Chapter04</title>

    <!-- WinJS references -->
    <link href="//Microsoft.WinJS.2.0/css/ui-dark.css" rel="stylesheet" />
    <script src="//Microsoft.WinJS.2.0/js/base.js"></script>
    <script src="//Microsoft.WinJS.2.0/js/ui.js"></script>

    <!-- Chapter04 references -->
    <link href="/css/default.css" rel="stylesheet" />
    <script src="declarative.js"></script>
</head>
<body>

    <div id="dateBirthday"
        data-win-control="WinJS.UI.DatePicker"></div>

</body>
</html>
```

In Listing 4.1, a DatePicker control is declared in the body of the HTML page. Notice that the page includes references to the ui-dark.css, base.js, and ui.js files: All of the file references required to use WinJS control.

The page also includes a reference to a file named declarative.js. This file contains the custom JavaScript code associated with the page. The contents of the declarative.js file are contained in Listing 4.2.

LISTING 4.2   Declaring a WinJS Control (declarative\declarative.js)

```
(function () {
    "use strict";

    function initialize() {
        WinJS.UI.processAll();
    }

    document.addEventListener("DOMContentLoaded", initialize);
})();
```

Listing 4.2 includes a call to the `WinJS.UI.processAll()` method. If you forget to call this method (which is very easy to do) then the controls declared in the HTML page are never converted into controls.

Notice that the call to `WinJS.UI.processAll()` happens within an `initialize()` method, which is not called until the `DOMContentLoaded` event is raised. The `DOMContentLoaded` event happens after an HTML document is loaded. You must wait until after the document is loaded before calling `WinJS.UI.processAll()` or there won't be anything yet to process.

Creating Controls Imperatively

In the previous section, I created an instance of the `DatePicker` control declaratively. I declared the control in the HTML markup of the page.

As an alternative to creating a WinJS control declaratively, you can also create a control imperatively. In other words, you can create the control entirely in your JavaScript code.

Consider the page in Listing 4.3. It contains a DIV element with an id of `dateBirthday`. This DIV element does not have a `data-win-control` attribute.

LISTING 4.3 Creating a WinJS Control Imperatively (controlImperative\controlImperative.html)

```
<!DOCTYPE html>
<html>
<head>
    <meta charset="utf-8" />
    <title>Chapter04</title>

    <!-- WinJS references -->
    <link href="//Microsoft.WinJS.2.0/css/ui-dark.css" rel="stylesheet" />
    <script src="//Microsoft.WinJS.2.0/js/base.js"></script>
    <script src="//Microsoft.WinJS.2.0/js/ui.js"></script>

    <!-- Chapter04 references -->
    <link href="/css/default.css" rel="stylesheet" />
    <script src="controlImperative.js"></script>
</head>
<body>

    <div id="dateBirthday"></div>

</body>
</html>
```

The code in Listing 4.4 creates a `DatePicker` control and associates the new control with the `dateBirthday` DIV element.

LISTING 4.4   Creating a WinJS Control Imperatively (controlImperative\controlImperative.js)

```
(function () {
    "use strict";

    function initialize() {
        var dateBirthday = document.getElementById("dateBirthday");
        var ctlBirthday = new WinJS.UI.DatePicker(dateBirthday);
    }

    document.addEventListener("DOMContentLoaded", initialize);
})();
```

The code in Listing 4.4 creates a new instance of the JavaScript `WinJS.UI.DatePicker()` class. The `DatePicker` class is created by passing the `dateBirthday` DIV element to the constructor for the `DatePicker` class. Notice that you do not need to call `WinJS.UI.processAll()` because you do not need to parse the document when creating WinJS controls imperatively.

The code in Listing 4.4 articulates the fact that a WinJS control is really just a JavaScript class. You can create this class declaratively with the `data-win-control` attribute or imperatively by instantiating the class in code. But, at the end of the day, it is a JavaScript class either way.

In this book, I take the declarative approach instead of the imperative approach to creating controls. There is nothing wrong with either approach. However, because the Microsoft samples favor the declarative approach, I will follow Microsoft's lead and use the declarative approach also.

Setting Control Options

Most controls support options. For example, when creating a `TimePicker` control, you want to be able to set the default time or the clock format (24-hour or 12-hour).

You can specify control options declaratively by taking advantage of the `data-win-options` attribute. For example, the following HTML fragment demonstrates how you can set the current time displayed by the `TimePicker` control to the time 3:04pm and the clock format to a 24-hour clock:

```
<div id="timeLunch"
    data-win-control="WinJS.UI.TimePicker"
    data-win-options="{
        current: '3:04pm',
        clock: '24HourClock'
    }"></div>
```

The options object passed to a control is a JavaScript object—hence the curly braces around the property names and value.

If you prefer, you can set these options imperatively. Here's how you can create an instance of the `TimePicker` control in code and set its current and clock options:

```
(function () {
    "use strict";

    function initialize() {
        var divLunch = document.getElementById("timeLunch");
        var ctrlLunch = new WinJS.UI.TimePicker(timeLunch, {
            current: '3:04pm',
            clock: '24HourClock'
        });
    }

    document.addEventListener("DOMContentLoaded", initialize);
})();
```

The options are passed to the `TimePicker` constructor as the second parameter. The current time and clock options are set.

> **NOTE**
>
> You can also take advantage of the `WinJS.UI.setOptions()` method to set control options imperatively. You can call the `setOptions()` method after the control is constructed.

Retrieving Controls from an HTML Document

When a control gets created, it is always associated with a DOM element. The DOM element is the "host" for the control.

You can retrieve a control from its associated DOM element by using the `winControl` property. Every DOM element that has an associated control has a `winControl` property that represents the control.

For example, if you declare a `DatePicker` control like this:

```
<div id="dateBirthday"
    data-win-control="WinJS.UI.DatePicker"></div>
```

Then you can retrieve the `DatePicker` control in your JavaScript code like this:

```
(function () {
    "use strict";

    function initialize() {
        WinJS.UI.processAll().done(function () {
            var ctlBirthday = document.getElementById("dateBirthday").winControl;
```

```
        ctlBirthday.current = "12/25/1966";
    });
}

document.addEventListener("DOMContentLoaded", initialize);
})();
```

When you call `document.getElementById()`, you retrieve a DOM element and not a control. However, after retrieving a DOM element with `document.getElementById()`, you can use the `winControl` property to get the associated WinJS control.

The `WinJS.UI.processAll()` method returns a promise. You should wait until all the controls created declaratively in a document are parsed and created before attempting to interact with the controls. In the preceding code, the `DatePicker` is retrieved when the promise returned by the `processAll()` method is done.

Using the `Tooltip` Control

You can use the WinJS `Tooltip` control to display a customizable tooltip over any HTML element (see Figure 4.4). When you hover over the element, the tooltip appears for a certain number of seconds. When you move your cursor away from the element, the tooltip disappears.

FIGURE 4.4   Displaying a tooltip with the `Tooltip` control (tooltip\tooltip.html)

You declare the `Tooltip` control in a page like this:

```
<button id="btnDelete"
    data-win-control="WinJS.UI.Tooltip"
    data-win-options="{
        innerHTML: 'Deletes the <b>record</b> from the database'
    }">Delete</button>
```

> **WARNING**
>
> Remember to call the `WinJS.UI.processAll()` method or the `Tooltip` control, just like any other WinJS control, won't appear.

Notice that you use the `innerHTML` option to set the text of the tooltip and this text can contain HTML such as B and IMG tags.

Using the `contentElement` **Property**

If you have a lot of HTML content to display (see Figure 4.5) then you can place the tooltip HTML content in a separate element like this:

```
<button id="btnDelete"
    data-win-control="WinJS.UI.Tooltip"
    data-win-options="{
        contentElement: select('#btnDeleteTooltip')
    }">Delete</button>

<div style="display:none">
    <div id="btnDeleteTooltip">
        Deletes the <b>record</b> from the database. Do you
        <i>really, really</i> want to do this? The record will
        be gone forever and you might weep.
    </div>
</div>
```

You use the `contentElement` option to specify a separate element that contains the HTML content for the tooltip. In the code, the content for the tooltip is contained in a DIV element with the ID `btnDeleteTooltip`.

Notice that the `btnDeleteTooltip` is surrounded by a DIV element that has a `style="display:none"` attribute. This outer DIV element is used to prevent the contents of the `btnDeleteTooltip` from being displayed in the page. You want the contents of the `contentElement` to appear only within the tooltip.

FIGURE 4.5   Showing a long tooltip

Styling a `Tooltip`

Because HTML already includes a tooltip attribute, you might be wondering why Microsoft introduced a WinJS `Tooltip` control. It is all about customization. Using the WinJS `Tooltip` control, you can create tooltips that match the style of your Windows Store app.

You can customize the appearance of the `Tooltip` control by modifying the `win-tooltip` Cascading Style Sheet class. For example, Figure 4.6 illustrates the appearance of the Tooltip control when you define the following `win-tooltip` style:

```
.win-tooltip {
    background-color: #ffd800;
    border: solid 2px red;
    border-radius: 15px;
}
```

FIGURE 4.6   Customizing the appearance of the tooltip

Using the `ToggleSwitch` Control

You can use the WinJS `ToggleSwitch` control in the same situations as you would use
a standard HTML checkbox (`<input type="checkbox">`). The difference between a
`ToggleSwitch` control and a checkbox control is a `ToggleSwitch` is more finger friendly:
You can swipe your finger across the `ToggleSwitch` to check or uncheck the `ToggleSwitch`
(see Figure 4.7 and Figure 4.8).

FIGURE 4.7   A `ToggleSwitch` that is checked

FIGURE 4.8   A `ToggleSwitch` that is unchecked

Here's how you can declare a `ToggleSwitch` control in a page:

```
<div
    data-win-control="WinJS.UI.ToggleSwitch"
    data-win-options="{
        title: 'Flux Capacitor State',
        labelOff: 'Disabled',
        labelOn: 'Enabled',
        checked: true
    }"></div>
```

Determining the State of a `ToggleSwitch`

You can detect whether a `ToggleSwitch` control is in a checked or unchecked state by reading the `ToggleSwitch` control's checked property. For example, the page in Listing 4.5 contains a `ToggleSwitch` control and a DIV element that displays different messages depending on the state of the `ToggleSwitch` control (see Figure 4.9).

FIGURE 4.9   Displaying a message depending on the state of a `ToggleSwitch`

LISTING 4.5   Using a `ToggleSwitch` Control (toggleSwitchChecked\toggleSwitchChecked.html)

```
<div id="togFlux"
    data-win-control="WinJS.UI.ToggleSwitch"
    data-win-options="{
        title: 'Flux Capacitor State',
        labelOff: 'Disabled',
        labelOn: 'Enabled',
        checked: true
    }"></div>

<div id="divMessage"></div>
```

The code in Listing 4.6 wires up a change event handler for the `ToggleSwitch` control. When you change the state of the `ToggleSwitch` control, the change event handler is invoked. This handler displays one of two messages in a DIV element.

LISTING 4.6   Using a `ToggleSwitch` Control (toggleSwitchChecked\toggleSwitchChecked.js)

```
(function () {
    "use strict";

    function initialize() {
        WinJS.UI.processAll().done(function () {

            var togFlux = document.getElementById("togFlux").winControl;
            var divMessage = document.getElementById("divMessage");

            togFlux.addEventListener("change", function (evt) {
                if (togFlux.checked) {
                    divMessage.innerHTML = "Flux Capacitor activated!";
                } else {
```

```
                     divMessage.innerHTML = "Flux Capacitor de-activated.";
                };
            })

        });
    }

    document.addEventListener("DOMContentLoaded", initialize);
})();
```

Remember to call `processAll()` before attempting to retrieve the `ToggleSwitch` control and modifying its properties (including wiring up an event handler). The `ToggleSwitch` control must exist before you can do anything with it.

Using the `Rating` Control

You can use the WinJS `Rating` control to collect and display user ratings. By default, the `Rating` control enables you to select between 1 and 5 stars to rate something (see Figure 4.10). You can change the rating by using your mouse, fingers, or by moving focus to the control and using your up/down or left/right arrow buttons.

FIGURE 4.10   Collecting a user rating

Here's how you declare a `Rating` control:

```
<div id="ratingProduct"
    data-win-control="WinJS.UI.Rating"></div>
```

There are a couple of options that you can set when declaring a `Rating` control: you can set the default rating (`averageRating`) and you can set whether a user is allowed to clear a rating (the default value is true).

```
<div id="ratingProduct"
    data-win-control="WinJS.UI.Rating"
    data-win-options="{
        averageRating:3,
        enableClear:false
    }"></div>
```

You clear a rating by swiping from right to left across the rating control. This results in no stars being selected.

> **WARNING**
>
> Remember to call `WinJS.UI.processAll()` or the `Rating` control will never become a `Rating` control.

Customizing the Ratings

You can control the number of ratings that are displayed and the tooltip displayed for each rating by setting the `maxRating` and `tooltipStrings` properties. For example, the following `Rating` control only displays three stars and the stars have the tooltips `bad`, `okay`, and `great!` (see Figure 4.11).

```
<div id="ratingProduct"
    data-win-control="WinJS.UI.Rating"
    data-win-options="{
        averageRating:2,
        maxRating:3,
        tooltipStrings: ['bad', 'okay', 'great!']
    }"></div>
```

FIGURE 4.11   Customizing `Rating` control ratings

Notice that the `tooltipStrings` property accepts a JavaScript array. Each item in the array corresponds to a star.

Submitting a Rating

The `Rating` control raises three events: preview, cancel, and change. The preview event is raised when you hover over a star. The cancel event is raised when you don't select a star after hovering over it. Finally, if you click a star, the change event is raised.

The page in Listing 4.7 contains a rating control and a DIV element. When you change the product rating, or even when you are considering changing the rating for the product, the message displayed in the DIV element is updated.

LISTING 4.7   Handling `Rating` Control Events (ratingSubmit\ratingSubmit.html)

```
<h1>Rate our Store!</h1>

<div id="ratingStore"
    data-win-control="WinJS.UI.Rating"
    data-win-options="{
        maxRating: 3
```

```
        }"></div>

<div id="divMessage"></div>
```

The code in Listing 4.8 contains event handlers for the `Rating` control's `previewchange`, `cancel`, and `change` events.

LISTING 4.8   Handling `Rating` Control Events (ratingSubmit\ratingSubmit.js)

```
(function () {
    "use strict";

    function initialize() {

        WinJS.UI.processAll().done(function () {
            var ratingStore = document.getElementById("ratingStore").winControl;
            var divMessage = document.getElementById("divMessage");

            ratingStore.addEventListener("previewchange", function (evt) {
                var tentativeRating = evt.detail.tentativeRating;

                switch (tentativeRating) {
                    case 1: divMessage.innerHTML = "Don't do it! That's just mean!";
                        break;
                    case 2: divMessage.innerHTML = "Okay, you sure? We'll try
harder!";
                        break;
                    case 3: divMessage.innerHTML = "Thanks!";
                        break;
                }
            });

            ratingStore.addEventListener("cancel", function (evt) {
                divMessage.innerHTML = "";
            });

            ratingStore.addEventListener("change", function (evt) {
                var userRating = ratingStore.userRating;

                switch (userRating) {
                    case 1: divMessage.innerHTML = "You gave us the worst rating.";
                        break;
                    case 2: divMessage.innerHTML = "You gave us an okay rating.";
                        break;
                    case 3: divMessage.innerHTML = "You gave us a good rating.";
                        break;
```

```
            }
        });

    });
}

document.addEventListener("DOMContentLoaded", initialize);
})();
```

As you hover your mouse over the rating stars, different messages are displayed by the `previewchange` event handler. (See Figure 4.12.) When you click a star, the change event is raised and the change handler displays a message.

FIGURE 4.12   Handling the `Rating` control's previewchange, cancel, and change events

Using the `DatePicker` Control

The WinJS `DatePicker` control—and, I hope you don't find this shocking—enables you to pick a date. It displays three select lists: month, day, and year (see Figure 4.13).

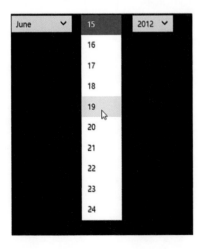

FIGURE 4.13   Displaying a `DatePicker` control

You declare a `DatePicker` like this:

```
<div id="dateBirthday"
    data-win-control="WinJS.UI.DatePicker"></div>
```

> **WARNING**
>
> Don't forget to call `WinJS.UI.processAll()` or your `DatePicker` will never become a `DatePicker`.

By default, the `DatePicker` control has today's date selected. You can assign a particular date to the `DatePicker` control by setting the control's `current` property like this:

```
<div id="dateBirthday"
    data-win-control="WinJS.UI.DatePicker"
    data-win-options="{
        current: '12/25/1966'
    }"></div>
```

The code causes the date '12/25/1966' to be selected as the default date in the `DatePicker` control.

Formatting the Year, Month, and Date

You can assign format strings to the `DatePicker` `yearPattern`, `monthPattern`, and `datePattern` properties to control the appearance of the year, month, and date. A format string can contain any characters. Within the format string, you can use one or more date format specifiers. A date format specifier is a magic string that displays part of a date using a particular format.

The `yearPattern` property accepts the following date format specifiers:

- `{year.full}`
- `{year.full(n)}`
- `{year.abbreviated}`
- `{year.abbreviated(n)}`
- `{era.abbreviated}`
- `{era.abbreviated(n)}`

The `monthPattern` property accepts the following date format specifiers:

- `{month.full}`
- `{month.abbreviated}`

▶ {month.abbreviated *(n)*}

▶ {month.solo.full}

▶ {month.solo.abbreviated}

▶ {month.solo.abbreviated *(n)*}

▶ {month.integer}

▶ {month.integer *(n)*}

Finally the `datePattern` property accepts the following date format specifiers:

▶ {day.integer}

▶ {day.integer *(n)*}

▶ {dayofweek.full}

▶ {dayofweek.abbeviated}

▶ {dayofweek.abbreviated *(n)*}

▶ {dayofweek.solo.full}

▶ {dayofweek.solo.abbeviated}

▶ {dayofweek.solo.abbeviated *(n)*}

Above the *(n)* refers to a number. For example, if you always want to display the day of the month using two digits (possibly including a leading zero) then you would use the date format specifier {day.integer(2)}.

Here's how you can display an integer for the, month, day and year:

```
<div id="dateBirthday"
    data-win-control="WinJS.UI.DatePicker"
    data-win-options="{
        monthPattern: '{month.integer(2)}',
        datePattern: '{day.integer(2)}',
        yearPattern: '{year.abbreviated}'
    }"></div>
```

Because the `datePattern` is set to the value {day.integer(2)}, a leading zero is displayed for single digit dates (see Figure 4.14).

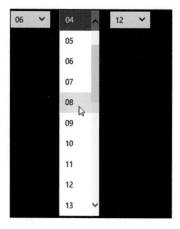

FIGURE 4.14   Formatting the month, day, and year

You can combine multiple format specifiers in a single format string. For example, if you want to display not only the day of the month but the day of the month and the day of the week, and not only the year but the year and the era, then you can declare the `DatePicker` like this:

```
<div id="dateBirthday"
    data-win-control="WinJS.UI.DatePicker"
    data-win-options="{
        monthPattern: '{month.integer(2)}-{month.full}',
        datePattern: '{day.integer(2)} {dayofweek.abbreviated}',
        yearPattern: '{year.full} {era.abbreviated}'
    }"></div>
```

Notice that the format string for the `monthPattern` includes a dash (-). You can throw in any extra characters that you need within a format string (see Figure 4.15).

FIGURE 4.15   Combining date format strings

NOTE

Under the covers, the `DatePicker` leverages the WinRT `Windows.Globalization.DateTimeFormatter` class to format dates. It uses the template strings used by that class.

Displaying Only Years, Months, or Days

Sometimes, you only want to enable a user to pick a month and not pick a year or a date. For example, you are creating a private jet reservation service and customers must reserve a jet for an entire month.

Listing 4.9 demonstrates how you can hide years and days and enable only months to be selected when using the DatePicker control.

LISTING 4.9   Displaying Only Months (datePickerMonthOnly\datePickerMonthOnly.html)

```
<!DOCTYPE html>
<html>
<head>
    <meta charset="utf-8" />
    <title>Chapter04</title>

    <!-- WinJS references -->
    <link href="//Microsoft.WinJS.2.0/css/ui-dark.css" rel="stylesheet" />
    <script src="//Microsoft.WinJS.2.0/js/base.js"></script>
    <script src="//Microsoft.WinJS.2.0/js/ui.js"></script>

    <!-- Chapter04 references -->
    <link href="/css/default.css" rel="stylesheet" />
    <script src="datePickerMonthOnly.js"></script>

    <style type="text/css">
        #dateBirthday .win-datepicker-date {
            display:none;
        }

        #dateBirthday .win-datepicker-year {
            display:none;
        }

    </style>

</head>
<body>

<div id="dateBirthday"
    data-win-control="WinJS.UI.DatePicker"
    data-win-options="{
        monthPattern: '{month.solo.full}'
```

```
    }"></div>


</body>
</html>
```

The page in Listing 4.9 includes two Cascading Style Sheet rules that hide the DatePicker control's date and year select lists (see Figure 4.16).

FIGURE 4.16   Displaying only the month select list

Capturing the Selected Date

The DatePicker control raises the same event when you change the month, day, or year: the change event. You can retrieve the currently selected date by handling this event.

For example, the HTML page in Listing 4.10 contains a DatePicker control and a DIV element that displays the selected date (see Figure 4.17).

FIGURE 4.17   Displaying the DatePicker current date

LISTING 4.10   Capturing the Selected Date (datePickerChange\datePickerChange.html)

```
<label>Birthday:</label>
<div id="dateBirthday"
    data-win-control="WinJS.UI.DatePicker"></div>

<div id="divMessage"></div>
```

The JavaScript file in Listing 4.11 illustrates how you can handle the change event so you can retrieve the selected date.

LISTING 4.11   Capturing the Selected Date (datePickerChange\datePickerChange.js)

```
(function () {
    "use strict";
```

```
    function initialize() {
        WinJS.UI.processAll().done(function () {
            var dateBirthday = document.getElementById("dateBirthday").winControl;
            var divMessage = document.getElementById("divMessage");

            dateBirthday.addEventListener("change", function (evt) {
                divMessage.innerHTML = "Your birthday is on "
                    + dateBirthday.current.toDateString();
            });

        });
    }


    document.addEventListener("DOMContentLoaded", initialize);
})();
```

Using the `TimePicker` Control

The WinJS `TimePicker` control enables you to select a time. (See Figure 4.18.) By default, the `TimePicker` displays three select lists that enable you to select the hour, minute, and period (AM/PM).

FIGURE 4.18   Using the `TimePicker` control

You declare a `TimePicker` control like this:

```
<div id="timeLunch"
    data-win-control="WinJS.UI.TimePicker"></div>
```

WARNING

Don't forget to call `WinJS.UI.processAll()` or the declaration of the `TimePicker` control will never get parsed and turned into a `TimePicker` control.

If you prefer military time (a 24-hour clock) then you can modify the `TimePicker`'s `clock` property like this:

```
<div id="timeLunch"
    data-win-control="WinJS.UI.TimePicker"
    data-win-options="{
```

```
    clock: '24HourClock'
}"></div>
```

Finally, if you want to display minutes in 15-minute increments (see Figure 4.19) instead of the default 1-minute increment then you can set the `minuteIncrement` property like this:

```
<div id="timeLunch"
    data-win-control="WinJS.UI.TimePicker"
    data-win-options="{
        minuteIncrement: 15
    }"></div>
```

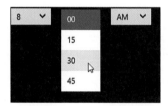

FIGURE 4.19   Changing the `TimePicker` control's minute increment

> **NOTE**
>
> If you have changed your computer's regional settings to display a 24-hour clock instead of a 12-hour clock then the `TimePicker` will default to displaying a 24-hour clock.

Getting and Setting the Current Time

By default, the `TimePicker` control displays the current time. You use the `current` property to get or set the time displayed by the `TimePicker` control.

For example, the page in Listing 4.12 contains a `TimePicker` control and a DIV element that displays a message (see Figure 4.20). The `TimePicker` control is declared so that it displays the time 12:00pm by default.

FIGURE 4.20   Displaying lunch time with the `TimePicker` control

LISTING 4.12   Setting the Current Time with the `TimePicker` Control
(timePickerSet\timePickerSet.html)

```
<label>Select a Lunch Time:</label>
<div id="timeLunch"
    data-win-control="WinJS.UI.TimePicker"
    data-win-options="{
        current: '12:00pm'
    }"></div>


<div id="divMessage"></div>
```

The JavaScript code in Listing 4.13 illustrates how you can capture a new time selected
with the `TimePicker` control. When a new time is selected, the message displayed by the
DIV element is updated.

LISTING 4.13   Setting the Current Time with the `TimePicker` Control
(timePickerSet\timePickerSet.html)

```
(function () {
    "use strict";

    function initialize() {
        WinJS.UI.processAll().done(function () {
            var timeLunch = document.getElementById("timeLunch").winControl;
            var divMessage = document.getElementById("divMessage");

            timeLunch.addEventListener("change", function (evt) {
                divMessage.innerHTML = "Lunch time is "
                    + timeLunch.current.toTimeString();
            });

        });
    }

    document.addEventListener("DOMContentLoaded", initialize);
})();
```

Because the JavaScript language does not have a separate `Time` data type, the `TimePicker`
control's current property returns both a date and a time. The `current` property represents
the current date and the selected time. In the code in Listing 4.13, the time portion is
extracted with the help of the JavaScript `toTimeString()` method.

Formatting the Hour, Minute, and Period

You can use template strings to format the appearance of the items which appear in the hour, minute, and period select lists. The template string can contain any characters that you want, but there are special format specifiers which you can use when displaying the different portions of a time.

You can use the following format specifiers with the `TimePicker hourPattern` property:

▶ `{hour.integer}`

▶ `{hour.integer` *(n)*`}`

You can use the following format specifiers with the `TimePicker minutePattern` property:

▶ `{minute.integer}`

▶ `{minute.integer` *(n)*`}`

You can use the following format specifiers with the `TimePicker periodPattern` property:

▶ `{period.abbreviated}`

▶ `{period.abbreviated` *(n)*`}`

The *n* refers to a number. For example, if you use `hour.integer(2)` then a leading 0 will appear for single digit hours.

The following declaration of a `TimePicker` control illustrates how you can customize the appearance of the hour, minute, and period select lists (see Figure 4.21).

```
<div id="timeLunch"
    data-win-control="WinJS.UI.TimePicker"
    data-win-options="{
        hourPattern: 'hour: {hour.integer(2)}',
        minutePattern: 'minute: {minute.integer(2)}',
        periodPattern: 'period: {period.abbreviated}'
    }"></div>
```

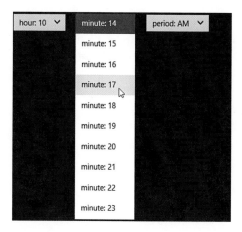

FIGURE 4.21   Formatting the hour, minute, and period

Using the Hub Control

The Hub control is new with WinJS 2.0. The control provides you with a way to organize the content in your app into different sections. Each section can have a custom layout.

For example, the Store app included in Windows 8.1 uses the Hub control (see Figure 4.22). When you open the store and view the home-page, you can see all of the available apps organized into different sections such as New Releases and Top Paid. These different sections were created with the Hub control.

> **NOTE**
>
> The Visual Studio 2013 Hub App project template uses the Hub control.

FIGURE 4.22   The Windows 8.1 Store uses the Hub control

Creating Hubs and Hub Sections

There are actually two Hub controls: the Hub control and the HubSection control. The page in Listing 4.14 illustrates how you can use these controls to organize a page into three sections.

LISTING 4.14   Using Hubs and Hub Sections (hub\hub.html)

```
<section id="hub" data-win-control="WinJS.UI.Hub">
    <div data-win-control="WinJS.UI.HubSection"
        data-win-options="{header:'Section A'}">
        Section A. Section A. Section A. <br />
        Section A. Section A. Section A. <br />
        Section A. Section A. Section A. <br />
    </div>
    <div data-win-control="WinJS.UI.HubSection"
        data-win-options="{header:'Section B'}">
        Section B. Section B. Section B. <br />
        Section B. Section B. Section B. <br />
        Section B. Section B. Section B. <br />
    </div>
    <div data-win-control="WinJS.UI.HubSection"
        data-win-options="{header:'Section C', isHeaderStatic:false}">
        Section C. Section C. Section C. <br />
        Section C. Section C. Section C. <br />
        Section C. Section C. Section C. <br />
    </div>
</section>
```

Listing 4.14 contains a Hub control with three child HubSection controls. The three HubSection controls are assigned the header text Section A, Section B, and Section C. You can see the header text at the top of each section in Figure 4.23.

FIGURE 4.23   A Hub with three sections

Notice that Section A and Section B but not Section C include a symbol indicating that the section headers are clickable. Section C is not clickable because it was declared with isHeaderStatic set to the value false.

Handling Hub Section Navigation

If you want to do something when someone clicks on the header for Section A or Section B then you can handle the Hub control's headerinvoked event. For example, you could handle this event and navigate the user to a new page with more detailed content for the section.

I discuss creating multipage apps and navigation in detail in Chapter 12, "Page Fragments and Navigation." Here, I just want to show you how you can handle the headerinvoked event and determine which section was clicked.

In Listing 4.15, the headerinvoked event is handled and the selected hub section index and header name is written to the Visual Studio JavaScript Console window.

LISTING 4.15   Using Hubs and Hub Sections (hub\hub.html)

```
(function () {
    "use strict";

    function initialize() {
        WinJS.UI.processAll().done(function () {
            var hub = document.getElementById("hub").winControl;
            hub.addEventListener("headerinvoked", function(e) {
                var section = e.detail.section;
                var sectionIndex = e.detail.index;

                // Display clicked section index and name
                console.log("You clicked on section " + section.header
                    + " with index " + sectionIndex);
            });
        });
    }

    document.addEventListener("DOMContentLoaded", initialize);
})();
```

Using the WebView Control

The WebView control (new in WinJS 2.0) enables you to embed a web page hosted on the Internet in your Windows Store app. There are several different scenarios in which it makes sense for you to use this control.

Imagine, for example, that you want to create a hybrid Windows Store app and website. You might want to implement your actual app using WinJS controls but host all of the help documentation for your app as web pages on a public website. In that case, you could use the `WebView` control to display your help documentation from the Internet.

Or, you might want to build an app that interacts with web pages hosted on the Internet. For example, you might want to build a Research app that enables you to take clippings or extract images from existing web pages hosted on the Internet. Again, the `WebView` control enables you to do this.

In this section, I explain how you can embed a `WebView` control in your Windows Store app and handle navigation events. I also demonstrate how you can capture screenshots from the pages hosted in the `WebView`.

> **NOTE**
>
> What about IFrames? There is already a standard technology to host one web page within another web page, so why did Microsoft need to reinvent the wheel?
>
> Unfortunately, IFrames have several limitations. Many websites are designed to bust out of IFrames using scripts or reject IFrames using the `X-Frame-Options` header (for example, Google.com). Also, IFrames do not support the navigation and capture application programming interfaces (APIs) that I discuss in the following sections. In general, you should use the `WebView` control instead of IFrames.

Hosting a Page from the Internet with the `WebView` Control

You declare a `WebView` control in a page in a different way than the other standard WinJS controls. Instead of using a `data-win-control` attribute, you declare a `WebView` control like this:

```
<x-ms-webview src="http://superexpertTraining.com"
    width="800" height="500"></x-ms-webview>
```

This `WebView` control displays the home page from SuperexpertTraining.com in the Windows Store app (see Figure 4.24). Furthermore, the control displays the external content in an 800px by 500px area.

FIGURE 4.24   Displaying a web page with the `WebView` control

Be aware that if the page being loaded into the `WebView` control contains JavaScript then the JavaScript might throw an error. Your app will display a dialog like the one in Figure 4.25.

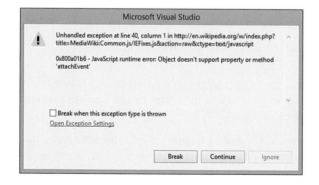

FIGURE 4.25   `WebView` control JavaScript error

Getting these errors is expected and your users won't see these errors when your app is deployed. If you don't want to see these JavaScript errors when running your app from Visual Studio then you can run your app outside the debugger by selecting the Visual Studio menu option Debug, Start Without Debugging.

WARNING

Clicking a link with a target attribute in the `WebView` control will cause the page to open outside of your app and in your default browser. This can be surprising to a user.

WARNING

The `WebView` control uses the Internet Explorer SmartScreen Filter to prevent phishing attacks. If you open a web page that SmartScreen finds suspicious then you get a pop-up warning message. You can test this feature by using the WebView control to open the page at malvertising.info (this page was created by Microsoft to test SmartScreen).

Handling Navigation and Navigation Events

You can use the methods exposed by the `WebView` control to handle navigation. For example, you can use the following three methods to display a web page:

▶ `navigate()`—Displays a remote HTML page represented by a URL

▶ `navigateToString()`—Displays an HTML page from an HTML string

▶ `NavigateToLocalStringUri`—Displays a local HTML page represented by a URL

The `WebView` control also exposes several useful events including

▶ `MSWebViewNavigationStarting`—Raised when a user starts navigating to a new URI

▶ `MSWebViewContentLoading`—Raised when new content is being loaded

▶ `MSWebViewDOMContentLoaded`—Raised when new content is finished loading

▶ `MSWebViewNavigationCompleted`—Raised when navigation is complete

You can use the `MSWebViewNavigationStarting` event to prevent a user from navigating somewhere where you don't want the user to go. For example, you might want to prevent a user from following links away from your website.

The page in Listing 4.16 contains a `WebView` control that displays the Minecraft entry from Wikipedia.org. You can click links in the page to navigate to other pages at Wikipedia.org but you cannot navigate away from Wikipedia.org to another website (see Figure 4.26).

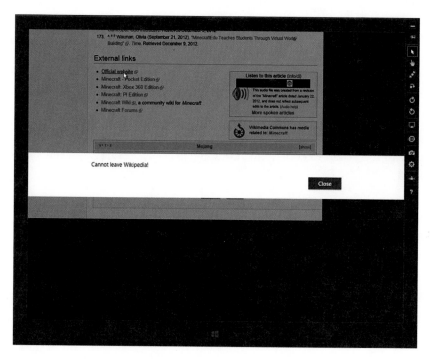

FIGURE 4.26   Preventing `WebView` navigation

LISTING 4.16   Controlling User Navigation (webViewNavigate\webViewNavigate.html)

```
<!DOCTYPE html>
<html>
<head>
    <meta charset="utf-8" />
    <title>Chapter04</title>

    <!-- WinJS references -->
    <link href="//Microsoft.WinJS.2.0/css/ui-dark.css" rel="stylesheet" />
    <script src="//Microsoft.WinJS.2.0/js/base.js"></script>
    <script src="//Microsoft.WinJS.2.0/js/ui.js"></script>

    <!-- Chapter04 references -->
    <link href="/css/default.css" rel="stylesheet" />
    <script src="webViewNavigation.js"></script>
</head>
<body>
```

```
<x-ms-webview id="webView1"
    width="800" height="500"></x-ms-webview>

</body>
</html>
```

The JavaScript code in Listing 4.17 prevents the user from navigating away from Wikipedia.org. An MSNavigationStarting event handler is used to check whether the user is navigating outside of the Wikipedia.org domain. Calling preventDefault() prevents the user from navigating.

LISTING 4.17   Controlling User Navigation (webViewNavigate\webViewNavigate.js)

```
(function () {
    "use strict";

    function initialize() {
        WinJS.UI.processAll().done(function () {

            // Get webview
            var webView1 = document.getElementById("webView1");

            // Navigate to wikipedia
            webView1.navigate("http://wikipedia.org/wiki/minecraft");

            // Display only wikipedia ages
            webView1.addEventListener("MSWebViewNavigationStarting", function (e) {
                var uri = new Windows.Foundation.Uri(e.uri);
                if (uri.domain !== "wikipedia.org") {
                    // prevent navigation
                    e.preventDefault();

                    // show a popup message
                    var md = new Windows.UI.Popups.MessageDialog("Cannot leave
➥Wikipedia!");
                    md.showAsync();
                }
            });

        });
    }

    document.addEventListener("DOMContentLoaded", initialize);
})();
```

Capturing `WebView` **Screenshots**

You can use the `WebView` control to capture images of web pages. For example, Figure 4.27 contains a `WebView` control next to an image. After you navigate to an Internet address and click the Capture! button, the web page displayed in the `WebView` control is captured as an image and displayed.

FIGURE 4.27   Capturing screenshots with the `WebView` control

When you capture a web page, an actual screenshot of the web page is captured including the scroll position of the page and any text entered into any of the form fields.

WARNING

Remember to run the app using Debug, Start Without Debugging or you will get several JavaScript exceptions when loading the remote page into the `WebView` control.

Here's how I created the app depicted in Figure 4.27. First, I created a page that contains a `WebView` control (see Listing 4.18).

LISTING 4.18   Capturing a Web Page (webViewCapture\webViewCapture.html)

```
<!DOCTYPE html>
<html>
<head>
    <meta charset="utf-8" />
    <title>Chapter04</title>

    <!-- WinJS references -->
    <link href="//Microsoft.WinJS.2.0/css/ui-dark.css" rel="stylesheet" />
    <script src="//Microsoft.WinJS.2.0/js/base.js"></script>
    <script src="//Microsoft.WinJS.2.0/js/ui.js"></script>

    <!-- Chapter04 references -->
    <link href="/css/default.css" rel="stylesheet" />
    <script src="webViewCapture.js"></script>
```

```
    <style>
        #inpAddress {
            width: 400px;
        }
    </style>

</head>
<body>
    <div>
        <input id="inpAddress" type="url" value="http://" />
        <button id="btnNavigate">Go!</button>
        <button id="btnCapture">Capture!</button>
    </div>

    <x-ms-webview id="webView1"
        width="800" height="500"></x-ms-webview>

    <img id="imgCapture" src="/images/placeholder.png" />

</body>
</html>
```

Next, I called the `WebView` control's `capturePreviewToBlobAsync()` method. This method returns a `captureOperation` that you can use to handle the capture. Notice that you must call the `start()` method on the `captureOperation` to actually perform the capture.

In Listing 4.19, I am displaying the captured web page with an HTML IMG element. Alternatively, I could save the captured image to the file system or do anything else that I can imagine with the image.

LISTING 4.19   Capturing a Web Page (webViewCapture\webViewCapture.js)

```
(function () {
    "use strict";

    function initialize() {
        WinJS.UI.processAll().done(function () {

            // Get elements
            var webView1 = document.getElementById("webView1");
            var imgCapture = document.getElementById("imgCapture");
            var inpAddress = document.getElementById("inpAddress");
            var btnNavigate = document.getElementById("btnNavigate");
            var btnCapture = document.getElementById("btnCapture");
```

```
                // Handle navigate
                btnNavigate.addEventListener("click", function () {
                    webView1.navigate(inpAddress.value);
                });

                // Handle capture
                btnCapture.addEventListener("click", function () {
                    var captureOperation = webView1.capturePreviewToBlobAsync();
                    captureOperation.oncomplete = function (e) {
                        // Get the capture
                        var image = e.target.result;

                        // Use HTML5 File API to create object URL to refer to the photo
➥file
                        var imageUrl = URL.createObjectURL(image);

                        // Show photo in IMG element
                        imgCapture.src = imageUrl;
                    };
                    captureOperation.start();
                });

            });
        }

    document.addEventListener("DOMContentLoaded", initialize);
})();
```

Summary

This chapter focused on the core controls contained in the WinJS library. I discussed the features of the `Tooltip`, `ToggleSwitch`, `Rating`, `DatePicker`, `TimePicker`, `Hub`, and `WebView` controls.

You learned how to create these controls both declaratively and imperatively. You also were provided with sample code that demonstrated how you can use these controls in different scenarios.

But there are more controls to discuss! More fun to be had! In latter chapters, I introduce you to additional WinJS controls such as the menu controls and the `ListView` control. First, however, we need to talk about forms.

CHAPTER 5

Creating Forms

I assume that anyone who is reading this book is already familiar with the basics of HTML, but I don't assume that you are familiar with the latest features of HTML5. In particular, I don't assume that you are familiar with the changes to HTML forms included in the HTML5 standard.

In the first section of this chapter, I describe how you can take advantage of HTML5 form validation in a Windows Store app. You learn how to use validation attributes—such as the `required` and `pattern` attribute—to enforce validation constraints.

Next, I discuss the new features of input elements included in HTML5. You learn how the new HTML5 input types enable you to control the type of data entered into a form field.

Finally, I talk about two other important new features of HTML5. I explain how you can take advantage of the `contenteditable` attribute to create input elements that accept rich text such as bold and italic text. I also discuss the new HTML5 progress element.

Using HTML5 Form Validation

In a Windows Store app, the easiest way to validate HTML form fields is to take advantage of the HTML5 validation attributes. Imagine, for example, that you want to create an HTML form that includes a form field for entering a Social Security number. In that case, you can use the `required` attribute to ensure that a value has been entered and you can use the `pattern` attribute to ensure that the value matches the pattern for a valid Social Security number.

Using the `required` Attribute

The following HTML form illustrates how you can use the `required` attribute:

```
<form>
    <div>
        <label>
            Social Security Number:
            <input id="ssn" required />
        </label>
    </div>
    <div>
        <input type="submit" />
    </div>
</form>
```

If you submit the form, and you do not enter a value for the `ssn` field, then you get the error message depicted in Figure 5.1. The input field has a red border surrounding it and a callout message is displayed.

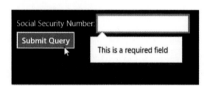

FIGURE 5.1   Using the `required` validation attribute

Using the `pattern` Attribute

You use the `pattern` attribute to validate the value entered into an input field against a regular expression pattern. For example, the following HTML form validates the Social Security number against a regular expression:

```
<form>
    <div>
        <label>
            Social Security Number:
            <input id="ssn"
                required
                pattern="^\d{3}-\d{2}-\d{4}$"
                title="###-##-####" />
        </label>
    </div>
    <div>
```

```
        <input type="submit" />
    </div>
</form>
```

Notice that the `ssn` field has both a `required` and `pattern` attribute. The `pattern` attribute is not triggered unless you enter a value.

Notice, furthermore, that the `ssn` field includes a `title` attribute. The `title` attribute contains the format displayed by the `pattern` error message.

If you enter an invalid Social Security number then you get the validation error message displayed in Figure 5.2.

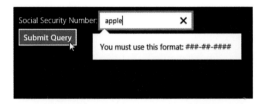

FIGURE 5.2   Using the `pattern` validation attribute

NOTE

My favorite site for finding regular expressions is located at http://regexlib.com.

Performing Custom Validation

If you need to add custom validation rules to a form element then you can take advantage of the JavaScript `setCustomValidity()` method. You can use this method to associate a custom validation error message with a form field.

Imagine, for example, that you have a complex set of rules for validating a username in a user registration form. For example, you want to ensure that the username is a certain length, unique in the database, and does not contain special characters. This is a good candidate for a custom validation.

The following HTML form includes a `userName` field:

```
<form>
    <div>
        <label>
            User Name:
            <input id="userName" required />
        </label>
    </div>
    <div>
```

```
        <input type="submit" />
    </div>
</form>
```

The following JavaScript code demonstrates how you can display a validation error message when the user name is too short:

```
var userName = document.getElementById("userName");

userName.addEventListener("input", function (evt) {
    // User name must be more than 3 characters
    if (userName.value.length < 4) {
        userName.setCustomValidity("User name too short!");
    } else {
        userName.setCustomValidity("");
    }
});
```

In the preceding code, an event listener for the input event is created. When the value of the input element is changed then the length of the value is checked. If the username is less than four characters then the setCustomValidity() method is used to invalidate the input element. Otherwise, the setCustomValidity() method is called with an empty string to clear any previous validation errors associated with the username element.

> **NOTE**
>
> The input event is raised as soon as the contents of an input element are changed. The input event differs from the change event because the change event is not raised until after the input element loses focus.

You must submit the form to see the validation error message. After you submit the form, you see the error in Figure 5.3.

FIGURE 5.3   Using custom validation

Customizing the Validation Error Style

By default, invalid HTML fields in a form appear with a red border. For example, if you submit an HTML form without entering a value in a required field then the field is displayed with a red border.

You can customize the appearance of form fields in different states of validity by using the following Cascading Style Sheet pseudo classes:

▶ `:valid`—Applies when an input element is valid

▶ `:invalid`—Applies when an input element is invalid

▶ `:required`—Applies when an input element is required (has the required attribute)

▶ `:optional`—Applies when an input element is not required (does not have the required attribute)

Imagine that you have created the following user registration form:

```
<form>
    <div>
        <label>
            First Name:
            <input id="firstName" required />
        </label>
    </div>
    <div>
        <label>
            Last Name:
            <input id="lastName" required />
        </label>
    </div>
    <div>
        <label>
            Company:
            <input id="company" />
        </label>
    </div>
    <div>
        <input type="submit" />
    </div>
</form>
```

The form contains required fields for the user first and last names. It also contains an optional field for the user company.

You can use the following style rules to control how the input elements are styled:

```
:valid {
    background-color: green;
}

:invalid {
```

```
    background-color: yellow;
}

:optional {
    border: 4px solid green;
}

:required {
    border: 4px solid red;
}
```

These rules cause valid fields to appear with a green background color and invalid fields to appear with a yellow background color. Optional fields appear with a green border and required fields appear with a red border.

Resetting a Form

After you successfully submit a form, it is a good idea to reset it so you can use the form again. For example, your app might include a form for adding new movies. Each time you add a new movie, you want the form to reset to its default state.

If you are using the validation attributes then you cannot reset a form simply by assigning empty strings to the form fields. If you assign an empty string to a required field then the field will be in an invalid state.

Instead, you should reset a form by calling the JavaScript reset() method. The reset() method throws a form back into its default state.

For example, here's a simple form for entering a movie title:

```
<form id="frmAdd">
    <div>
        <label>
            Title:
            <input id="inpTitle" required />
        </label>
    </div>
    <div>
        <input type="submit" />
    </div>
</form>
```

Here's the JavaScript code that you can use for handling the form submit event:

```
(function () {
    "use strict";

    function initialize() {
```

```
        var frmAdd = document.getElementById("frmAdd");
        var inpTitle = document.getElementById("inpTitle");

        frmAdd.addEventListener("submit", function (evt) {
            evt.preventDefault();
            var newMovie = {
                title: document.getElementById("inpTitle").value
            };
            addMovieToDb(newMovie).done(function () {
                frmAdd.reset();
            });
        });

        function addMovieToDb(newMovie) {
            return new WinJS.Promise(function (complete) {
                // Add to database
                complete();
            });
        }
    }

    document.addEventListener("DOMContentLoaded", initialize);
})();
```

The preceding code adds the movie title to an IndexedDB database and then resets the form so the form returns to its default state. The `reset()` method is used to return the form to its default state.

> **WARNING**
>
> If you neglect to call `evt.preventDefault()` in your form submit handler then the page will be submitted and reloaded. You don't want to do this. In a Windows Store App, you want to avoid ever submitting back to the server.

Using HTML5 Input Elements

If you have worked with HTML then you are most likely very familiar with the standard input element types such as `<input type="text" />` and `<input type="checkbox" />`. Different input types have different appearances and accept different types of data.

The HTML5 recommendation adds several new input types:

▶ search

▶ tel

▶ url

- ▶ email
- ▶ datetime
- ▶ date
- ▶ month
- ▶ week
- ▶ time
- ▶ datetime-local
- ▶ number
- ▶ range
- ▶ color

You can take advantage of these new input types to enforce validation rules. For example, an `<input type="number" />` element will accept only numerals and not other types of characters. And an `<input type="url" />` will accept only valid (absolute) URLs.

You also can take advantage of these new input types to control the user interface for entering a value into a field. For example, when using the touch keyboard, an `<input type="email" />` field displays a specialized keyboard for entering email addresses, which includes specialized keys such as @ and .com (see Figure 5.4).

FIGURE 5.4   Specialized email touch keyboard

In this section, you learn how to take advantage of the new features of HTML5 input elements.

NOTE

As I write this, not all features of HTML5 forms are supported by Windows Store apps. In particular, the date, time, and color types are not supported.

Labeling Form Fields

First off, you need to know the proper way to label HTML form fields. Providing proper labels is important for making your app accessible to users with disabilities—so adding labels is the right thing to do.

There are two ways that you can use a label element to label a form element. If you want the label to appear right next to the form element then you can include the form element inside the label's opening and closing tags like this:

```
<label>
  Title:
  <input id="inpTitle" required />
</label>
```

If the label is separated from the element being labeled in the page then you can associate the label and the form element explicitly by using the label's `for` attribute like this.

```
<label for="inpTitle">
  Title:
</label>
... Other Content ...
<input id="inpTitle" required />
```

You should always label all of your form elements to make your apps more accessible to people with disabilities (screen readers need these labels). However, if you need to provide additional hints about the appropriate input value for a form element then you can take advantage of the new HTML5 `placeholder` attribute. When used in a Windows Store app, the `placeholder` attribute creates a watermark.

For example, the following HTML form contains a field for entering a product activation code:

```
<label>
    Activation Code:
    <input id="activationCode"
        size="10"
        placeholder="##-####-##" />
</label>
```

The form includes a placeholder attribute which displays the text ##-####-## (see Figure 5.5). As soon as you start typing a value into the field, the placeholder text disappears.

FIGURE 5.5   Using the `placeholder` attribute

NOTE

You can use the Cascading Style Sheet `:-ms-input-placeholder` pseudo class to style the text displayed by a `placeholder` attribute.

Entering a Number

If you want to prevent a user from entering anything except a number into an input field then you should use the `type="number"` attribute like this:

```
<label>
    Favorite Number:
    <input id="inpFavNumber"
        type="number"
        placeholder="###" />
</label>
```

When the input type has the value number, and you enter anything that is not a number, then the value disappears as soon as the field loses focus. This can be confusing to the user. So it is a good idea to include a placeholder attribute or instruction text that indicates that the field only accepts numbers (no dollar signs, just numbers).

You can use the `min` and `max` attributes to specify a minimum and maximum value for the input field like this:

```
<label>
    Quantity:
    <input id="inpQuantity"
        type="number"
        placeholder="###"
        min="1"
        max="10" />
</label>
```

If you enter a number that does not fall into the specified range then a validation error message is displayed (see Figure 5.6).

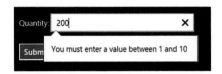

FIGURE 5.6   A number out of range

By default, you can only enter an integer value into an `<input type="number" />` field. If you want to enter a noninteger value, such as 1.5, then you need to modify the `step` attribute like this:

```
<input id="inpFavNumber"
    type="number"
    step="0.5"
    placeholder="###" />
```

The `step` attribute determines the allowable increment between numbers.

When you use a number field in a Windows Store app, and you are using the touch keyboard, you get a special keyboard for entering numbers automatically (see Figure 5.7).

FIGURE 5.7   Entering a number with the touch keyboard

Entering a Value from a Range of Values

If you want to display a slider, then you can create an `<input type="range" />` element. For example, the following HTML form displays a slider that enables you to select a quantity of candy to buy:

```
<label>
    Quantity of Candy:
    <input id="quantity"
        type="range"
        min="10"
        max="100"
        step="5"
        value="30"/>
</label>
```

The slider displays a range of values between 10 and 100 with 5-unit increments. The default value is set to 30 (see Figure 5.8).

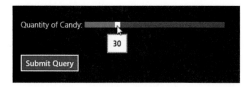

FIGURE 5.8   Displaying a slider

Entering Email Addresses, URLs, Telephone Numbers, and Search Terms

You can use the input types email, url, tel, and search to enable users to enter email addresses, URLs, telephone numbers, and search terms.

If you use `<input type="email" />`, and you are using the touch keyboard, then you get the specialized keyboard which includes @ and .com keys in Figure 5.9.

FIGURE 5.9   Touch keyboard for email

Using `<input type="email" />` also gives you automatic validation. You must enter a valid email address or you get the validation error message in Figure 5.10.

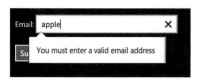

FIGURE 5.10   Validation for email

Using `<input type="url" />` creates a special input field for entering URLs. You get the touch keyboard in Figure 5.11 which includes special / and .com keys.

NOTE

The touch keyboard only appears when you don't have a keyboard attached to your machine or you explicitly open the touch keyboard.

FIGURE 5.11   Touch keyboard for URL

An `<input type="url" />` field requires you to enter a valid absolute URL. For example, the URL http://Superexpert.com and the URL ftp://Superexpert.com are valid, but the URL superexpert.com and the URL www.superexpert.com are not because they are not absolute URLs (see Figure 5.12).

FIGURE 5.12   Validating a URL

You use the `<input type="tel" />` element to enter telephone numbers. Because there are so many different formats for telephone numbers, this input type does not perform any validation. Instead, you can use `<input type="tel" />` to display a specialized touch keyboard for telephone numbers (see Figure 5.13).

FIGURE 5.13   Entering a telephone number

Finally, there is `<input type="search" />`. An `<input type="search" />` element behaves identically to an `<input type="text" />` element. The only difference is that you get a keyboard with a Search key instead of an Enter key.

Entering a Value from a List of Values

You can use the new HTML5 list attribute to provide an auto-complete experience for your users. For example, the following code provides a list of three suggestions for your car make:

```
<label>
    Car Make:
    <input id="inpCarMake"
        list="dlCarMakes" />
    <datalist id="dlCarMakes">
        <option>BMW</option>
        <option>Ford</option>
        <option>Tesla</option>
    </datalist>
</label>
```

The list attribute points at an HTML5 datalist element which contains the list of suggestions. When you start entering text into the input element then you get the suggestions displayed in Figure 5.14.

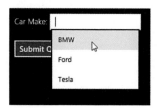

FIGURE 5.14   Getting a list of suggestions

You are not forced to select from the list. Using the list attribute makes an input element work more like a combo box than a select list.

Selecting Files

You can use `<input type="file" />` to create a file picker. For example, you can use `<input type="file" />` to enable a user to select a picture file from their hard drive.

The following HTML page includes an `<input type="file" />` element and a DIV element with the ID imgPicture. After you select a picture from your hard drive, the picture appears in the img element (see Figure 5.15).

```
<form id="frmAdd">
    <div>
        <label>
            Picture:
            <input id="inpFile" type="file" accept="image/*" />
        </label>
```

```
            <input type="submit" />
        </div>
    </form>

    <img id="imgPicture" />
```

When you use the `<input type="file" />` element, you can use the `accept` attribute to restrict the type of files that can be uploaded. For example, in the preceding markup, the `accept` element has the value `"image/*"`, which prevents any file except image files from being selected.

FIGURE 5.15　Selecting a picture file

The following JavaScript code is used to handle the form submit event. This code grabs the selected picture file from the input elements files collection and displays the picture in the IMG element:

```
(function () {
    "use strict";

    function initialize() {
        var frmAdd = document.getElementById("frmAdd");

        frmAdd.addEventListener("submit", function (evt) {
            evt.preventDefault();

            var imgPicture = document.getElementById("imgPicture");
            var inpFile = document.getElementById("inpFile");

            if (inpFile.files.length > 0) {
```

```
                     // Use HTML5 File API to create object URL to refer to the photo
➥file
                     var pictureUrl = URL.createObjectURL(inpFile.files[0]);

                     // Show photo in IMG element
                     imgPicture.src = pictureUrl;
                 }
            });

     }

   document.addEventListener("DOMContentLoaded", initialize);
})();
```

Creating a Rich Text Editor

If you want to create a form field that accepts rich text—such as bold, italic, or underlined text—then you can use the contenteditable attribute. Imagine, for example, that you want to enable a user to enter a college admissions essay. In that case, you can use the following HTML form:

```
<form>
    <label for="inpEssay">
        College Admissions Essay:
    </label>

    <div id="inpEssay" contenteditable="true" class="win-textarea richtext"></div>

    <br />
    <input type="submit" />
</form>
```

In the form, the contenteditable attribute is applied to a DIV element with the ID inpEssay. The contenteditable attribute makes the content of the DIV element editable (see Figure 5.16).

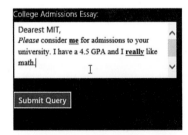

FIGURE 5.16   Creating a rich text editor

You can use Ctrl-B to make the text bold, Ctrl-I to make the text italic, and Ctrl-U to make the text underlined.

Notice that the DIV element with the `contenteditable` attribute has two CSS classes applied to it named `win-textarea` and `richtext`. The `win-textarea` class is included as part of the WinJS library and this class applies the standard Windows Store app styles to the editor.

The `richtext` class is defined like this:

```
.richtext {
  width:300px;
  height:100px;
  white-space:pre-wrap;
}
```

The HTML5 recommendation recommends that you should always use `white-space:pre-wrap` with a `contenteditable` DIV element, and who am I to question the wisdom of the editors of the HTML5 recommendation? For this reason, I always use `white-space:pre-wrap` with a `contenteditable` DIV.

Displaying Progress

The HTML5 recommendation includes a new element—named the progress element—that enables you to display a progress indicator. There are two basic types of progress indicators: an indeterminate and a determinate progress indicator.

You use an indeterminate progress indicator when you want to show a busy wait indicator, and you do not know how much longer a task will take. Here's how you declare an indeterminate progress indicator:

```
<progress id="progress1"></progress>
```

In a Windows Store app, the default progress indicator displays a set of animated dots moving horizontally (see Figure 5.17).

FIGURE 5.17   Displaying indeterminate progress

If you want to display a determinate progress indicator then you need to supply values for the progress element's `max` and `value` attributes. For example, here's how you would create a progress indicator that shows progress between the values 0 and 100:

```
<progress id="progress1"
    max="20"
    value="1">
</progress>
```

And, here is JavaScript code which updates the progress every 1 second:

```
(function () {
    "use strict";

    function initialize() {
        var progress1 = document.getElementById("progress1");
        var ivlProgress = window.setInterval(updateProgress, 1000);

        function updateProgress() {
            progress1.value = ++progress1.value;
            if (progress1.value === 20) {
                window.clearInterval(ivlProgress);
            }
        }
    }
    document.addEventListener("DOMContentLoaded", initialize);
})();
```

Declaring a progress element in this way gives you a traditional progress bar (see Figure 5.18).

FIGURE 5.18   Displaying determinate progress

There are some style options that you can use with a progress element in a Windows Store app. When creating an indeterminate progress indicator, you can use the win-ring class to display an animated ring of dots instead of the default animated horizontal dots (see Figure 5.19):

```
<progress id="progress2" class="win-ring">
</progress>
```

FIGURE 5.19   Displaying an animated ring of dots

If you want to control the size of an indeterminate progress indicator then you can use the `win-medium` or `win-large` classes. For example, the following page contains three progress indicators of increasing size:

```
<progress id="progressRing1"
    class="win-ring">
</progress>

<br /><br />
<progress id="progressRing2"
    class="win-ring win-medium">
</progress>

<br /><br />
<progress id="progressRing3"
    class="win-ring win-large">
</progress>
```

Summary

The focus of this chapter was on creating HTML5 forms for Windows Store apps. In the first section, I explained how you can take advantage of the new form validation features included in HTML5. You learned how to use the `required` and `pattern` attributes to perform basic validation and the `setCustomValidity()` method to perform advanced validation.

Next, I described how you can take advantage of the new HTML5 input types. You learned how to accept numbers by using the number and range types. You also learned how to accept email addresses, URLs, telephone numbers, and search terms. I also demonstrated how you can select files from your computer hard drive by using `<input type="file" />`.

Finally, I demonstrated how you can create a rich text editor with the `contenteditable` attribute and a progress indicator with the new HTML5 progress element.

CHAPTER 6

Menus and Flyouts

This chapter focuses on the topics of flyouts, menus, toolbars, settings, and dialogs. You learn how to throw options at users and get their responses.

I start by explaining how you can use the `Flyout` and `Menu` controls to display options within the body of a page. You learn how to display buttons, toggles, flyouts, and separators with a `Menu` control.

Next, I discuss app bars and nav bars. The app bar is the standard location for placing application commands and the nav bar is the standard location for displaying navigation links in a Windows Store app.

You also learn how to configure your app settings. You learn how to take advantage of the `SettingsFlyout` control to extend the standard settings displayed by the Settings charm.

Finally, I show you how you can create modal dialogs with the `MessageDialog` class. You learn how to create warning dialogs and Yes/No dialogs.

Using the `Flyout` Control

You use a `Flyout` control to display a popup in a page. The popup disappears just as soon as you click outside of the popup (or press the Esc key). You can use the `Flyout` control to display information, display warnings, or gather input.

> **NOTE**
>
> The `Flyout` control supports *light dismiss*. When you click outside the `Flyout` control, the control disappears automatically.

A common use for flyouts is to display warnings. For example, if your app happens to include a Delete All Data Forever button then it would be a good idea to use a flyout to warn the user before all of the user data is deleted.

Another common use for flyouts is for displaying forms that appear inline in a page. For example, the page in Listing 6.1 contains a `Flyout` control that enables you to select a typeface (see Figure 6.1).

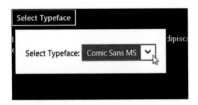

FIGURE 6.1   Displaying a flyout

LISTING 6.1   Displaying a Flyout (flyout\flyout.html)

```
<!-- Flyout Control -->
<div id="flyTypeface"
    data-win-control="WinJS.UI.Flyout">
    <label>Select Typeface:</label>
    <select id="selectTypeface">
        <option>Arial</option>
        <option>Impact</option>
        <option>Comic Sans MS</option>
    </select>
</div>

<!-- Button which opens FlyOut -->
<button id="btnTypeface">Select Typeface</button>

<!-- The text to style -->
<p id="pText">
    Lorem ipsum dolor sit amet, consectetuer adipiscing elite
    Maecenas porttitor congue massa. Fusce posuere, magna sed
    pulvinar ultricies, purus lectus malesuada libero, sit amet
    commodo magna eros quis urna.
</p>
```

The page in Listing 6.1 contains a button that opens a flyout. The flyout displays a select list of typefaces. When you select a typeface, the lorem ipsum text is modified to appear with the selected typeface.

The JavaScript code in Listing 6.2 demonstrates how you can wire-up a button so it opens a flyout. The button click handler calls the `Flyout` control's `show()` method to display the flyout.

When you call the `show()` method, you should pass an anchor element. The anchor element determines where the flyout will appear in the page. In Listing 6.2, the flyout is anchored to the button.

After you pick a typeface, the `hide()` method is used to hide (programmatically dismiss) the flyout. If you don't call `hide()`, the flyout remains open.

LISTING 6.2   Displaying a Flyout (flyout\flyout.js)

```javascript
(function () {
    "use strict";

    function initialize() {
        WinJS.UI.processAll().done(function () {
            var btnTypeface = document.getElementById("btnTypeface");
            var flyTypeface = document.getElementById("flyTypeface").winControl;
            var selectTypeface = document.getElementById("selectTypeface");
            var pText = document.getElementById("pText");

            // Wire-up handler to show FlyOut
            btnTypeface.addEventListener("click", function () {
                flyTypeface.show(btnTypeface);
            });

            // Wire-up handler for typeface select
            selectTypeface.addEventListener("change", function () {
                pText.style.fontFamily = selectTypeface.value;

                // Hide the flyout
                flyTypeface.hide();
            });

        });
    }

    document.addEventListener("DOMContentLoaded", initialize);
})();
```

WARNING

Remember to call `WinJS.UI.processAll()` when using the `Flyout` control or the `Flyout` control will never fly out.

Using the `Menu` Control

The WinJS `Menu` control is derived from the `Flyout` control—so it has a lot of features in common. Like the `Flyout` control, the `Menu` control appears in a popup and the menu disappears automatically when you click outside of the menu area.

However, unlike the `Flyout` control, the `Menu` control is specifically designed to display menu commands. You can place only menu commands in a `Menu` control and not other types of controls or HTML elements. The `Menu` control supports the following types of menu commands:

- ▶ `button`—You click the menu item to do something.

- ▶ `toggle`—You toggle the menu item.

- ▶ `flyout`—Clicking the menu item displays a flyout.

- ▶ `separator`—A separator between different groups of menu commands.

Listing 6.3 illustrates how you can declare the `Menu` control so it uses each of these menu commands.

LISTING 6.3   Displaying a Menu (menu\menu.html)

```
<!-- Clicking this button shows the Menu -->
<button id="btnEdit">Edit</button>

<!-- The Menu control -->
<div id="menuEdit"
    data-win-control="WinJS.UI.Menu">
    <button
        data-win-control="WinJS.UI.MenuCommand"
        data-win-options="{
            id:'menuCommandDelete',
            label:'Delete',
            type: 'button'
        }"></button>
    <hr
        data-win-control="WinJS.UI.MenuCommand"
        data-win-options="{
            type: 'separator'
        }" />
    <button
        data-win-control="WinJS.UI.MenuCommand"
        data-win-options="{
            id:'menuCommandBold',
            label:'Bold',
            type: 'toggle'
        }"></button>
```

```
        <button
            data-win-control="WinJS.UI.MenuCommand"
            data-win-options="{
                id:'menuCommandItalic',
                label:'Italic',
                type: 'toggle'
            }"></button>
        <button
            data-win-control="WinJS.UI.MenuCommand"
            data-win-options="{
                id:'menuCommandTypeface',
                label:'Typeface',
                type: 'flyout',
                flyout: select('#flyTypeface')
            }"></button>

</div>

<!-- Flyout Control -->
<div id="flyTypeface"
        data-win-control="WinJS.UI.Flyout">
        <label>Select Typeface:</label>
        <select id="selectTypeface">
            <option>Arial</option>
            <option>Impact</option>
            <option>Comic Sans MS</option>
        </select>
</div>

<!-- The text to style -->
<p id="pText">
    Lorem ipsum dolor sit amet, consectetuer adipiscing elite
    Maecenas porttitor congue massa. Fusce posuere, magna sed
    pulvinar ultricies, purus lectus malesuada libero, sit amet
    commodo magna eros quis urna.
</p>
```

The page in Listing 6.3 contains a chunk of lorem ipsum text. You use the Menu control to modify the appearance of the text (see Figure 6.2).

FIGURE 6.2   Using a Menu control

This menu contains five menu commands (instances of the WinJS.UI.MenuCommand class). It contains a button, separator, two toggle, and a flyout command.

The button command deletes all of the text. This command is wired-up to a click event handler in the JavaScript file in Listing 6.3.

The separator command does absolutely nothing at all. It just displays a separator between different groups of commands on the menu (a horizontal line).

The two toggle commands enable you to toggle the text between bold/normal and italic/normal. Click handlers for these commands are included in Listing 6.4.

Finally, the flyout command displays a Flyout control. The Flyout control is included in the HTML page in Listing 6.3 with the name flyTypeface. The flyout enables you to select a typeface for the text (see Figure 6.3). When the flyout appears, the menu disappears.

LISTING 6.4   Displaying a Menu (menu\menu.js)

```
(function () {
    "use strict";

    function initialize() {
        WinJS.UI.processAll().done(function () {
            var btnEdit = document.getElementById("btnEdit");
            var menuEdit = document.getElementById("menuEdit").winControl;
            var selectTypeface = document.getElementById("selectTypeface");
            var flyTypeface = document.getElementById("flyTypeface").winControl;
            var pText = document.getElementById("pText");

            // When you click Edit then show the Menu
            btnEdit.addEventListener("click", function () {
                menuEdit.show(btnEdit);
            });

            // Wire-up menu commands
            document.getElementById("menuCommandDelete").addEventListener("click",
➥function (evt) {
```

```
                pText.innerHTML = "[deleted]";
            });
            document.getElementById("menuCommandBold").addEventListener("click",
function (evt) {
                var toggleState = document.getElementById("menuCommandBold").
winControl.selected;
                if (toggleState) {
                    pText.style.fontWeight = 'bold'
                } else {
                    pText.style.fontWeight = 'normal'
                }
            });
            document.getElementById("menuCommandItalic").addEventListener("click",
function (evt) {
                var toggleState = document.getElementById("menuCommandItalic").
winControl.selected;
                if (toggleState) {
                    pText.style.fontStyle = 'italic'
                } else {
                    pText.style.fontStyle = 'normal'
                }
            });
            selectTypeface.addEventListener("change", function () {
                pText.style.fontFamily = selectTypeface.value;
                flyTypeface.hide();
            });

        });
    }

    document.addEventListener("DOMContentLoaded", initialize);
})();
```

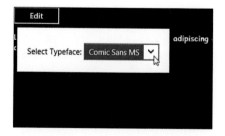

FIGURE 6.3   Using a Menu control to display a flyout

Using the `AppBar` Control

Windows Store apps have a standard location for application commands: the app bar. The app bar typically appears at the bottom of an app, and it does not appear until you swipe from either the bottom or top of the page or right-click when using a mouse.

For example, Figure 6.4 illustrates the appearance of the app bar when using the standard Windows 8.1 Photos app. The app bar is highlighted in a red box. If you click on the page, this app bar disappears and you get a full screen experience.

FIGURE 6.4   Internet Explorer app bar

Creating a Simple App Bar

You use the WinJS `AppBar` control to add an app bar to your Windows Store app. For example, here is how you would declare an app bar which appears on the bottom of your app:

```
<div id="appBar1"
    data-win-control="WinJS.UI.AppBar">

    <button data-win-control="WinJS.UI.AppBarCommand"
        data-win-options="{
            id:'cmdPlay',
            label:'Play',
```

```
            icon:'play',
            tooltip:'Play Song'
        }">
    </button>
    <button data-win-control="WinJS.UI.AppBarCommand"
        data-win-options="{
            id:'cmdPause',
            label:'Pause',
            icon:'pause',
            tooltip:'Pause Song'
        }">
    </button>


</div>
```

> **NOTE**
>
> For every project template except the Blank App template, the app bar control is included in the default.html page by default—but it's commented out.

This app bar contains two buttons: Play Song and Pause Song. Each button has both a label and an icon (see Figure 6.5).

FIGURE 6.5   A simple app bar

If you want to create an app bar that appears on the top of your app then you need to set the AppBar placement property like this:

```
<div id="appBar1"
    data-win-control="WinJS.UI.AppBar"
    data-win-options="{
        placement:'top'
    }">
```

```
<button data-win-control="WinJS.UI.AppBarCommand"
    data-win-options="{
        id:'cmdSave',
        label:'Save',
        icon:'save',
        tooltip:'Save Song List'
    }">
</button>

</div>
```

The `placement` property defaults to the value `"bottom"`. In the preceding code, I set the property to the value `"top"` so the app bar appears at the top of the app (see Figure 6.6).

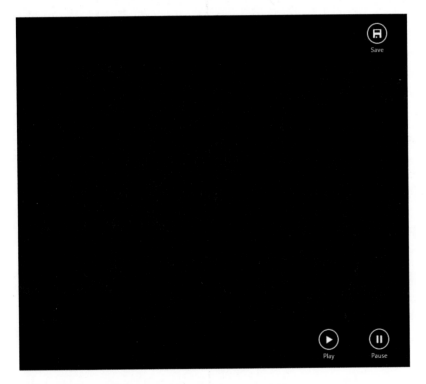

FIGURE 6.6   Creating both bottom and top app bars

Using App Bar Commands

There are four types of app bar commands:

▶ `button`—Creates a button which performs some action

▶ `toggle`—Creates a toggle button which switches between two states

▶ **flyout**—Creates a flyout that you can use to display a form

▶ **separator**—Creates a separator (vertical line) between other commands

▶ **Content**—Enables you to add any custom content to the app bar

Listing 6.5 contains a sample of an app bar that contains all five of these commands.

LISTING 6.5   Using Different Types of App Bar Commands

```
<div id="appBar1"
    data-win-control="WinJS.UI.AppBar">

    <!-- AppBar Commands -->
    <button data-win-control="WinJS.UI.AppBarCommand"
        data-win-options="{
            id:'cmdPlay',
            label:'Play',
            icon:'play',
            tooltip:'Play Song'
        }">
    </button>
    <button data-win-control="WinJS.UI.AppBarCommand"
        data-win-options="{
            id:'cmdMute',
            type: 'toggle',
            label:'Mute',
            icon:'mute',
            tooltip:'Mute Song'
        }">
    </button>
    <hr data-win-control="WinJS.UI.AppBarCommand"
        data-win-options="{
            type: 'separator'
        }" />
    <button data-win-control="WinJS.UI.AppBarCommand"
        data-win-options="{
            id:'cmdAddSong',
            type: 'flyout',
            label:'Add',
            icon:'add',
            tooltip:'Add Song',
            flyout: select('#flyAddSong')
        }">
    </button>
    <div data-win-control="WinJS.UI.AppBarCommand"
        data-win-options="{
```

6

```
            id:'cmdSearchSongs',
            type: 'content',
            label:'Search',
            icon:'search',
            tooltip:'Search Songs'
        }">
        <input id="inpSearch" />
    </div>
</div>

<!-- Add Song Flyout -->
<div id="flyAddSong"
    data-win-control="WinJS.UI.Flyout">
    <form>
        <input id="inpNewSong" required />
        <input type="submit" value="Add" />
    </form>
</div>
```

When you swipe or right-click then you get the app bar depicted in Figure 6.7.

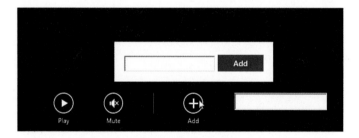

FIGURE 6.7   An app bar with different types of commands

The most common app bar command is the button command. You can create a click handler for a button command and do some action in response to clicking the button. For example, here is how you would create a click handler for the cmdPlay button:

```
(function () {
    "use strict";

    function initialize() {
        WinJS.UI.processAll().done(function () {
            var cmdPlay = document.getElementById("cmdPlay");
            cmdPlay.addEventListener("click", function () {
                console.log("Play song");
            });
```

```
        });
    }

    document.addEventListener("DOMContentLoaded", initialize);
})();
```

The button command includes both a `label` and `icon` property that you can use to control the appearance of the button in the app bar. You can either point the `icon` property to a custom PNG image or you can use one of the dozens of built-in icons represented by the `WinJS.UI.AppBarIcon` enumeration.

The toggle command displays a button that looks just like a button command. However, when you click the button, the button toggles between a highlighted and not highlighted state.

Here's how you can use the `selected` property to determine whether a toggle button is selected:

```
(function () {
    "use strict";

    function initialize() {
        WinJS.UI.processAll().done(function () {

            var cmdMute = document.getElementById("cmdMute");
            cmdMute.addEventListener("click", function () {
                console.log(cmdMute.winControl.selected);
            });

        });
    }

    document.addEventListener("DOMContentLoaded", initialize);
})();
```

The separator command creates a vertical bar between commands so you can group them. Use an HR element instead of a BUTTON element when creating a separator command.

The flyout command displays a `Flyout` control. In Listing 6.5, the `cmdAdd` command displays a flyout that contains a form for entering the title of a new song.

Finally, the content command displays an input box. You can use a content command to display anything you want within an app bar.

Showing Contextual Commands

Some app bar commands apply to the entire app. Other app bar commands apply only when an item is selected. For example, it might make sense to always display an Add button in the app bar. Displaying a Delete or Edit button, on the other hand, makes sense only when an item is selected.

The app bar has two built-in sections named `"global"` and `"selection"`. By default, when you add commands to the app bar, the commands appear in the global section. These commands appear on the right-hand side of the app bar.

You also have the option of adding commands to the selection section. These commands appear on the left-hand side of the app bar. Commands in the selection section should appear only when something is selected.

Imagine that you want to display a list of tasks by using a `ListView` control. You want users to be able to add new tasks and delete existing tasks. In that case, it makes sense to place the Add button in the app bar global section and the Delete button in the app bar selection section (see Figure 6.8).

FIGURE 6.8   Global versus selection app bar sections

Here's how you can declare your app bar so it contains Add and Delete commands:

```
<div id="appBar1"
    data-win-control="WinJS.UI.AppBar" data-win-options="{sticky:true}">
    <button data-win-control="WinJS.UI.AppBarCommand"
        data-win-options="{
            id:'cmdAdd',
            label:'Add',
            icon:'add',
            tooltip:'Add Task',
```

```
            type: 'flyout',
            flyout: select('#flyAdd'),
            section: 'global'
        }">
    </button>
    <button data-win-control="WinJS.UI.AppBarCommand"
        data-win-options="{
            id:'cmdDelete',
            label:'Delete',
            icon:'delete',
            tooltip:'Delete Task',
            section: 'selection',
            extraClass:'appBarSelection'
        }">
    </button>
</div>
```

Notice that the Add command is placed in the global section of the app bar. You don't really need to be explicit about this—global is the default value.

The Delete command is placed in the selection section. Notice, furthermore, that an additional CSS class named appBarSelection is associated with the Delete command. I'll take advantage of that class in a moment to hide and display the Delete command.

Here's the JavaScript code for hiding and displaying the app bar commands:

```
// Hide selection commands by default
appBar1.hideCommands(document.querySelectorAll('.appBarSelection'));

// When ListView item selected, display app bar
lvTasks.addEventListener("selectionchanged", function () {
    if (lvTasks.selection.count() == 1) {
        appBar1.showCommands(document.querySelectorAll('.appBarSelection'));
        appBar1.show();
    } else {
        appBar1.hideCommands(document.querySelectorAll('.appBarSelection'));
    };
});
```

When the app first starts, you want to hide the Delete command because nothing is selected. In the preceding code the hideCommands() method is used to hide every command associated with the appBarSelection CSS class.

Next, the code handles the selectonchanged event raised by the ListView control. When you select an item in the ListView (by swiping or right-clicking the item) then the selection commands are displayed with the help of the showCommands() method.

Because the app bar is hidden by default, you might not notice the Delete command. For that reason, the preceding code calls the `show()` method to force the app bar to be displayed. That way, when you select an item in the `ListView`, the app bar is displayed automatically and you know that you can delete an item.

> **NOTE**
>
> You can force the app bar to continue to appear after calling `show()` by using the app bar control's `sticky` property. When the `sticky` property has the value true then the app bar does not disappear automatically.

Using the `NavBar` Control

The `NavBar` control—which is new in WinJS 2.0—is the standard place to display navigation links for your Windows Store app. Typically, the nav bar appears at the top of your app and it only appears when you swipe from the top of your app or right-click your app.

Figure 6.9 illustrates the appearance of the nav bar in the standard Windows 8.1 Bing News app. The nav bar contains two levels of navigation links. It contains links to news Topics, Sources, and Videos. It also contains links to different news sources such as ABC News, *The New York Times*, and Fox News.

FIGURE 6.9   The nav bar in the Windows 8.1 Bing News app

Creating a Simple Nav Bar

You need to work with three WinJS controls to create a nav bar: the `NavBar` control, the `NavBarContainer` control, and the `NavBarCommand` control. Here is how you can create a simple nav bar that contains a single row of navigation links:

```
<!-- Nav Bar Control -->
<div id="navBar1"
    data-win-control="WinJS.UI.NavBar"
    data-win-options="{
        placement:'top'
    }">


    <!-- Nav Bar Container -->
    <div data-win-control="WinJS.UI.NavBarContainer">

        <!-- Nav Bar Commands -->
        <div data-win-control="WinJS.UI.NavBarCommand"
            data-win-options="{
                label:'Home',
                icon:'home',
                location: '/pages/home/home.html'
            }">
        </div>
        <div data-win-control="WinJS.UI.NavBarCommand"
            data-win-options="{
                label:'Videos',
                icon:'video',
                location: '/pages/videos/videos.html'
            }">
        </div>
        <div data-win-control="WinJS.UI.NavBarCommand"
            data-win-options="{
                label:'Settings',
                icon:'settings',
                location: '/pages/settings/settings.html'
            }">
        </div>

    </div>

</div>
```

WARNING

When creating `NavBarCommand` controls, don't use HTML BUTTON elements. Use DIV elements instead or you won't navigate.

Notice that each `NavBarCommand` has three options. The label and icon options are used for displaying each navigation link (see Figure 6.10). The location option determines where you navigate in a multi-page app.

NOTE

We discuss multi-page apps in detail in Chapter 12, "Page Fragments and Navigation." If you drop a `NavBar` control into the default page of a multi-page app created from the Navigation App template, the bar will appear on all content pages and will allow the user to navigate between them without additional code.

FIGURE 6.10   A simple nav bar

Configuring App Settings

Windows Store apps have a standard location for users to configure app settings. You access app settings from the Settings charm in the charm bar which you can open by

▶ Moving your mouse to the bottom right of your screen

▶ Swiping with your finger from the right edge of the screen

▶ Pressing the Windows logo key + I

The first two methods open the Charms panel from which you can select Settings. The last method opens the Settings panel directly.

By default, System settings—such as network and volume settings—appear at the bottom of the Settings window (see Figure 6.11). Permission settings also appear automatically. Finally, if you did in fact get your Windows Store app from the Windows Store then the Settings window will also include Rate and Review settings.

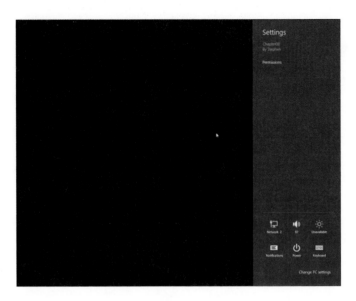

FIGURE 6.11   Default settings

You can add custom settings to the Settings window for your app. These custom settings can be configuration settings such as user preferences. The custom settings might also include information about your app including Help, About, and Privacy Policy pages.

You create custom app settings with the help of the SettingsFlyout control. For each app settings section that you want to create, you create a separate HTML file that contains a SettingsFlyout. I'll demonstrate how this works by creating both About Page settings and Personal settings.

Creating About Page Settings

Most apps include an About Page that provides information about the company that built the application. The About Page is purely informational (see Figure 6.12).

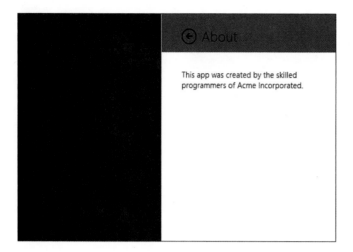

FIGURE 6.12   Creating About settings

If you want to create an About settings in your Settings window then you first need to create a new HTML file that contains a `SettingsFlyout` control. The HTML page in Listing 6.6 illustrates how you can create an About settings.

LISTING 6.6   About Settings

```
<!DOCTYPE html>
<html>
    <head>
        <title>About</title>
    </head>
    <body>
        <div id="divAbout"
            data-win-control="WinJS.UI.SettingsFlyout"
            data-win-options="{
                width:'narrow'
            }">
            <div class="win-header"
                style="background-color:#464646">
                <button
                    onclick="WinJS.UI.SettingsFlyout.show()"
                    class="win-backbutton"></button>
                <div class="win-label">About</div>
            </div>
            <div class="win-content">
                This app was created by the skilled programmers of Acme
                Incorporated.
            </div>
```

```
        </div>
    </body>
</html>
```

The page in Listing 6.6 contains a single WinJS `SettingsFlyout` control. Notice that the `SettingsFlyout` control is declared with a "narrow" width. When you open settings with a narrow width, the settings take up the same size as the Settings window. Alternatively, you can set the width to the value "wide" to create a larger space for displaying settings.

You can place whatever content that you please within the flyout and the content will appear when you open the settings. However, there are some guidelines from Microsoft. The `SettingsFlyout` control in Listing 6.6 contains a back button so you can get back to the Settings window. The content also takes advantage of several standard WinJS style classes such as `win-label` and `win-content`.

Before you can use the About settings, you must register the settings by handling the `WinJS.Application` settings event like this:

```
(function () {
    "use strict";
    WinJS.Application.onsettings = function (e) {
        e.detail.applicationcommands = {
            "divAbout": { href: "aboutSettings.html", title: "About" }
        };
        WinJS.UI.SettingsFlyout.populateSettings(e);
    }
    WinJS.Application.start();
})();
```

You assign a collection of settings commands to the `e.details.applicationcommands` object. In the code, the path and title of the About settings are assigned to the collection of application commands.

> **WARNING**
>
> When creating settings, you must call `WinJS.Application.start()` or the settings event will never be raised.

Creating Personal Settings

Imagine that you want to enable users to enter their first and last names in the app settings for a Windows Store app (see Figure 6.13). You are building a friendly app and you want to address the user by name.

FIGURE 6.13   Collecting Personal settings

The HTML page in Listing 6.7—named personalSettings.html—contains a `SettingsFlyout` that contains an HTML form. The form has two form fields named `inpFirstName` and `inpLastName`, and both form fields are required.

LISTING 6.7   `SettingsFlyout` for Personal Settings

```
<!DOCTYPE html>
<html>
    <head>
        <title>Security</title>
        <script type="text/javascript" src="personalSettings.js"></script>
    </head>
    <body>
        <div id="divPersonal"
            data-win-control="WinJS.UI.SettingsFlyout"
            data-win-options="{
                width:'narrow'
            }">
            <div class="win-header"
                style="background-color:#464646">
                <button
                    onclick="WinJS.UI.SettingsFlyout.show()"
                    class="win-backbutton"></button>
                <div class="win-label">Personal</div>
            </div>
            <div class="win-content">
            <form id="frmPersonal">
                <div>
```

```
                <label>
                    First Name: <br />
                    <input id="inpFirstName" required />
                </label>
            </div>
            <div>
                <label>
                    Last Name: <br />
                    <input id="inpLastName" required />
                </label>
            </div>
            <div>
                <input type="submit" value="Save" />
            </div>
        </form>
        </div>
    </div>
    </body>
</html>
```

Notice that the page in Listing 6.7 refers to a JavaScript file named personalSettings.js. The personalSettings.js file is contained in Listing 6.8. This JavaScript file is responsible for both loading and saving the user first and last names.

LISTING 6.8   Loading and Saving Personal Settings

```
(function () {
    "use strict";

    WinJS.UI.Pages.define("personalSettings.html",
    {
        processed: function (element, options) {
            var roamingSettings = Windows.Storage.ApplicationData.current.
➥roamingSettings;
            var divPersonal = document.getElementById("divPersonal").winControl;
            var frmSecurity = document.getElementById("frmPersonal");
            var inpFirstName = document.getElementById("inpFirstName");
            var inpLastName = document.getElementById("inpLastName");

            // Read the first and last name
            divPersonal.addEventListener("beforeshow", function () {
                inpFirstName.value = roamingSettings.values["firstName"] || "";
                inpLastName.value = roamingSettings.values["lastName"] || "";
            });

            // Save first and last names
```

```
        frmSecurity.addEventListener("submit", function () {
            roamingSettings.values["firstName"] = inpFirstName.value;
            roamingSettings.values["lastName"] = inpLastName.value;
        });


    }
  });
}());
```

The JavaScript code in Listing 6.8 includes an event handler for the `SettingsFlyout` beforeshow event. This event is raised right before the `SettingsFlyout` is displayed. In Listing 6.8, the user's first and last name is loaded from roaming settings and assigned to the two form fields.

The code in Listing 6.8 also includes an event handler for the form submit event. This handler saves the user's first and last name to roaming settings. The first and last name is saved permanently on the computer so the settings are available whenever the user runs the app again in the future. Because the settings are stored in roaming storage, the settings are also available across different computers associated with the same user account.

> **NOTE**
>
> Roaming settings are stored in the computer registry and synchronized across devices. Currently, Microsoft limits you to storing 100KB in roaming storage (use the `ApplicationDate.RoamingStorageQuota` property to view the limit).

To use the Personal settings in a page, you must register the settings in the JavaScript file associated with the page. The following code registers both the About Page settings (from the previous section) and the Personal settings:

```
(function () {
    "use strict";
    WinJS.Application.onsettings = function (e) {
        e.detail.applicationcommands = {
            "divPersonal": { href: "personalSettings.html", title: "Personal" },
            "divAbout": { href: "aboutSettings.html", title: "About" }
        };
        WinJS.UI.SettingsFlyout.populateSettings(e);
    }
    WinJS.Application.start();
})();
```

Displaying Windows Dialogs

Sometimes, nothing beats a good old-fashioned modal dialog. A modal dialog blocks all user interaction with your app until the modal dialog gets its answer.

Modal dialogs are necessary when your app will not work without some crucial information. For example, a Weather app cannot display the weather without knowing your location. So it makes sense to use a modal dialog to ask for the user's location when the app first runs.

You also can use modal dialogs in the same situations in which you would use JavaScript alerts: when you really need to get in a user's face to convey critical warnings or information. You should use modal dialogs sparingly.

NOTE

JavaScript alerts do not work in Windows Store apps written with JavaScript. Because I consider JavaScript alerts to be closely related to the (deprecated) HTML blink tag, this is a good thing.

You create modal dialogs by using the `MessageDialog` class. Here's how you can open a dialog with the message, "Did you know that your fly is unzipped?" (see Figure 6.14).

```
var message = new Windows.UI.Popups.MessageDialog(
    "Did you know that your fly is unzipped?"
);
message.showAsync();
```

FIGURE 6.14   Using a message dialog

You can customize the appearance of the dialog by supplying commands. For example, here is how you would create a Yes/No dialog:

```
// Create dialog
var message = new Windows.UI.Popups.MessageDialog(
    "Did you know that your fly is unzipped?",
    "Warning!!!"
);

// Add commands
message.commands.append(new Windows.UI.Popups.UICommand("&Yes"));
message.commands.append(new Windows.UI.Popups.UICommand("&No"));

// Show dialog
message.showAsync().done(function (answer) {
    if (answer.label === "&Yes") {
        console.log("You picked yes");
    } else {
        console.log("You picked no");
    }
});
```

The code appends two `UICommand` objects to the message dialog that are labeled Yes and No (see Figure 6.15). You can use the promise returned by the `showAsync()` method to determine which of the two buttons was clicked.

FIGURE 6.15   A yes/no dialog

NOTE

Notice that the buttons' labels are "&Yes" and "&No". The & is used to specify the keyboard shortcut for invoking the button. You can press Alt-Y to invoke the Yes button and Alt-No to invoke the No button. When you hold down the Alt key, the shortcuts appear with underlines.

Summary

The chapter was all about flyouts, menus, settings, toolbars, and dialogs. I started by discussing how you can use the `Flyout` control to make simple ephemeral popups which can contain any HTML content at all.

Next, I explained how you can use the `Menu` control to display menu commands. You learned how to include buttons, flyouts, toggles, and separators in a menu.

I also discussed the app bar and nav bar. You learned how the app bar is the standard location in a Windows Store app for placing commands, and the nav bar is the standard location in a Windows Store app for placing navigation links.

You also learned how to take advantage of the `SettingsFlyout` control to extend the settings displayed in your Windows Store app's Settings window. You learned how to store and retrieve settings from roaming settings.

Finally, I showed you how you can create modal dialogs by taking advantage of the `MessageDialog` class. We created warning dialogs and Yes/No dialogs.

Stay tuned. In the next chapter, we jump into a discussion of how you can display collections of data in your app.

CHAPTER 7

Using the ItemContainer, Repeater, and FlipView Controls

The focus of this chapter is on three controls related to working with collections of data: the ItemContainer, Repeater, and FlipView controls.

The ItemContainer control enables you to create invokable, selectable, and draggable content—things you can interact with. Although the ItemContainer control can be used on its own, the ItemContainer control is most often used with the Repeater and ListView controls.

The Repeater control is a very flexible control for displaying a collection of data. You can use a Repeater control to display a collection of data using any format you want.

Finally, the FlipView control is a useful control for displaying one item from a collection of items at a time. You can use the FlipView control, for example, to display individual news articles in a list of articles.

Using the ItemContainer Control

Let me start by discussing the ItemContainer control. After you wrap content in an ItemContainer control, you can invoke, select, or drag-and-drop the content.

Here's a simple example. The following markup includes three ItemContainer controls, which represent three options labeled Option 1, Option 2, and Option 3:

```
<div id="optionList">

    <div data-win-control="WinJS.UI.ItemContainer">
        Option 1
    </div>
```

```
<div data-win-control="WinJS.UI.ItemContainer">
    Option 2
</div>

<div data-win-control="WinJS.UI.ItemContainer">
    Option 3
</div>

</div>
```

When this markup is displayed, you can click an option to invoke it (the ItemContainer control works like a button) or you can right-click an option to select it. For example, in Figure 7.1, Option 2 and Option 3 are selected.

FIGURE 7.1   Selecting from ItemContainer options

Styling an ItemContainer

The ItemContainer control does not impose any styling on its content. For example, if you wrap a DIV element with an ItemContainer then the DIV element will continue to render as a DIV element. The element will work as a block element and expand across the entire page.

If you want to style the content which appears in an ItemContainer then you have to work with one or more of the standard Cascading Style Sheet classes built into the WinJS library.

The ItemContainers that appear in Figure 7.1 were styled with the following win-* CSS classes:

```
#optionList .win-itemcontainer
{
    width:100px;
    height:100px;
    margin:10px;
    float:left;
}

#optionList .win-itembox {
    background-color: gray;
```

```
}

#optionList .win-item
{
    padding:10px;
}
```

Notice that each CSS rule is qualified with #optionList. In CSS, more specific rules override less specific rules. Without the #optionList qualifier, the earlier CSS rules would be ignored because they would be overridden by the default ItemContainer styles defined in the WinJS ui-dark.css or ui-light.css file.

The win-itemcontainer class applies to the outermost DIV element rendered by the ItemContainer. The win-itemcontainer class provides the DIV element with a fixed width and height of 100 pixels. It also floats the DIV elements so the options appear next to one another horizontally.

The win-itembox applies to a DIV element that is nested inside the win-itemcontainer. This is a good place to set the background color of the DIV.

The win-item class applies to the innermost DIV element rendered by the ItemContainer. The win-item class above adds some padding to each option element.

When an ItemContainer is rendered, three nested DIV elements are rendered. For example, the Option 1 ItemContainer renders the following three DIV elements:

```
<div class="win-disposable win-vertical win-swipeable win-itemcontainer
➡win-container" data-win-control="WinJS.UI.ItemContainer">
    <div class="win-itembox">
        <div class="win-item">
            Option 1
        </div>
    </div>
    <div></div>
</div>
```

If you select an ItemContainer—by right-clicking the ItemContainer or swiping it—then some additional DIV elements are rendered. These additional DIV elements are responsible for displaying the check mark that appears at the top right of a selected ItemContainer:

```
<div class="win-disposable win-vertical win-swipeable win-itemcontainer
➡win-container win-selected" data-win-control="WinJS.UI.ItemContainer">
    <div class="win-itembox win-selected">
        <div class="win-selectionbackground"></div>
        <div class="win-item">
```

```
        Option 2
    </div>
    <div class="win-selectionborder"></div>
    <div class="win-selectioncheckmarkbackground"></div>
    <div class="win-selectioncheckmark"></div>
    </div>
    <div></div>
</div>
```

You can override any of these CSS classes to control the appearance of an `ItemContainer`. For example, you can customize the `win-selectionborder` class to change the appearance of a selected `ItemContainer`.

Interacting with an `ItemContainer`

The whole point of the `ItemContainer` is that it makes it content interactive; you can invoke, select, and drag `ItemContainers`.

By default, when you click an `ItemContainer` then the `iteminvoked` event is raised. Imagine that you have created the three options in Listing 7.1.

LISTING 7.1   Invoking an `ItemContainer` (itemInvoke\itemInvoke.html)

```
<div class="option" data-option="option 1" data-win-control="WinJS.
➥UI.ItemContainer">
    Option 1
</div>

<div class="option" data-option="option 2" data-win-control="WinJS.
➥UI.ItemContainer">
    Option 2
</div>

<div class="option" data-option="option 3" data-win-control="WinJS.
➥UI.ItemContainer">
    Option 3
</div>
```

Notice that I added a `data-option` attribute to each `ItemContainer`. That way, I have a unique identifier for each option.

> **NOTE**
>
> HTML5 enables you to add a `data-*` attribute to any element. You can use `data-*` attributes to associate custom information with an HTML element.

I can detect when an `ItemContainer` is clicked by handling the invoked event like I do in Listing 7.2.

LISTING 7.2   Invoking an `ItemContainer` (itemContainerInvoked\itemContainerInvoked.js)

```
(function () {
    "use strict";

    function initialize() {

        var options = WinJS.Utilities.query(".option");

        WinJS.UI.processAll().done(function () {

            options.listen("invoked", function (e) {
                var md = new Windows.UI.Popups.MessageDialog(e.target.
➥dataset["option"]);
                md.showAsync();
            });

        });

    }



    document.addEventListener("DOMContentLoaded", initialize);
})();
```

When you click any of the `ItemContainers` then a dialog pops up that displays the identity of the selected option (see Figure 7.2). The identity of the clicked option is retrieved from the `ItemContainer` data-option attribute. The value of the data-option attribute is represented by the element's `dataset["option"]` property. (If you added a `data-something` attribute then you would get the value of this attribute with `dataset["something"]`.)

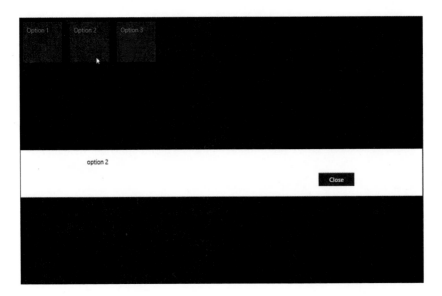

FIGURE 7.2   Invoking an `ItemContainer`

By default, an `ItemContainer` can be both invoked and selected. You can change this
default behavior by modifying the `tapBehavior` and `swipeBehavior` properties.

The `tapBehavior` property accepts the following values:

▶ `directSelect`—Tapping an item both invokes and selects it

▶ `toggleSelect`—Tapping an item selects/deselects it

▶ `invokeOnly`—Tapping an item invokes but does not select it

▶ `None`—Tapping an item neither invokes nor selects it

The `swipeBehavior` property accepts the following two values:

▶ `select`—Swiping an item selects it

▶ `None`—Swiping an item does not select it

Selecting an `ItemContainer`

Selecting an `ItemContainer` raises both a `selectionchanging` and `selectionchanged` event.
You can handle these events to detect when an `ItemContainer` is selected.

Imagine, for example, that you want to create a set of options that work like radio
buttons. When you select one option, all of the other options are unselected automatically
so that you can select only one option at a time.

Listing 7.3 contains three `ItemContainers` that represent the three options.

LISTING 7.3   Selecting an `ItemContainer` (ItemContainerSelection\ItemContainerSelection.html)

```
<div class="option" data-win-control="WinJS.UI.ItemContainer">
    Option 1
</div>


<div class="option" data-win-control="WinJS.UI.ItemContainer">
    Option 2
</div>


<div class="option" data-win-control="WinJS.UI.ItemContainer">
    Option 3
</div>
```

And, Listing 7.4 contains the JavaScript code that ensures that only one option is selected at a time.

LISTING 7.4   Selecting an `ItemContainer` (ItemContainerSelection\ItemContainerSelection.js)

```
(function () {
    "use strict";

    function initialize() {
        var options = WinJS.Utilities.query(".option");

        WinJS.UI.processAll().done(function () {

            // When an option state is changed
            options.listen("selectionchanged", function (e) {
                // If selected then unselect all of the other options
                var isSelected = e.target.winControl.selected;
                if (isSelected) {
                    options.forEach(function (option) {
                        if (option != e.target) {
                            option.winControl.selected = false;
                        }
                    })
                }
            });


        });
    }


    document.addEventListener("DOMContentLoaded", initialize);
})();
```

In Listing 7.4, a `selectionchanged` event handler is added to all of the `ItemContainers` on the page. When the `selectionchanged` event is raised, and a new option is selected, each option (other than the option that raised the event) is unselected. This ensures that only one option is selected at a time.

> **WARNING**
>
> Be careful about infinite recursion here. Setting the `ItemContainer selected` property raises the `selectionchanging` and `selectionchanged` events. Therefore, if you are not careful about when you set the `selected` property within either of these events then you can crash your app.

Creating Drag-and-Drop Items

The `ItemContainer` is compatible with standard HTML5 drag and drop. You enable drag and drop for an `ItemContainer` by setting the draggable option to the value true like this:

```
<div data-win-control="WinJS.UI.ItemContainer" data-win-options="{draggable:true}">
    Item 1
</div>
```

After you enable drag and drop for an `ItemContainer`, you can handle the standard HTML5 drag and drop events:

▶ `dragstart`—Raised when you start dragging a draggable `ItemContainer`.

▶ `dragover`—Raised when you drag an `ItemContainer` over an element. Handle this event to enable an `ItemContainer` to be dropped on a particular element.

▶ `dragenter`—Raised when you drag an `ItemContainer` over a new element. Handle this event to create a visual indication of possible drop targets.

▶ `dragleave`—Raised when drag an `ItemContainer` out of a element. Handle this event to create a visual indication of possible drop targets.

▶ `dragend`—Raised when a drag and drop operation completes. Handle this event to do any clean up.

Imagine, for example, that you want to be able to drag a list of items onto a drop target. When you drag an item onto the drop target, you want the drop target to display the identity of the item dropped (see Figure 7.3).

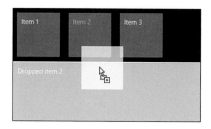

FIGURE 7.3   Dragging and dropping `ItemContainers`

The page in Listing 7.5 contains three `ItemContainer` controls with drag and drop enabled. The page also contains a DIV element which acts as the drop target.

LISTING 7.5   Dragging an `ItemContainer` (itemContainerDrag\itemContainerDrag.html)

```
<!DOCTYPE html>
<html>
<head>
    <meta charset="utf-8" />
    <title>Chapter07</title>

    <!-- WinJS references -->
    <link href="//Microsoft.WinJS.2.0/css/ui-dark.css" rel="stylesheet" />
    <script src="//Microsoft.WinJS.2.0/js/base.js"></script>
    <script src="//Microsoft.WinJS.2.0/js/ui.js"></script>

    <link href="/css/default.css" rel="stylesheet" />
    <script src="itemContainerDrag.js"></script>

    <style>

        #draggables .win-itemcontainer {
            width: 100px;
            height: 100px;
            margin: 10px;
            float: left;
        }

        #draggables .win-itembox {
            background-color: gray;
        }

        #draggables .win-item {
            padding: 10px;
        }
```

```css
        #dropTarget {
            border:double white 2px;
            padding:10px;
            min-width:500px;
            min-height:300px;
            background-color:gray;
        }

        #dropTarget.hiLite {
            background-color: lightgray;
        }
    </style>

</head>
<body>
    <div id="draggables">
        <div data-item="item 1" data-win-control="WinJS.UI.ItemContainer" data-win-
options="{draggable:true}">
            Item 1
        </div>

        <div data-item="item 2" data-win-control="WinJS.UI.ItemContainer" data-win-
options="{draggable:true}">
            Item 2
        </div>

        <div data-item="item 3" data-win-control="WinJS.UI.ItemContainer" data-win-
options="{draggable:true}">
            Item 3
        </div>
    </div>
    <br style="clear:both" />

    <div id="dropTarget"></div>

</body>
</html>
```

The JavaScript in Listing 7.6 contains event handlers for the standard HTML5 drag and drop events.

LISTING 7.6   Dragging an `ItemContainer` (itemContainerDrag\itemContainerDrag.js)

```javascript
(function () {
    "use strict";
```

```
    function initialize() {
        var dragMeItem = null;
        var dropTarget = document.getElementById("dropTarget");

        WinJS.UI.processAll().done(function () {
            // Handle drag start - called when you start dragging an ItemContainer
            WinJS.Utilities.query("#draggables>div").listen("dragstart", function
➥(e) {
                dragMeItem = e.target;
            });

            // Handle dragover to indicate valid drop targets
            // Call preventDefault() when over valid target
            dropTarget.addEventListener("dragover", function (e) {
                e.preventDefault();
            });


            // Handle dragenter/dragleave to highlight drop target
            dropTarget.addEventListener("dragenter", function () {
                dropTarget.classList.add("hiLite");
            });
            dropTarget.addEventListener("dragleave", function () {
                dropTarget.classList.remove("hiLite");
            });

            // Handle drop to perform the drop
            dropTarget.addEventListener("drop", function (e) {
                // Get value of data-item and show it
                dropTarget.innerHTML = "Dropped " + dragMeItem.parentElement.
➥dataset["item"];
            });

            // Handle dragend to clean up
            document.addEventListener("dragend", function (e) {
                dropTarget.classList.remove("hiLite");
            });

        });

    }


    document.addEventListener("DOMContentLoaded", initialize);
})();
```

When you start dragging an `ItemContainer`, the `dragstart` handler is called. This handler assigns the `ItemContainer` being dragged to the `dragMeItem` variable.

As you drag the `ItemContainer` around the page, the `dragover`, the `dragenter`, and the `dragleave` events are raised. The `dragover` event is used to determine where the `ItemContainer` can be dropped. The `dragover` event handler in Listing 7.6 enables the `ItemContainer` to be dropped only when the `ItemContainer` is dragged over the `dropTarget` DIV element.

You can (optionally) handle the `dragenter` and `dragleave` events to make a change in the user interface to indicate valid drop locations. In the code in Listing 7.6, the `dropTarget` DIV element is highlighted when you drag an `ItemContainer` over it.

The drop handler is responsible for handling the actual drop. In Listing 7.6, the drop handler simply displays the identity of the dropped `ItemContainer` in the `dropTarget`.

Finally, the `dragend` handler performs clean up. In Listing 7.6, the `dragend` handler is used to ensure that the `dropTarget` is no longer highlighted after the drag-and-drop operation completes.

> **NOTE**
>
> The `ListView` control implements all of the HTML5 drag-and-drop event handlers for you. In other words, if you want to implement drag and drop with very little work then just use a `ListView` control. We discuss drag and drop using the `ListView` in the next chapter.

Using the `Repeater` Control

The `Repeater` control is the most flexible control included in the WinJS library for displaying a collection of data. You can use the `Repeater` control to render a variety of different types of elements including bulleted lists, select lists, checkbox lists, and tables.

Let me start with a simple example. Listing 7.7 contains a `Repeater` control that renders an HTML table of products (see Figure 7.4).

Product Id	Product Name	Product Price
1	Milk	2.2
2	Eggs	1.19
3	Fish	2.33
4	Peanut Butter	5.2

FIGURE 7.4   Rendering an HTML table with a `Repeater` control

LISTING 7.7   Using the `Repeater` Control (repeater\repeater.html)

```
<table>
    <thead>
        <tr>
            <th>Product Id</th>
            <th>Product Name</th>
            <th>Product Price</th>
        </tr>
    </thead>
    <tbody id="repeater1" data-win-control="WinJS.UI.Repeater">
        <tr>
            <td data-win-bind="textContent:id"></td>
            <td data-win-bind="textContent:name"></td>
            <td data-win-bind="textContent:price"></td>
        </tr>
    </tbody>
</table>
```

In Listing 7.7, the TBODY element is converted into a `Repeater` control with the help of the `data-win-control="WinJS.UI.Repeater"` attribute. The inner content of the `Repeater` is used as the Repeater template. Each item from the Repeater data source is displayed as a row in the TBODY.

> **NOTE**
>
> I used a little bit of CSS to style the HTML table so you can see the table borders.
>
> ```
> table {
>   border-collapse:collapse;
> }
>
> th, td {
>     border: solid 1px gray;
>     padding:10px;
> }
> ```

Listing 7.8 contains the JavaScript code for associating a data source with the `Repeater`.

LISTING 7.8   Using a `Repeater` control (repeater\repeater.js)

```
(function () {
    "use strict";

    function initialize() {
```

```
        WinJS.UI.processAll().done(function () {

            var repeater1 = document.getElementById("repeater1").winControl;

            // Create a List of products
            var listProducts = new WinJS.Binding.List([
                { id: 1, name: "Milk", price: 2.20 },
                { id: 2, name: "Eggs", price: 1.19 },
                { id: 3, name: "Fish", price: 2.33 },
                { id: 4, name: "Peanut Butter", price: 5.20 }
            ]);

            // Bind the list of products to the ListView
            repeater1.data = listProducts;
        });
    }


    document.addEventListener("DOMContentLoaded", initialize);
})();
```

You can bind a `Repeater` control to a `WinJS.Binding.List`. In Listing 7.8, the `Repeater` is bound to a list named `listProducts` which represents a list of products. The `Repeater` is bound to the list with the help of the `Repeater` control's data property.

NOTE

I talked about the `WinJS.Binding.List` object in Chapter 3, "Observables, Bindings, and Templates."

Using an External Template

Most of the time, the easiest option is to define a `Repeater` template as the inner content of the `Repeater` as I did in the previous section. However, you also have the option of creating an external `Repeater` template.

Here's an example. Listing 7.9 contains two controls: a `Repeater` control and a separate `Template` control. The `Repeater` is associated with the template through its `template` property.

LISTING 7.9   Repeater with an External Template (repeaterExternal\repeaterExternal.html)

```
<table style="display:none">
<tbody id="productRowTemplate" data-win-control="WinJS.Binding.Template">
    <tr>
        <td data-win-bind="textContent:id"></td>
        <td data-win-bind="textContent:name"></td>
        <td data-win-bind="textContent:price"></td>
    </tr>
</tbody>
</table>

<table>
    <thead>
        <tr>
            <th>Product Id</th>
            <th>Product Name</th>
            <th>Product Price</th>
        </tr>
    </thead>
    <tbody id="repeater1" data-win-control="WinJS.UI.Repeater" data-win-
➥options="{template: select('#productRowTemplate')}">
    </tbody>
</table>
```

The Repeater in Listing 7.9 renders an HTML table. Each row is rendered with the
productRowTemplate template.

Notice that the external template is wrapped in an HTML table element hidden with
display:none. A template exists in the page and because it exists in the page, it must be
valid markup.

> **WARNING**
>
> Make sure that you declare the Template control before the Repeater control on the
> page. Otherwise, the Repeater control won't find it.

Using a Nested Template

One reason to create an external template is so that you can create nested Repeaters.
Imagine, for example, that you want to create an evil organization chart used by a
company that specializes in producing evil (see Figure 7.5).

FIGURE 7.5   An evil org chart

The JavaScript file in Listing 7.10 contains the data for the org chart. Notice that the data follows a pattern. The data is a list of employees. Each employee can have a `minions` property that represents another list of employees. An org chart can be arbitrarily deep.

LISTING 7.10   Using Nested `Repeaters` (repeaterNested\repeaterNested.js)

```
(function () {
    "use strict";

    function initialize() {

        WinJS.UI.processAll().done(function () {

            var repeater1 = document.getElementById("repeater1").winControl;

            // Create a List of evil employees
            var listEmployees = new WinJS.Binding.List([
                {
                    name: "Dr Evil", salary: "billions", minions: new WinJS.Binding.
➥List([

                        { name: "Bad Guy 1", salary: "4 dollars" },
                        { name: "Bad Guy 2", salary: "zero dollars" },
                        { name: "Bad Guy 3", salary: "100 dollars", minions: new
➥WinJS.Binding.List([
```

```
                            { name: "Henchman 1", salary: "14 dollars" },
                            { name: "Henchman 2", salary: "1 dollar" }
                    ])}
                ])
            }
        ]);

        // Bind the list of products to the ListView
        repeater1.data = listEmployees;
    });
}


    document.addEventListener("DOMContentLoaded", initialize);
})();
```

So now that we have nested data, we can show it with the help of nested Repeaters. The page in Listing 7.11 contains a Repeater control named repeater1 that refers to a separate Template control named employeeTemplate. The employeeTemplate displays the name and salary of the current employee. However, the employeeTemplate also contains a second Repeater control that displays the employee's minions.

The minions are bound to the nested Repeater control with the help of the data-win-bind="winControl.data: minions" attribute. Because the nested Repeater refers to the employeesTemplate, the org chart can nest as deeply as required by the data source.

LISTING 7.11   Using Nested Repeaters (repeaterNested\repeaterNested.html)

```
<h1>Evil Org Chart</h1>

<ul id="employeeTemplate" data-win-control="WinJS.Binding.Template">
    <li>
        Name: <span data-win-bind="textContent:name"></span>
        /Salary: <span data-win-bind="textContent:salary"></span>
        <ul data-win-control="WinJS.UI.Repeater" data-win-options="{template:
➡select('#employeeTemplate')}" data-win-bind="winControl.data: minions">
        </ul>
    </li>
</ul>

<ul id="repeater1" data-win-control="WinJS.UI.Repeater" data-win-options="{template:
➡select('#employeeTemplate')}">
</ul>
```

Using the `Repeater` with the `ItemContainer`

If you want the items displayed by a `Repeater` control to be invokable, selectable, or drag-gable then you can use the `Repeater` control with the `ItemContainer` control.

Listing 7.12 contains a simple example. The `Repeater` in Listing 7.12 is bound to a list of three items. The `Repeater` renders an `ItemContainer` for each of the items.

LISTING 7.12   Using a `Repeater` with an `ItemContainer` (repeaterItemContainer\
repeaterItemContainer.html)

```
<div id="repeater1" data-win-control="WinJS.UI.Repeater">
    <div data-win-control="WinJS.UI.ItemContainer" data-win-bind="dataset.
➥name:name">
        <span data-win-bind="textContent:name"></span>
    </div>
</div>
```

Notice that the `ItemContainer` includes a `data-win-bind="dataset.name:name"` attribute. This attribute associates the name of each data item with the `ItemContainer`.

The `Repeater` is bound to the list of items in the JavaScript file in Listing 7.13.

LISTING 7.13   Using a `Repeater` with an `ItemContainer` (repeaterItemContainer\
repeaterItemContainer.js)

```
(function () {
    "use strict";

    function initialize() {

        WinJS.UI.processAll().done(function () {

            var repeater1 = document.getElementById("repeater1").winControl;

            // Create a List of options
            var listOptions = new WinJS.Binding.List([
                { name: "Option 1" },
                { name: "Option 2" },
                { name: "Option 3" }
            ]);

            // Bind the list of products to the ListView
            repeater1.data = listOptions;

            // Handle invoking a Repeater item
            repeater1.addEventListener("invoked", function (e) {
                var optionName = e.target.dataset.name;
```

```
            var md = new Windows.UI.Popups.MessageDialog(optionName);
            md.showAsync();
        });

    });
}


    document.addEventListener("DOMContentLoaded", initialize);
})();
```

When you open the page, the list of three items is rendered by the `Repeater`. If you click an item then a message box is displayed with the name of the invoked item (see Figure 7.6).

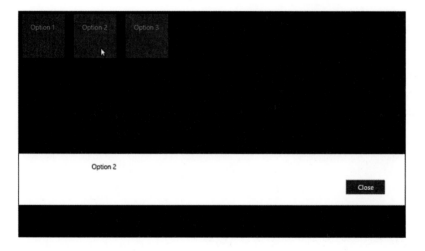

FIGURE 7.6   Invoking an item in a `Repeater` control

Using the `FlipView` Control

The `FlipView` control can be used to display a collection of items. Unlike the `Repeater` or `ListView` controls, the `FlipView` only displays a single item from a collection at a time.

The `FlipView` control is ideal for displaying a photo gallery—one picture at a time. It can also be used for swiping through a list of magazine or newspaper articles.

When you use a `FlipView`, only a single item from a data source is displayed. However, arrows are displayed so you can move to the next or previous item in the data source.

For example, the JavaScript file in Listing 7.14 includes a collection of three articles. Each article has a `title`, `author`, and `articleText` property.

LISTING 7.14   A List of Articles

```
(function () {
    "use strict";

    // Create List of articles
    var listArticles = new WinJS.Binding.List([
        {
            title: "Why Dogs are Better than Cats",
            author: "Arnold Wiggles",
            articleText: "Pellentesque habitant morbi tristique senectus et netus \
    et malesuada fames ac turpis egestas. Proin pharetra nonummy pede. Mauris et
➥orci."
        },
        {
            title: "Why Dogs are Better than Fish",
            author: "Jane Rubble",
            articleText: "Lorem ipsum dolor sit amet, consectetuer adipiscing elit. \
    Maecenas porttitor congue massa. Fusce posuere, magna sed pulvinar \
    ultricies, purus lectus malesuada libero, sit amet commodo magna \
    eros quis urna."
        },
        {
            title: "Why Dogs are Better than Mice",
            author: "Eric Alexander",
            articleText: "Lorem ipsum dolor sit amet, consectetuer adipiscing elit. \
    Maecenas porttitor congue massa. Fusce posuere, magna sed pulvinar \
    ultricies, purus lectus malesuada libero, sit amet commodo magna \
    eros quis urna."
        }
    ]);



    WinJS.Namespace.define("MyData",
    {
        listArticles: listArticles
    });


})();
```

Now imagine that you want to display the articles, one article at a time, in your Windows Store app. The page in Listing 7.15 illustrates how you can use a `FlipView` control to display individual articles from a list of articles (see Figure 7.7).

Notice that the page includes a reference to the articles.js file from Listing 7.10, which contains the data for the `FlipView`.

FIGURE 7.7   Displaying articles with a `FlipView` control

LISTING 7.15   Displaying an Article with a `FlipView` (flipView\flipView.html)

```
<!DOCTYPE html>
<html>
<head>
    <meta charset="utf-8" />
    <title>Chapter04</title>

    <!-- WinJS references -->
    <link href="//Microsoft.WinJS.2.0/css/ui-dark.css" rel="stylesheet" />
    <script src="//Microsoft.WinJS.2.0/js/base.js"></script>
    <script src="//Microsoft.WinJS.2.0/js/ui.js"></script>

    <!-- Chapter07 references -->
    <link rel="stylesheet" type="text/css" href="flipView.css" />
    <script src="articles.js"></script>
    <script src="flipView.js"></script>
</head>
<body>

    <div id="tmplArticle"
        data-win-control="WinJS.Binding.Template">
        <div class="articleItem">
            <h2 data-win-bind="innerText:title"></h2>
            Author: <span data-win-bind="innerText:author"></span>
            <p data-win-bind="innerText:articleText"></p>
```

```
        </div>
    </div>



    <div id="fvArticles"
        data-win-control="WinJS.UI.FlipView"
        data-win-options="{
            itemDataSource: MyData.listArticles.dataSource,
            itemTemplate: select('#tmplArticle')
    }"></div>

</body>
</html>
```

The `FlipView` control is declared with the following HTML:

```
<div id="fvArticles"
    data-win-control="WinJS.UI.FlipView"
    data-win-options="{
        itemDataSource: MyData.listArticles.dataSource,
        itemTemplate: select('#tmplArticle')
    }"></div>
```

The `FlipView` is bound to the list of articles with the help of the `itemDataSource` property. You can bind a `FlipView` to any data source which implements the `IListDataSource` interface. There are only two objects in the WinJS library which implement this interface: the `WinJS.Binding.List` object and the `WinJS.UI.StorageDataSource` object.

In the markup above, the `FlipView` is bound to the list of articles which is a `WinJS.Binding.List`. In particular, the `FlipView` is bound to the dataSource property of the `listArticles` List object. The `dataSource` property returns the object that implements the `IListDataSource`.

The `FlipView` control's `itemTemplate` property points to a `Template` control with the id `tmplArticle` that is declared earlier in the page. The `Template` control contains the template used to format the article displayed by the `FlipView`.

> **WARNING**
>
> Make sure that you declare the `Template` control before the `FlipView` control and not after in the page or you will get a mysterious error and spend hours trying to debug it.

> **WARNING**
>
> As always, remember to call `WinJS.UI.processAll()` or the `FlipView` won't become a `FlipView`.

Displaying Page Numbers

When swiping through items displayed by a `FlipView`, it can be useful to know which item you are viewing out of how many items. In other words, you might want to display a page number (see Figure 7.8).

FIGURE 7.8   Displaying a page number with a `FlipView`

You can use the `FlipView` control's `currentPage` property to retrieve the current page (the index of the current item) displayed by the `FlipView`. You can use the `count()` method to get the total number of pages (the total number of items) contained in the data source associated with the `FlipView`.

The page in Listing 7.16 contains a `FlipView` and a DIV element. The DIV element displays both the current page and the total number of pages.

LISTING 7.16   Displaying the Current Page Number with a `FlipView` (flipViewPageNumber\ flipViewPageNumber.html)

```
<div id="tmplArticle"
    data-win-control="WinJS.Binding.Template">
    <div class="articleItem">
        <h2 data-win-bind="innerText:title"></h2>
        Author: <span data-win-bind="innerText:author"></span>
        <p data-win-bind="innerText:articleText"></p>
    </div>
</div>


<div id="fvArticles"
    data-win-control="WinJS.UI.FlipView"
    data-win-options="{
```

```
    itemDataSource: MyData.listArticles.dataSource,
    itemTemplate: select('#tmplArticle')
}"></div>
```

```
<div id="divPageNumber"></div>
```

The page number and page count displayed in the HTML page is updated with the `updatePageNumber()` function contained in Listing 7.17. This function updates the `divPageNumber` DIV element in the page.

LISTING 7.17   Displaying the Current Page Number with a `FlipView` (flipViewPageNumber\
flipViewPageNumber.js)

```
(function () {
    "use strict";

    function initialize() {
        WinJS.UI.processAll().done(function () {
            var fvArticles = document.getElementById("fvArticles").winControl;
            var divPageNumber = document.getElementById("divPageNumber");

            // Show Page Number and Page Count
            function updatePageNumber() {
                var currentPage = fvArticles.currentPage + 1;
                fvArticles.count().done(function (count) {
                    divPageNumber.innerHTML = "Page " + currentPage
                        + " of " + count;
                });
            }
            updatePageNumber();

            // Update Page Number when new page selected
            fvArticles.addEventListener("pageselected", updatePageNumber);

        });
    }

    document.addEventListener("DOMContentLoaded", initialize);
})();
```

Notice that the `FlipView` `count()` method does not directly return a page count. Instead, it returns a promise that returns a page count when the promise completes. This makes the `updatePageNumber()` function slightly more complicated.

Creating Custom `FlipView` Buttons

You might want to create custom buttons for navigating back and forth through the items in a `FlipView`. The default arrows which appear for navigating through a `FlipView` are subtle; they don't appear unless you hover your mouse over the control. You might want to bang the user over the head with more explicit navigation buttons (see Figure 7.9).

FIGURE 7.9   Custom `FlipView` buttons

You can take advantage of two methods of the `FlipView` control to control navigation programmatically: the `previous()` and `next()` methods.

For example, the page in Listing 7.18 includes two buttons named `btnPrevious` and `btnNext`.

LISTING 7.18   A `FlipView` with Custom Buttons (flipViewButtons\flipViewButtons.html)

```
<div id="tmplArticle"
    data-win-control="WinJS.Binding.Template">
    <div class="articleItem">
        <h2 data-win-bind="innerText:title"></h2>
        Author: <span data-win-bind="innerText:author"></span>
        <p data-win-bind="innerText:articleText"></p>
    </div>
</div>


<div id="fvArticles"
    data-win-control="WinJS.UI.FlipView"
    data-win-options="{
        itemDataSource: MyData.listArticles.dataSource,
        itemTemplate: select('#tmplArticle')
    }"></div>


<div id="divNavigation">
    <button id="btnPrevious">Previous</button>
    <button id="btnNext">Next</button>
</div>
```

The JavaScript code in Listing 7.19 contains the code to wire up the `btnPrevious` and `btnNext` buttons to event handlers. When you click the `btnPrevious` button, the `previous()` method is called; when you click the `btnNext` button, the `next()` method is called.

LISTING 7.19   A `FlipView` with Custom Buttons (flipViewButtons\flipViewButtons.js)

```javascript
(function () {
    "use strict";

    function initialize() {
        WinJS.UI.processAll().done(function () {
            var fvArticles = document.getElementById("fvArticles").winControl;
            var btnPrevious = document.getElementById("btnPrevious");
            var btnNext = document.getElementById("btnNext");

            // Setup Buttons
            btnPrevious.addEventListener("click", function () {
                fvArticles.previous();
            });
            btnNext.addEventListener("click", function () {
                fvArticles.next();
            });
        });
    }

    document.addEventListener("DOMContentLoaded", initialize);
})();
```

Summary

In this chapter, you were introduced to three controls related to working with collections. First, I described how you can wrap content in an `ItemContainer` control to make the content invokable, selectable, or draggable.

I also discussed the `Repeater` control. You saw how you can use the `Repeater` control to render a collection of data as an HTML table. I demonstrated how you can use the `Repeater` and `ItemContainer` controls together.

Finally, I talked about the `FlipView` control. You learned how to use the `FlipView` to display one item from a collection. I showed you how you can page through news articles from a collection of articles.

In the next chapter, I tackle the most important and feature-rich control in the WinJS library: the `ListView` control.

CHAPTER 8

Using the `ListView` Control

This entire chapter is devoted to one control: the `ListView` control. This is the single most important control included in the WinJS library. If you need to efficiently display an interactive list or grid of items—for example, a list of products, a list of movies, a list of files, a list of photos—then the `ListView` control is the control to use.

The `ListView` control is used in many of the standard Windows 8.1 apps. For example, the `ListView` is used in the Windows 8.1 Mail app to display the list of messages in your inbox (see Figure 8.1). The control has been designed to perform well when displaying thousands of items.

In this chapter, I explain how you can take advantage of all of the most important features of the `ListView` control. You learn the basics, including how to select, sort, filter, and group items in a `ListView`.

I also discuss more advanced features of the `ListView` control. In particular, you learn how to use the `ListView` control with semantic zoom to generate different representations of the same data. You also learn how to take advantage of drag and drop with a `ListView`.

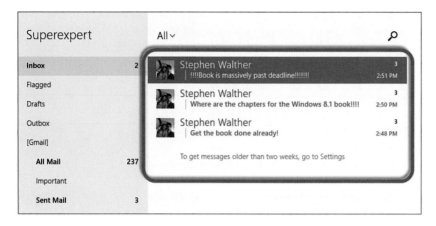

FIGURE 8.1 `ListView` in the Mail app

Introduction to the `ListView` Control

Let's start with the basics. You can bind a `ListView` control to any data source that implements the JavaScript `IListDataSource` interface. The WinJS library includes two objects that implement this data source:

▶ `WinJS.Binding.List`—Enables you to represent a JavaScript array as a data source.

▶ `WinJS.UI.StorageDataSource`—Enables you to represent files from your computer hard drive as a data source. For example, you can use the `WinJS.UI.StorageDataSource` with the `ListView` control to display a list of pictures retrieved from your computer's Pictures library.

In this chapter, we focus on using the `WinJS.Binding.List` data source because this is the most flexible data source. You can create an instance of the `WinJS.Binding.List` data source from any JavaScript array.

For example, you can perform an Ajax request against a remote server and retrieve an array of products. You can then display the array of products by using the `List` data source with the `ListView` control.

NOTE

Instead of using either the `WinJS.Binding.List` or `WinJS.UI.StorageDataSource` data sources, you can create a custom data source and use it with the `ListView` control. You might want to create a custom data source, for example, if you need to display data from an IndexedDB database with a `ListView` control. We create several custom data sources—including an `IndexedDB` data source—in the next chapter.

Let's look at how you can use the `ListView` control with a `WinJS.Binding.List` data source. The page in Listing 8.1 contains a `ListView` control that displays a set of products (see Figure 8.2).

LISTING 8.1   Binding to a `List` Data Source (simple\simple.html)

```
<div id="tmplProduct"
    data-win-control="WinJS.Binding.Template">
    <div class="productItem">
        <h2 data-win-bind="innerText:name"></h2>
        Price: <span data-win-bind="innerText:price"></span>
    </div>
</div>

<div id="lvProducts"
    data-win-control="WinJS.UI.ListView"
    data-win-options="{
        itemTemplate: select('#tmplProduct')
    }"></div>
```

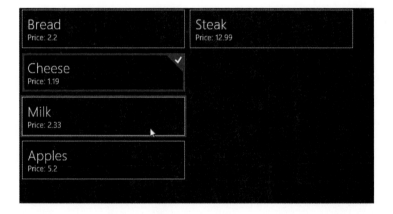

FIGURE 8.2   Displaying a list of products

The `ListView` control in Listing 8.1 uses a template to render each product. The template is contained in a `Template` control with the id `tmplProduct`.

> **WARNING**
>
> Make sure that you declare the `Template` control in the page before the `ListView` control or you will get a mysterious and hard-to-debug exception.

The JavaScript file in Listing 8.2 contains the array of products. A `WinJS.Binding.List` object is created from the array of products and the `List` object is bound to the `ListView` control with the help of the `itemDataSource` property. When you view the page, you see the list of products from the JavaScript array.

LISTING 8.2   Binding to a `List` Data Source (simple\simple.js)

```javascript
(function () {
    "use strict";

    function initialize() {
        WinJS.UI.processAll().done(function () {
            // Get reference to ListView control
            var lvProducts = document.getElementById("lvProducts").winControl;

            // Create a List of products
            var listProducts = new WinJS.Binding.List([
                { name: "Bread", price: 2.20 },
                { name: "Cheese", price: 1.19 },
                { name: "Milk", price: 2.33 },
                { name: "Apples", price: 5.20 },
                { name: "Steak", price: 12.99 }
            ]);

            // Bind the list of products to the ListView
            lvProducts.itemDataSource = listProducts.dataSource;

        });
    }

    document.addEventListener("DOMContentLoaded", initialize);
})();
```

NOTE

I used a tiny bit of CSS with Listing 8.1 to create borders around each of the products:

```css
#lvProducts .productItem {
  border: solid 1px white;
  padding: 10px;
  width: 300px;
}
```

You can stick just about anything in a JavaScript array: the results of a database query, the results of an Ajax call, the Fibonacci series. For this reason, when you bind a `ListView` control to a `List`, you can bind to almost any type of data.

For example, the `ListView` in Listing 8.3 displays a list of blog posts retrieved from a blog feed, as shown in Figure 8.3.

LISTING 8.3   Binding to a Blog Feed (blog\blog.html)

```
<div id="tmplBlog"
    data-win-control="WinJS.Binding.Template">
    <div>
        <span data-win-bind="innerHTML: title.text WinJS.Binding.oneTime"></span>
    </div>
</div>

<div id="lvBlog"
    data-win-control="WinJS.UI.ListView"
    data-win-options="{
        itemTemplate: select('#tmplBlog')
    }"></div>
```

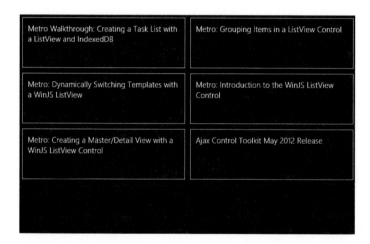

FIGURE 8.3   Displaying a list of blog posts

The list of blog posts is retrieved from an RSS feed located at http://StephenWalther.com (hey, that's my blog) with the help of the WinRT SyndicationClient class. Listing 8.4 contains the code which grabs the feed and binds it to the ListView control.

LISTING 8.4   Binding to a Blog Feed (blog\blog.js)

```
(function () {
    "use strict";

    function initialize() {
        WinJS.UI.processAll().done(function () {
            // Get reference to ListView control
            var lvBlog = document.getElementById("lvBlog").winControl;
```

8

```
            // Use WinRT SyndicationClient to get blog feed
            var client = new Windows.Web.Syndication.SyndicationClient();
            var feedURI = new Windows.Foundation.Uri("http://stephenwalther.com/
➡feed");

            client.retrieveFeedAsync(feedURI).done(function (feed) {

                // Convert feed items to a List
                var listItems = new WinJS.Binding.List(feed.items);

                // Bind list to ListView
                lvBlog.itemDataSource = listItems.dataSource;
            });

        });
    }

    document.addEventListener("DOMContentLoaded", initialize);
})();
```

The SyndicationClient returns an instance of the SyndicationFeed class. The SyndicationFeed class has an items property that contains the blog entries.

The blog entries are passed to the constructor for the WinJS.Binding.List class and the List class is bound to the ListView control.

WARNING

By default, a ListView control will try to make each of its list items into an observable by calling the WinJS.Binding.as() method. Unfortunately, this does not work on WinRT objects such as the items returned by the SyndicationClient class. You'll get an exception if you try to bind WinRT objects to a ListView control.

There are two ways to get around this problem. If you look closely at the template in Listing 8.3 then you will notice that the blog title is bound using the WinJS.Binding. oneTime() binding converter. When you use the WinJS.Binding.oneTime() converter, the ListView control does not attempt to convert the items bound to it into observables.

Another solution to this problem would be to copy the array of WinRT objects into a new JavaScript array of JavaScript objects before binding to the ListView control. JavaScript objects, unlike WinRT objects, are happy to be made into observables.

Using Different ListView Layouts

The overall appearance of a ListView is determined by its layout. The ListView control supports three different layouts:

▶ **Grid Layout**—ListView items are displayed in a multiple column grid.

▶ **Cell Spanning Layout**—Same as grid layout but supports multiple column cells.

▶ **List Layout**—ListView items are displayed in a single list.

Each layout corresponds to a JavaScript object—the `GridLayout`, `CellSpanningLayout`, `ListLayout` objects—that has its own properties and methods. Let me discuss each of these layout options in detail.

Using Grid Layout

The default layout is grid layout. When a `ListView` displays items in grid layout, the items are displayed in multiple columns. If there are too many items to fit in the `ListView` then you scroll to the right to view the additional items (see Figure 8.4).

> **NOTE**
>
> Under the covers, grid layout uses the W3C CSS 3 Grid Layout recommendation. You can read the details here at http://dev.w3.org/csswg/css3-grid-layout/.

FIGURE 8.4   `ListView` in grid layout

When the `ListView` uses grid layout, you can set the `maximumRowsOrColumns` property to set the maximum number of grid rows that should be displayed. Here's how you would set the `maximumRowsOrColumns` property so a `ListView` displays only one row (see Figure 8.5):

```
<div id="lvProducts"
    data-win-control="WinJS.UI.ListView"
    data-win-options="{
        itemTemplate: select('#tmplProduct'),
        layout: {type:WinJS.UI.GridLayout, maximumRowsOrColumns:1}
    }"></div>
```

FIGURE 8.5   Setting the `GridLayout maximumRowsOrColumns` property

Finally, if you prefer to scroll your `ListView` vertically instead of horizontally then you can set the grid layout orientation option to vertical like this:

```
<div id="lvProducts"
    data-win-control="WinJS.UI.ListView"
    data-win-options="{
        itemTemplate: select('#tmplProduct'),
        layout: {type: WinJS.UI.GridLayout, orientation: 'vertical'}
    }"></div>
```

When you switch orientations, the scrollbar appears on the right of the `ListView` instead of across the bottom of the `ListView` (see Figure 8.6).

FIGURE 8.6   Vertical scrolling `ListView`

Using List Layout

The second layout mode that you can use with a `ListView` control is list layout. In list layout mode, the items are displayed in a single vertical list. If all of the items do not fit in the `ListView` then you can scroll the `ListView` (see Figure 8.7).

FIGURE 8.7   A `ListView` control that uses list layout

Here's how you can declare a `ListView` so it uses list layout:

```
<div id="lvProducts"
    data-win-control="WinJS.UI.ListView"
    data-win-options="{
        itemTemplate: select('#tmplProduct'),
        layout: {type:WinJS.UI.ListLayout}
    }"></div>
```

When `ListView` items are rendered with list layout then the items are not actually displayed using HTML UL and LI elements as the name of the layout might imply. Instead, DIV elements are rendered for each item.

Using Cell Spanning Layout

The final layout mode is called *cell spanning layout*. Cell spanning layout is similar to grid layout but, unlike grid layout, cell spanning layout enables you to create grid items with different sizes. For example, you can make a tile screen that contains different size tiles like the Windows 8.1 start screen.

Unfortunately, great power also requires lots of math. So, if you want to create different size grid items then you will need to get out your calculator to figure out the sizes of the different items.

Imagine that you want to create the page in Figure 8.8. Notice that the figure includes three sizes of tiles: normal, wide, and tall.

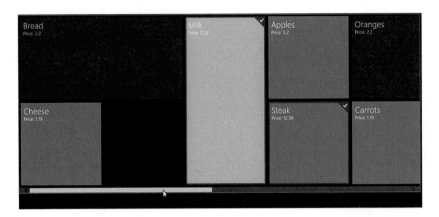

FIGURE 8.8   Creating different size tiles

Listing 8.5 contains a page with cell spanning layout enabled.

LISTING 8.5   Using Cell Spanning Layout (layoutCellSpanning\layoutCellSpanning.html)

```html
<!DOCTYPE html>
<html>
<head>
    <meta charset="utf-8" />
    <title>ListView</title>

    <!-- WinJS references -->
    <link href="//Microsoft.WinJS.2.0.Preview/css/ui-dark.css" rel="stylesheet" />
    <script src="//Microsoft.WinJS.2.0.Preview/js/base.js"></script>
    <script src="//Microsoft.WinJS.2.0.Preview/js/ui.js"></script>

    <!-- Chapter references -->
    <script src="layoutCellSpanning.js"></script>

    <style>

    .win-listview {
        margin: 5px;
        border: 2px solid gray;
        height: 580px;
    }


    .normal {
        width: 250px;
        height: 250px;
        padding: 10px;
```

```
            background-color: gray;
    }

    .tall {
        width: 250px;
        height: 530px;
        padding: 10px;
        background-color: orange;
    }


    .wide {
        width: 530px;
        height: 250px;
        padding: 10px;
        background-color: navy;
    }

    </style>
</head>
<body>

    <div id="tmplProduct" data-win-control="WinJS.Binding.Template">
        <div data-win-bind="className: tileSize" >
            <h2 data-win-bind="innerText:name"></h2>
            Price: <span data-win-bind="innerText:price"></span>
        </div>
    </div>

    <div id="lvProducts"
        data-win-control="WinJS.UI.ListView"
        data-win-options="{
            itemTemplate: select('#tmplProduct'),
            layout: {type: WinJS.UI.CellSpanningLayout}
        }"></div>

</body>
</html>
```

Notice that the layout property for the ListView control is set to the value WinJS. UI.CellSpanningLayout.

Notice, furthermore, that the page includes three CSS classes that set the width and height for normal, tall, and wide ListView items. Each class also defines a different background color.

The different CSS classes are used by the `Template` control in the body of the page. This template contains an inner DIV element with the attribute `data-win-bind="className: tileSize"`. The CSS class rendered for each `ListView` item is determined by each data item's `tileSize` property.

Listing 8.6 contains the code for binding the `ListView` to a set of products.

LISTING 8.6 Using Cell Spanning Layout (layoutCellSpanning\layoutCellSpanning.js)

```
(function () {
    "use strict";

    function initialize() {
        WinJS.UI.processAll().done(function () {
            // Get reference to ListView control
            var lvProducts = document.getElementById("lvProducts").winControl;

            // Create a List of products
            var listProducts = new WinJS.Binding.List([
                { name: "Bread", price: 2.20, tileSize:"wide" },
                { name: "Cheese", price: 1.19, tileSize:"normal" },
                { name: "Milk", price: 2.33, tileSize: "tall" },
                { name: "Apples", price: 5.20, tileSize: "normal" },
                { name: "Steak", price: 12.99, tileSize: "normal" },
                { name: "Oranges", price: 2.20, tileSize: "wide" },
                { name: "Carrots", price: 1.19, tileSize: "normal" },
                { name: "Yogurt", price: 2.33, tileSize: "normal" },
                { name: "Eggs", price: 5.20, tileSize: "normal" },
                { name: "Soda", price: 12.99, tileSize: "normal" },
                { name: "Steak", price: 12.99, tileSize: "normal" },
                { name: "Oranges", price: 2.20, tileSize: "normal" },
                { name: "Carrots", price: 1.19, tileSize: "normal" },
                { name: "Yogurt", price: 2.33, tileSize: "normal" },
                { name: "Eggs", price: 5.20, tileSize: "normal" },
                { name: "Soda", price: 12.99, tileSize: "normal" }

            ]);

            lvProducts.layout.groupInfo = function(groupInfo) {
                return {
                    enableCellSpanning: true,
                    cellWidth: 270,
                    cellHeight: 270
                };
            };
```

```
lvProducts.layout.itemInfo = function (itemIndex) {
    var item = listProducts.getItem(itemIndex);

    var size = null;
    switch (item.data.tileSize) {
        case "normal":
            size = {
                width: 270,
                height: 270
            };
            break;
        case "wide":
            size = {
                width: 550,
                height: 270
            };
            break;
        case "tall":
            size = {
                width: 270,
                height: 550
            };
            break;
    }
    return size;
};




    // Bind the list of products to the ListView
    lvProducts.itemDataSource = listProducts.dataSource;

    });
}

document.addEventListener("DOMContentLoaded", initialize);
})();
```

In Listing 8.6, each product has a `tileSize` property of normal, wide, or tall. This property determines how each product is rendered.

Two functions are associated with the `ListView` control's layout: a `groupInfo` and `itemInfo` function. The groupInfo function enables variable size cells by setting `enableCellSpanning` to the value true. The `groupInfo` function also defines the default size of `ListView` items to be 270 pixels by 270 pixels.

The `itemInfo` function is called for each data item displayed by the `ListView`. The `itemInfo` function determines whether a normal, wide, or tall tile is displayed for each data item.

The only tricky thing about getting all of this to work is making sure that the size of the `ListView` items specified by the CSS classes matches the size of the `ListView` items specified by both the `GroupInfo()` and `itemInfo()` functions. What makes this extra tricky is that you must take into account the padding and margins between the `ListView` elements when calculating the width and height of items in the `GroupInfo()` and `itemInfo()` functions.

Invoking Items in a `ListView` Control

Under the covers, a `ListView` control renders `ItemContainer` controls for each `ListView` item. This is the exact same `ItemContainer` control that we discussed in the previous chapter. Therefore, `ListView` items support the same events and styling as `ItemContainer` controls.

You can handle the `ListView` control's `iteminvoked` event to detect when a particular `ListView` item is clicked. The page in Listing 8.7 contains a standard `ListView` control (nothing special about it).

LISTING 8.7   Invoking a `ListView` Item (itemInvoked\itemInvoked.html)

```
<div id="tmplProduct"
    data-win-control="WinJS.Binding.Template">
    <div class="productItem">
        <h2 data-win-bind="innerText:name"></h2>
        Price: <span data-win-bind="innerText:price"></span>
    </div>
</div>

<div id="lvProducts"
    data-win-control="WinJS.UI.ListView"
    data-win-options="{
        itemTemplate: select('#tmplProduct')
    }"></div>
```

When you click one of the items displayed by the `ListView`, a dialog appears that displays the index and name of the item invoked (see Figure 8.9).

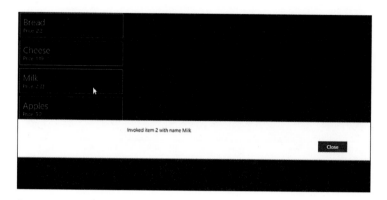

FIGURE 8.9   Invoking a `ListView` item

The `iteminvoked` handler is contained in Listing 8.8. Information about the item clicked is retrieved from the event handler's detail property.

LISTING 8.8   Invoking a `ListView` Item (itemInvoked\itemInvoked.html)

```
(function () {
    "use strict";

    function initialize() {
        WinJS.UI.processAll().done(function () {
            // Get reference to ListView control
            var lvProducts = document.getElementById("lvProducts").winControl;

            // Create a List of products
            var listProducts = new WinJS.Binding.List([
                { name: "Bread", price: 2.20 },
                { name: "Cheese", price: 1.19 },
                { name: "Milk", price: 2.33 },
                { name: "Apples", price: 5.20 }
            ]);

            // Wire up item invoked handler
            lvProducts.addEventListener("iteminvoked", function (e) {
                var itemIndex = e.detail.itemIndex;
                e.detail.itemPromise.then(function (item) {
                    var message = "Invoked item " + itemIndex
                        + " with name " + item.data.name;
                    var md = new Windows.UI.Popups.MessageDialog(message);
                    md.showAsync();
                });
            });
        });
```

8

```
        // Bind the list of products to the ListView
        lvProducts.itemDataSource = listProducts.dataSource;


    });
}


document.addEventListener("DOMContentLoaded", initialize);
})();
```

Selecting Items in a `ListView` Control

You can use the `ListView` control's `selectionchanging` and `selectionchanged` events to detect when an item is selected in a `ListView`. Imagine, for example, that you want to create a master/detail page: You want to display a list of product categories and, when a user selects a product category, display a list of matching products (see Figure 8.10).

FIGURE 8.10   Selecting ListView items

The page in Listing 8.9 contains two `ListView` controls: a `ListView` that displays the categories and a `ListView` that displays the matching products.

LISTING 8.9   Creating a Master/Detail Page (masterDetail\masterDetail.html)

```
<!-- Templates -->
<div id="tmplCategory"
    data-win-control="WinJS.Binding.Template">
    <div class="categoryItem">
        <h2 data-win-bind="innerText:categoryName"></h2>
    </div>
</div>

<div id="tmplProduct"
    data-win-control="WinJS.Binding.Template">
    <div class="productItem">
        <h2 data-win-bind="innerText:productName"></h2>
        Price: <span data-win-bind="innerText:price"></span>
```

```
        </div>
    </div>

    <div id="container">

        <!-- Master ListView for Categories -->
        <div id="lvCategories"
            data-win-control="WinJS.UI.ListView"
            data-win-options="{
                itemTemplate: select('#tmplCategory'),
                selectionMode: 'single',
                tapBehavior: 'directSelect',
                swipBehavior: 'select',
                layout: {type: WinJS.UI.ListLayout}
            }"></div>

        <!-- Details ListView for Products -->
        <div id="lvProducts"
            data-win-control="WinJS.UI.ListView"
            data-win-options="{
                itemTemplate: select('#tmplProduct'),
                selectionMode: 'none',
                layout: {type: WinJS.UI.ListLayout}
            }"></div>

    </div>
```

The logic for the master/detail page is contained in Listing 8.10. The categories and products are represented with an array named `products`. This array is bound to the categories `ListView`.

When you select a category then the `selectionchanged` event is raised. In Listing 8.10, the `selectionchanged` event handler is used to retrieve the list of matching products from the selected category and display the products in the second `ListView` control.

LISTING 8.10   Creating a Master/Detail Page (masterDetail\masterDetail.html)

```
(function () {
    "use strict";

    function initialize() {
        WinJS.UI.processAll().done(function () {
            // Get references to ListView controls
            var lvProducts = document.getElementById("lvProducts").winControl;
            var lvCategories = document.getElementById("lvCategories").winControl;
```

```
// Create array of categories and products
var products = [
    {
        categoryName: "Beverages",
        products: [
            { productName: "Pepsi", price: 4.00 },
            { productName: "Milk", price: 2.11 },
            { productName: "Moxie", price: 1.33 }
        ]
    },
    {
        categoryName: "Meat",
        products: [
            { productName: "Steak", price: 34.33 },
            { productName: "Chicken", price: 2.01 }
        ]
    },
    {
        categoryName: "Fruit",
        products: [
            { productName: "Apples", price: 2.88 },
            { productName: "Oranges", price: 7.01 }
        ]
    }
];

// Create a List of categories and products
var listProducts = new WinJS.Binding.List(products);

// Bind the list to the Categories ListView
lvCategories.itemDataSource = listProducts.dataSource;

// Handle the selectionchanged event
lvCategories.addEventListener("selectionchanged", function () {
    if (lvCategories.selection.count() > 0) {
        lvCategories.selection.getItems().done(function (items) {
            // Get products for first selected item
            var selectedProducts = items[0].data.products;

            // Convert to list
            var listSelectedProducts = new WinJS.Binding.
➥List(selectedProducts);

            // Bind to Products ListView
            lvProducts.itemDataSource = listSelectedProducts.dataSource;
        });
    }
```

```
        });


    });
  }

    document.addEventListener("DOMContentLoaded", initialize);
})();
```

Sorting Items in a `ListView` Control

You can sort the items displayed with a `ListView` control by sorting the items in the
`ListView` control's data source. For example, you might want to sort a list of products in
order of the product name or price (see Figure 8.11).

FIGURE 8.11   Sorting `ListView` items

The `WinJS.Binding.List` object supports the `createSorted()` method. This method
accepts a sort function that returns a new `WinJS.Binding.List` sorted according to the
function.

For example, the following code sorts a list of products in order of the product name:

```
// Create a List of products
var listProducts = new WinJS.Binding.List([
    { name: "Bread", price: 2.20 },
    { name: "Cheese", price: 1.19 },
    { name: "Milk", price: 2.33 },
    { name: "Apples", price: 5.20 },
    { name: "Steak", price: 12.99 }
]);


// Sort the products
var sortedListProducts = listProducts.createSorted(function (item1, item2) {
    return item1.name > item2.name ? 1 : -1;
});
```

```
// Bind the list of products to the ListView
lvProducts.itemDataSource = sortedListProducts.dataSource;
```

The preceding code uses the `createSorted()` method to create a new sorted data source based on the original unsorted products data source. The `ListView` is bound to the new data source instead of the original data source.

In the preceding code, the products are sorted with the following sort function:

```
function (item1, item2) {
    return item1.name > item2.name ? 1 : -1;
}
```

A sort function sorts items by returning one of three possible values:

- ▶ 0—When the two items should be sorted in the same order
- ▶ -1—When the first item should be sorted before the second item
- ▶ 1—When the first item should be sorted after the second item

The `sortedListProducts` data source is a live data source. If you add a new item to the `listProducts` data source then the new item will appear in the `ListView` in the right order. Changes to the `listProducts` data source are picked up automatically.

NOTE

You can use the same types of sort functions with the WinJS `createSorted()` method as you would use with the standard JavaScript array `sort()` method.

Filtering Items in a `ListView` Control

You can filter the items displayed in a `ListView` by filtering the items in the data source associated with the `ListView`. For example, when browsing through a large set of products, you might want to enable a user to filter the products by only showing products that match a filter string (see Figure 8.12).

FIGURE 8.12   Filtering a list of products

You can take an existing `WinJS.Binding.List` and create a new filtered `WinJS.Binding.List` by calling the `createFiltered()` method. This method accepts a filter function that returns either the value true or false depending on whether an item from the original list should be included in the new list.

The code in Listings 8.11 and 8.12 illustrate how you can use the `createFiltered()` method to create a keyup search form. The page in Listing 8.11 contains an input box and a `ListView` control.

LISTING 8.11   Filtering a List of Products (filtering\filtering.html)

```
<div>
    <input id="inputFilter" />
</div>
<div id="tmplProduct"
    data-win-control="WinJS.Binding.Template">
    <div class="productItem">
        <h2 data-win-bind="innerText:name"></h2>
        Price: <span data-win-bind="innerText:price"></span>
    </div>
</div>


<div id="lvProducts"
    data-win-control="WinJS.UI.ListView"
    data-win-options="{
        itemTemplate: select('#tmplProduct')
    }"></div>
```

The JavaScript code in Listing 8.12 includes a function named `filterProducts()`. This function accepts a `ListView` and a filter string and filters the `ListView` so it only displays products that match the filter string.

LISTING 8.12   Filtering a List of Products (filtering\filtering.js)

```
(function () {
    "use strict";

    // Create a List of products
    var listProducts = new WinJS.Binding.List([
        { name: "Bread", price: 2.20 },
        { name: "Broccoli", price: 1.19 },
        { name: "Bananas", price: 2.33 },
        { name: "Apples", price: 5.20 },
        { name: "Apple Sauce", price: 12.99 }
    ]);
```

```
function initialize() {

    WinJS.UI.processAll().done(function () {
        // Get references to DOM elements and Controls
        var lvProducts = document.getElementById("lvProducts").winControl;
        var inputFilter = document.getElementById("inputFilter");

        // Bind the unfiltered list of products to the ListView
        lvProducts.itemDataSource = listProducts.dataSource;

        inputFilter.addEventListener("keyup", function () {
            filterProducts(lvProducts, inputFilter.value);
        });

    });
}


function filterProducts(listViewToFilter, filter) {
    // Filter the data source
    var filteredListProducts = listProducts.createFiltered(function (item) {
        var result = item.name.toLowerCase().indexOf(filter);
        return item.name.toLowerCase().indexOf(filter) == 0;
    });

    // Bind the list of products to the ListView
    listViewToFilter.itemDataSource = filteredListProducts.dataSource;
}

    document.addEventListener("DOMContentLoaded", initialize);
})();
```

Here's the filter function used by the createFiltered() method:

```
function (item) {
    var result = item.name.toLowerCase().indexOf(filter);
    return item.name.toLowerCase().indexOf(filter) == 0;
}
```

This function returns an item when the item name does not start with the filter string. Depending on what the user types into the input box, different results are displayed. This is a live filter, so the results change as the user types.

Grouping Items in a `ListView` Control

You can group the items that appear in a `ListView` control. For example, instead of displaying a flat list of products, you can group products by product category (see Figure 8.13).

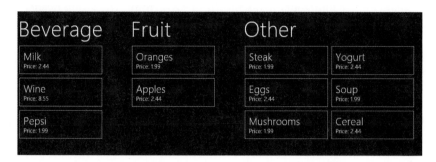

FIGURE 8.13   Grouping `ListView` items

If you want to take advantage of groups, then you need to create a grouped data source. You create a grouped data source by calling the `WinJS.Binding.List createGrouped()` method.

The code in Listing 8.13 and Listing 8.14 illustrates how you can use the `createGrouped()` method to group products by categories.

LISTING 8.13   Grouping `ListView` Items (grouped\grouped.html)

```
<!-- Templates -->
<div id="tmplProductGroupHeader" data-win-control="WinJS.Binding.Template">
    <div class="productGroupHeader">
        <h1 data-win-bind="innerText: title"></h1>
    </div>
</div>


<div id="tmplProduct"
    data-win-control="WinJS.Binding.Template">
    <div class="productItem">
        <h2 data-win-bind="innerText:name"></h2>
        Price: <span data-win-bind="innerText:price"></span>
    </div>
</div>


<!-- Products ListView -->
<div id="lvProducts"
    data-win-control="WinJS.UI.ListView"
    data-win-options="{
```

```
        itemTemplate: select('#tmplProduct'),
        groupHeaderTemplate: select('#tmplProductGroupHeader')
    }"></div>
```

The HTML page in Listing 8.13 contains two templates: one template for the group header and one template for the individual items shown in each group. The group header template is associated with the ListView control declaratively with the ListView control's groupHeaderTemplate property.

LISTING 8.14   Grouping ListView Items (grouped\grouped.js)

```
(function () {
    "use strict";

    function initialize() {
        WinJS.UI.processAll().done(function () {
            // Get reference to ListView control
            var lvProducts = document.getElementById("lvProducts").winControl;

            // Create a List of products
            var listProducts = new WinJS.Binding.List([
                        { name: "Milk", price: 2.44, category: "Beverages" },
                        { name: "Oranges", price: 1.99, category: "Fruit" },
                        { name: "Wine", price: 8.55, category: "Beverages" },
                        { name: "Apples", price: 2.44, category: "Fruit" },
                        { name: "Steak", price: 1.99, category: "Other" },
                        { name: "Eggs", price: 2.44, category: "Other" },
                        { name: "Mushrooms", price: 1.99, category: "Other" },
                        { name: "Yogurt", price: 2.44, category: "Other" },
                        { name: "Soup", price: 1.99, category: "Other" },
                        { name: "Cereal", price: 2.44, category: "Other" },
                        { name: "Pepsi", price: 1.99, category: "Beverages" }
            ]);

            // Create grouped data source
            var groupListProducts = listProducts.createGrouped(
                function (dataItem) {
                    return dataItem.category;
                },
                function (dataItem) {
                    return { title: dataItem.category };
                },
                function (group1, group2) {
                    return group1 > group2 ? 1 : -1;
```

```
                }
            );

            // Bind the list of products to the ListView
            lvProducts.groupDataSource = groupListProducts.groups.dataSource;
            lvProducts.itemDataSource = groupListProducts.dataSource;


        });
    }

    document.addEventListener("DOMContentLoaded", initialize);
})();
```

The JavaScript code in Listing 8.14 is used to create both the grouped data source and the item data source. The grouped data source is created by calling the `createGrouped()` method.

Notice that the `createGrouped()` method requires three functions as arguments:

- ▶ `groupKey`—This function associates each list item with a group. The function accepts a data item and returns a key that represents a group. In the preceding code, we return the value of the category property for each product.

- ▶ `groupData`—This function returns the data item displayed by the group header template. For example, in the preceding code, the function returns a title for the group that is displayed in the group header template.

- ▶ `groupSorter`—This function determines the order in which the groups are displayed. The preceding code displays the groups in alphabetical order: Beverages, Fruit, Other.

The two data sources—the grouped and the item data sources—are bound to the `ListView` control with the following two lines of code:

```
// Bind the list of products to the ListView
lvProducts.groupDataSource = groupListProducts.groups.dataSource;
lvProducts.itemDataSource = groupListProducts.dataSource;
```

The grouped data source is a live data source—so the groups displayed by the `ListView` change when you change the data source. Furthermore, you can use the grouped data source with a filtered data source.

Switching Views with Semantic Zoom

Semantic Zoom is a feature of Windows 8 that enables you to view data at two different zoom levels. For example, the Windows 8 Start screen takes advantage of Semantic Zoom. By default, when you open the Start screen, you see a close-up view of your apps (see Figure 8.14). However, you can zoom out to see a more far away view of your apps (see Figure 8.15).

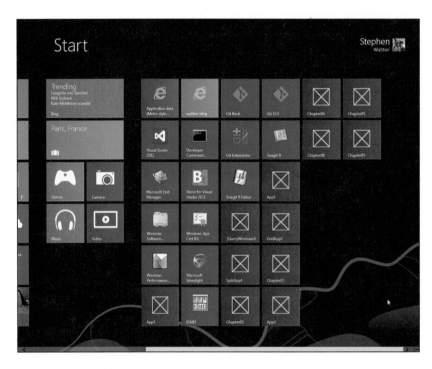

FIGURE 8.14   Default Start screen

When using the mouse, you can zoom out by clicking the – button, which appears at the bottom right of the screen. When using touch, you can zoom in and out by using pinch and stretch gestures.

You can implement Semantic Zoom in your Windows app by taking advantage of the WinJS SemanticZoom control. When used with the ListView control, the SemanticZoom control enables you to provide two different views of the same data: the hundred-foot view and the ten-foot view.

FIGURE 8.15   Zoomed-out Start screen

Imagine that you are working with a lot of products and the products can be grouped by category. To make it easier for a user to navigate to different categories, you can take advantage of Semantic Zoom. By default, you see the products grouped into categories (see Figure 8.16). However, if you zoom out, then you see only the list of categories without the products (see Figure 8.17).

FIGURE 8.16   Using semantic zoom (ten-foot view)

FIGURE 8.17   Using semantic zoom (hundred-foot view)

The HTML page in Listing 8.15 illustrates how you can implement Semantic Zoom. The page contains a SemanticZoom control that has two child ListView controls. The different ListViews are displayed at different zoom levels.

LISTING 8.15   Zooming with Semantic Zoom (semanticZoom\semanticZoom.html)

```html
<!-- Zoom In Template -->
<div id="tmplProductGroupHeader" data-win-control="WinJS.Binding.Template">
    <div class="productGroupHeader">
        <h1 data-win-bind="innerText: title"></h1>
    </div>
</div>


<div id="tmplProduct"
    data-win-control="WinJS.Binding.Template">
    <div class="productItem">
        <h2 data-win-bind="innerText:name"></h2>
        Price: <span data-win-bind="innerText:price"></span>
    </div>
</div>


<!-- Zoom Out Template -->
<div id="tmplCategory"
    data-win-control="WinJS.Binding.Template">
    <div class="categoryItem">
        <h2 data-win-bind="innerText:title"></h2>
    </div>
</div>



<!-- SemanticZoom and ListViews -->
<div id="divSemanticZoom" data-win-control="WinJS.UI.SemanticZoom">
    <!-- Zoom In ListView (Products) -->
    <div id="lvProducts"
        data-win-control="WinJS.UI.ListView"
```

```
        data-win-options="{
            itemTemplate: select('#tmplProduct'),
            groupHeaderTemplate: select('#tmplProductGroupHeader')
        }"></div>

    <!-- Zoom Out ListView (Categories) -->
    <div id="lvCategories"
        data-win-control="WinJS.UI.ListView"
        data-win-options="{
            itemTemplate: select('#tmplCategory')
        }"></div>
</div>
```

Here are the lines of code from Listing 8.15 where the `SemanticZoom` control is used:

```
<div id="divSemanticZoom" data-win-control="WinJS.UI.SemanticZoom">
    <!-- Zoom In ListView (Products) -->
    <div id="lvProducts"
        data-win-control="WinJS.UI.ListView"
        data-win-options="{
            itemTemplate: select('#tmplProduct'),
            groupHeaderTemplate: select('#tmplProductGroupHeader')
        }"></div>

    <!-- Zoom Out ListView (Categories) -->
    <div id="lvCategories"
        data-win-control="WinJS.UI.ListView"
        data-win-options="{
            itemTemplate: select('#tmplCategory')
        }"></div>
</div>
```

The `SemanticZoom` control contains the two `ListView` controls with the different zoom levels. The `SemanticZoom` control switches between these two `ListView` controls displaying one zoom level or the other.

The JavaScript file in Listing 8.16 contains the code for implementing Semantic Zoom. A data source representing a list of products is bound to the zoomed-in `ListView` control. Additionally, a grouped data source is bound to both the zoomed-in and zoomed-out `ListView` controls.

8

LISTING 8.16   Zooming with Semantic Zoom (semanticZoom\semanticZoom.js)

```
(function () {
    "use strict";

    function initialize() {
        WinJS.UI.processAll().done(function () {
            // Get reference to ListView control
            var lvProducts = document.getElementById("lvProducts").winControl;
            var lvCategories = document.getElementById("lvCategories").winControl;

            // Create a List of products
            var listProducts = new WinJS.Binding.List([
                { name: "Milk", price: 2.44, category: "Beverages" },
                { name: "Oranges", price: 1.99, category: "Fruit" },
                { name: "Wine", price: 8.55, category: "Beverages" },
                { name: "Apples", price: 2.44, category: "Fruit" },
                { name: "Steak", price: 1.99, category: "Other" },
                { name: "Eggs", price: 2.44, category: "Other" },
                { name: "Mushrooms", price: 1.99, category: "Other" },
                { name: "Yogurt", price: 2.44, category: "Other" },
                { name: "Soup", price: 1.99, category: "Other" },
                { name: "Cereal", price: 2.44, category: "Other" },
                { name: "Pepsi", price: 1.99, category: "Beverages" }
            ]);

            // Create grouped data source
            var groupListProducts = listProducts.createGrouped(
                function (dataItem) {
                    return dataItem.category;
                },
                function (dataItem) {
                    return { title: dataItem.category };
                },
                function (group1, group2) {
                    return group1 > group2 ? 1 : -1;
                }
            );

            // Bind the list of products to the Zoom In ListView
            lvProducts.itemDataSource = groupListProducts.dataSource;
            lvProducts.groupDataSource = groupListProducts.groups.dataSource;

            // Bind the list of categories to the Zoom Out ListView
            lvCategories.itemDataSource = groupListProducts.groups.dataSource;
```

```
    });


    }

    document.addEventListener("DOMContentLoaded", initialize);
})();
```

Switching a `ListView` Template Dynamically

You can assign a function to the `ListView` control's `itemTemplate` property. This is great, because it means that you can switch the template used to render a `ListView` item at runtime.

Imagine, for example, that you want to display products using two templates: one template for normal products and one template for on-sale products (see Figure 8.18). The HTML page in Listing 8.17 includes the two templates.

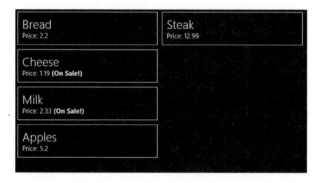

FIGURE 8.18   Switching templates dynamically

LISTING 8.17   Switching Templates Dynamically (dynamicTemplate\dynamicTemplate.js)

```html
<div id="tmplProduct"
    data-win-control="WinJS.Binding.Template">
    <div class="productItem">
        <h2 data-win-bind="innerText:name"></h2>
        Price: <span data-win-bind="innerText:price"></span>
    </div>
</div>

<div id="tmplProductOnSale"
    data-win-control="WinJS.Binding.Template">
    <div class="productItem">
```

```
        <h2 data-win-bind="innerText:name"></h2>
        Price: <span data-win-bind="innerText:price"></span>
        <b>(On Sale!)</b>
    </div>
</div>


<div id="lvProducts"
    data-win-control="WinJS.UI.ListView"></div>
```

The only difference between the normal product template and the on sale template is that the on sale template includes the message On Sale!

Notice that the item template used by the ListView control is not set declaratively. Instead, we set the template imperatively in the JavaScript file in Listing 8.18.

LISTING 8.18   Switching Templates Dynamically (dynamicTemplate\dynamicTemplate.js)

```
(function () {
    "use strict";

    function initialize() {
        WinJS.UI.processAll().done(function () {
            // Get reference to ListView control
            var lvProducts = document.getElementById("lvProducts").winControl;

            // Create a List of products
            var listProducts = new WinJS.Binding.List([
                { name: "Bread", price: 2.20 },
                { name: "Cheese", price: 1.19, onSale: true },
                { name: "Milk", price: 2.33, onSale: true },
                { name: "Apples", price: 5.20 },
                { name: "Steak", price: 12.99 }
            ]);


            // Assign an item template function
            lvProducts.itemTemplate = function (itemPromise) {
                return itemPromise.then(function (item) {
                    // Select either normal product template or on sale template
                    var itemTemplate = document.getElementById("tmplProduct");
                    if (item.data.onSale) {
                        itemTemplate = document.getElementById("tmplProductOnSale");
                    };

                    // Render selected template to DIV container
```

```
                var container = document.createElement("div");
                itemTemplate.winControl.render(item.data, container);
                return container;
            });
        };

        // Bind the list of products to the ListView
        lvProducts.itemDataSource = listProducts.dataSource;
    });
}

document.addEventListener("DOMContentLoaded", initialize);
})();
```

The dynamic template switching happens in the following chunk of code, which requires some explanation:

```
lvProducts.itemTemplate = function (itemPromise) {
    return itemPromise.then(function (item) {
        // Select either normal product template or on sale template
        var itemTemplate = document.getElementById("tmplProduct");
        if (item.data.onSale) {
            itemTemplate = document.getElementById("tmplProductOnSale");
        };

        // Render selected template to DIV container
        var container = document.createElement("div");
        itemTemplate.winControl.render(item.data, container);
        return container;
    });
};
```

When each ListView item is rendered, a promise is passed to the itemTemplate function. The data item associated with the ListView item is not available until the promise completes. Notice that the item parameter passed to the function includes a data property that represents the data item associated with the ListView item. You can use the item.data.onSale property to determine whether a product is on sale.

When the promise completes, you can return the HTML fragment that will be rendered for the ListView item. In the preceding code, the HTML fragment is rendered with the help of either the tmplProduct template (for a normal product) or the tmplProductOnSale template (for an on-sale product). The template is rendered to a DOM element named container that is returned from the function.

Using Drag and Drop

The `ListView` control natively supports HTML5 drag and drop. You can reorder the items in a `ListView` by dragging the items in the `ListView`. You also can drag and drop items into and out of a `ListView`.

Reordering Items in a `ListView`

Enabling users to re-order the items in a `ListView` is super simple. You just need to assign the value true to the `ListView` control's `itemsReorderable` property. The page in Listing 8.19 has reordering enabled.

LISTING 8.19   Reordering Items in a `ListView` (itemsReorderable\itemsReorderable.html)

```
<div id="tmplProduct"
    data-win-control="WinJS.Binding.Template">
    <div class="productItem">
        <h2 data-win-bind="innerText:name"></h2>
        Price: <span data-win-bind="innerText:price"></span>
    </div>
</div>

<div id="lvProducts"
    data-win-control="WinJS.UI.ListView"
    data-win-options="{
        itemsReorderable:true,
        itemTemplate: select('#tmplProduct')
    }"></div>


<div id="divMessage"></div>
```

When you enable item reordering for a `ListView`, the `ListView` handles updating its data source when the order of its items changes. In other words, the `ListView` control moves the items in its data source automatically.

The JavaScript code in Listing 8.20 demonstrates how you can handle the `WinJS.Binding.List itemmoved` event to detect when an item in a `List` has been moved. The event handler writes a message to the page (see Figure 8.19).

LISTING 8.20   Reordering Items in a `ListView` (itemsReorderable\itemsReorderable.js)

```
(function () {
    "use strict";

    function initialize() {
        WinJS.UI.processAll().done(function () {
            // Get references to elements and controls
```

```
        var lvProducts = document.getElementById("lvProducts").winControl;
        var divMessage = document.getElementById("divMessage");

        // Create a List of products
        var listProducts = new WinJS.Binding.List([
            { name: "Bread", price: 2.20 },
            { name: "Cheese", price: 1.19 },
            { name: "Milk", price: 2.33 },
            { name: "Apples", price: 5.20 }
        ]);


        listProducts.addEventListener("itemmoved", function (e) {
            var product = e.detail.value;
            var oldIndex = e.detail.oldIndex;
            var newIndex = e.detail.newIndex;

            var message = "item " + product.name
                + " moved from " + oldIndex
                + " to " + newIndex;

            divMessage.innerHTML = message;
        });



        // Bind the list of products to the ListView
        lvProducts.itemDataSource = listProducts.dataSource;

    });
    }

    document.addEventListener("DOMContentLoaded", initialize);
})();
```

FIGURE 8.19   Reordering items in a ListView

Dragging Items from `ListViews`

You also can drag and drop items in and out of a `ListView` control. Imagine, for example, that you are using a `ListView` control to display a list of products and you want users to be able to drag products from the `ListView` into a shopping cart (see Figure 8.20).

FIGURE 8.20   Dragging items from a `ListView` to a shopping cart

In that case, you can create the page in Listing 8.21. This page contains a `ListView` that represents the list of products and a DIV element that represents the shopping cart.

LISTING 8.21   Dragging and Dropping with a `ListView` (dragDrop\dragDrop.html)

```
<!DOCTYPE html>
<html>
<head>
    <meta charset="utf-8" />
    <title>ListView</title>

    <!-- WinJS references -->
    <link href="//Microsoft.WinJS.2.0/css/ui-dark.css" rel="stylesheet" />
    <script src="//Microsoft.WinJS.2.0/js/base.js"></script>
    <script src="//Microsoft.WinJS.2.0/js/ui.js"></script>

    <!-- Chapter references -->
    <script src="dragDrop.js"></script>

    <style>

        #container {
            width: 800px;
            position: relative;
        }
```

```
            #lvProducts {
                width: 400px;
            }

            .productItem {
                background-color:navy;
                border: solid 1px white;
                padding: 10px;
            }

            #divCart {
                position:absolute;
                top:0px;
                right:0px;
                width:350px;
                background-color: orange;
                padding: 10px;
            }

            #divCart.hiLite {
                color:black;
                background-color:yellow;
            }

    </style>
</head>
<body>

    <div id="tmplProduct"
        data-win-control="WinJS.Binding.Template">
        <div class="productItem">
            <h2 data-win-bind="innerText:name"></h2>
            Price: <span data-win-bind="innerText:price"></span>
        </div>
    </div>

    <div id="container">
        <h2>Products</h2>
        <div id="lvProducts"
            data-win-control="WinJS.UI.ListView"
            data-win-options="{
                itemsDraggable:true,
                itemTemplate: select('#tmplProduct'),
                layout: {type:WinJS.UI.ListLayout}
            }"></div>
```

```
        <div id="divCart">
            <h2>Shopping Cart</h2>
            <ul id="ulCart"></ul>
        </div>
    </div>

</body>
</html>
```

Notice that the `ListView` control includes a `itemsDraggable` property that is set to the value true. You need to enable this property to drag items out of the `ListView`.

The logic for handling drag and drop is contained in Listing 8.22.

LISTING 8.22   Dragging and Dropping with a `ListView` (dragDrop\dragDrop.js)

```
(function () {
    "use strict";

    function initialize() {
        WinJS.UI.processAll().done(function () {
            // Get references to elements and controls
            var lvProducts = document.getElementById("lvProducts").winControl;
            var divCart = document.getElementById("divCart");
            var ulCart = document.getElementById("ulCart");

            // Create a List of products
            var listProducts = new WinJS.Binding.List([
                { name: "Bread", price: 2.20 },
                { name: "Cheese", price: 1.19 },
                { name: "Milk", price: 2.33 },
                { name: "Apples", price: 5.20 }
            ]);


            // Bind the list of products to the ListView
            lvProducts.itemDataSource = listProducts.dataSource;

            lvProducts.addEventListener("itemdragstart", function (e) {
                var selectedIndex = e.detail.dragInfo.getIndices()[0];
                e.detail.dataTransfer.setData("Text", JSON.
➥stringify(selectedIndex));
            });

            // Allow drop on cart
            divCart.addEventListener("dragover", function (e) {
```

```
                e.preventDefault();
            });


            // highlight cart on hover
            divCart.addEventListener("dragenter", function (e) {
                divCart.classList.add("hiLite");
            });


            // unhighlight when leave hover
            divCart.addEventListener("dragleave", function (e) {
                divCart.classList.remove("hiLite");
            });


            // handle drop
            divCart.addEventListener("drop", function (e) {
                var selectedIndex = JSON.parse(e.dataTransfer.getData("Text"));
                listProducts.dataSource.itemFromIndex(selectedIndex).then(function
➡(selectedItem) {
                    ulCart.innerHTML += "<li>" + selectedItem.data.name + "</li>";
                });
            });


            // cleanup
            divCart.addEventListener("dragend", function (e) {
                divCart.classList.remove("hiLite");
            });


        });
    }

    document.addEventListener("DOMContentLoaded", initialize);
})();
```

Listing 8.22 contains event handlers for the following events:

- ▶ **itemdragstart**—Handle this event to store the identity of the item being dragged.
  The `e.detail.dragInfo` property contains methods that enable you to retrieve information about the `ListView` item being dragged.

- ▶ **dragover**—Handle this event to specify valid drop targets. If you don't call
  `preventDefault()` when you hover over an element, then you cannot perform a
  drop over the element.

- ▶ **dragenter**—Handle this event to show a visual indicator of a valid drop target. In
  the preceding code, I add a CSS class to the shopping cart that changes the background color to yellow.

▶ **dragleave**—Handle this event to show a visual indicator of a valid drop target. In the preceding code, I remove the CSS class which changes the background color of the shopping cart.

▶ **drop**—Handle this event to perform the drop. In the preceding code, I retrieve the name of the product dropped and display the name in the shopping cart.

▶ **dragend**—Handle this event to perform any cleanup associated with the drag-and-drop operation.

Notice that, with the exception of the `itemdragstart` event handler, all of the event handlers are standard HTML5 drag-and-drop event handlers. The `ListView` control, and the `ItemContainer` controls that it renders, follows the HTML5 standard.

Summary

This chapter was all about the `ListView` control. You learned how to take advantage of this control to display a collection of items in either a list or a grid.

First, I explained the basic features of this control. You learned how select, sort, filter, and group items in a `ListView`. I also discussed several advanced features of the control including how to switch `ListView` item templates dynamically and how to drag and drop `ListView` items.

In the next chapter, I show you how you can use a `ListView` control with different types of custom data sources including an `IndexedDB` data source.

CHAPTER 9

Creating Data Sources

The WinJS library includes two objects that you can use as data sources—the `List` and the `StorageDataSource` objects. If you need to use a `ListView` or `FlipView` with other types of data then you need to write a custom data source.

The goal of this chapter is to explain how you can write custom data sources. In this chapter, I explain how you can create three custom data sources:

▶ `FileDataSource`—The file data source stores data on the local file system.

▶ `WebServiceDataSource`—The web service data source enables you to use a remote web service to retrieve and store data.

▶ `IndexedDBData Source`—The IndexedDB data source enables you to retrieve and store data using an IndexedDB database.

The full source of these data sources are contained in the GitHub project for this book (https://github.com/StephenWalther/Windows8.1AppsUnleashed).

Creating Custom Data Sources

Let me start by giving you an overview of how you can create a custom data source. In this section, I'll explain how you can implement the methods of a custom data source that uses a JavaScript array to store data. I'll walk through creating the constructor for this data source as well as the most important methods for this data source. After discussing this (overly simple) data source in this section, we'll dive into building more practical data sources in latter sections, such as the Web service data source and IndexedDB data source.

Creating the Data Source Class

The easiest way to create a custom data source is to derive a new class from the base VirtualizedDataSource class. For example, you can use the following code to create a new data source named MyDataSource:

```
var MyDataSource = WinJS.Class.derive(
    WinJS.UI.VirtualizedDataSource,
    // Constructor
    function () {
        this._adapter = new MyDataAdapter();
        this._baseDataSourceConstructor(this._adapter);
    }
);
```

In the preceding code, two arguments are passed to the `WinJS.Class.derive()` method to create the new `MyDataSource` class: a base class (`WinJS.UI.VirtualizedDataSource`) and a constructor for the new class.

In the constructor for your derived `VirtualizedDataSource` class, you call the `_baseDataSourceContructor()` method with a data adapter. The bulk of the work that goes into building a custom data source goes into creating this data adapter class.

Creating a Data Adapter

You create a data adapter by implementing the `IListDataAdapter` interface. This interface has the following methods:

▶ change()

▶ getCount()

▶ insertAfter()

▶ insertAtEnd()

▶ insertAtStart()

▶ insertBefore()

▶ itemsFromDescription()

▶ itemsFromEnd()

▶ itemsFromIndex()

▶ itemsFromKey()

- ▶ itemsFromStart()

- ▶ itemSignature()

- ▶ moveAfter()

- ▶ moveBefore()

- ▶ moveToEnd()

- ▶ moveToStart()

- ▶ remove()

- ▶ setNotificationHandler()

The interface also includes the following property:

- ▶ compareByIdentity

Fortunately, you don't need to actually implement all of these methods and properties. You can implement only the methods that you actually need.

For example, if you want to create a simple, read-only data source then you only need to implement the getCount() and itemsFromIndex() methods. If you want to create a more complicated, read-write data source then you need to also implement the change(), insertAtEnd(), and remove() methods.

In the following sections, I describe how you can implement several of these methods such as the getCount() and itemsFromIndex() methods.

Implementing the getCount() Method

The getCount() method should return the total number of records represented by the data source. For example, if you are storing items in a JavaScript array, then the getCount() method should return the length of the array:

```
getCount: function () {
    return WinJS.Promise.wrap(this._arrayData.length);
}
```

The getCount() method must return a promise. Therefore, you either need to wrap the return value in a promise using WinJS.Promise.wrap() or you need to create a new promise object.

Implementing the itemsFromIndex() Method

The itemsFromIndex() method returns a set of items from the data source. Three arguments are passed to this method:

- ▶ **requestIndex**—The index of the first item to retrieve from the data source

▶ **countBefore**—The number of items before the requested index to retrieve from the data source

▶ **countAfter**—The number of items after the requested index to retrieve from the data source

The `countBefore` and `countAfter` parameters are intended to be interpreted as hints. You can return more than the `countBefore` or `countAfter` number of items if you wish.

Here's a simple implementation of the `itemsFromIndex()` method. This method returns a portion of JavaScript array.

```
itemsFromIndex: function (requestIndex, countBefore, countAfter) {
    var startIndex = Math.max(0, requestIndex - countBefore);
    var subItems = this._arrayData.slice(startIndex);
    return WinJS.Promise.wrap({
        items: subItems,
        offset: requestIndex - startIndex,
        totalCount: this._arrayData.length
    });
}
```

The `itemsFromIndex()` method should return an object that implements the `IFetchResult` interface. In the preceding code, three properties of the `IFetchResult` interface are returned: `items`, `offset`, and `totalCount`.

The `items` property represents the array of items returned by the `itemsFromIndex()` method. Each item in the items array must implement the `IListItem` interface. At the very minimum, each item must have a key and a data property.

The `offset` property represents the position of the item which corresponds to the `requestIndex` in the items array. If you return items before the requested index then the offset will be greater than 0.

Finally, the `totalCount` property returns the total number of items represented by the data source and not just the number of items being returned.

Each item in the items array returned by `itemsFromIndex` must implement the `IListItem` interface. Here's a sample of the data returned from the `itemsFromIndex()` method:

```
{
  items: [
    {key:"1", data: {name: "wake up"}},
    {key:"3", data: {name: "get out of bed"}},
    {key:"4", data: {name: "drag the comb across my head"}}
  ]
  offset: 0,
  totalCount: 3
}
```

NOTE

In addition to the `itemsFromIndex()` method, you also can implement the
`itemsFromDescription()`, `itemsFromEnd()`, `itemsFromKey()`, or `itemsFromStart()`
methods. Implementing these additional methods for fetching data is optional.

Implementing the `insertAtEnd()` Method

If you want to support creating new items then you should implement the `insertAtEnd()`
method. Two arguments are passed to this method, the key of the new item and the
actual new item.

Here is a sample which illustrates how you can use the `insertAtEnd()` method to add a
new item to a JavaScript array.

```
insertAtEnd: function (unused, data) {
    var newItem = {
        key: (++this._maxKey).toString(),
        data: data
    };
    this._arrayData.push(newItem);
    return WinJS.Promise.wrap(newItem);
},
```

Typically, you don't provide a key and you let the data source generate the key for you.
Therefore, typically, you ignore the key argument passed to the `insertAtEnd()` method
and you generate the key yourself. In the preceding code, the key is generated by adding
one to the previously generated key and converting the result into a string.

WARNING

Data source keys must be strings.

Notice that the `insertAtEnd()` method returns the new item including its key. The object
that is returned conforms to the `IItem` interface wrapped in a promise.

Implementing the `remove()` Method

If you need the ability to delete an item from a data source then you need to implement
the `remove()` method. The key of the item being removed is passed to the method and the
method returns nothing if the item is removed.

Here's some sample code that removes an item from an array:

```
remove: function (key) {
    var i = this._getIndexFromKey(key);
    this._arrayData.splice(i, 1);
    return WinJS.Promise.wrap(null);
```

```
},

_getIndexFromKey:function(key) {
    for (var i = 0; i < this._arrayData.length; i++) {
        if (this._arrayData[i].key == key) {
            return i;
        }
    }
}
}
```

Implementing the `change()` Method

If you need to support editing items in a data source then you need to implement the `change()` method. Three arguments are passed to the `change()` method: the key of the item being edited, the new value of the item being edited, and the index of the item being edited.

Here's some sample code for implementing the `change()` method:

```
change: function (key, data, indexHint) {
    var index = this._getIndexFromKey(key);
    this._arrayData[index] = data;
    var newItem = {
        key: key,
        index: index,
        data: data
    };
    return new WinJS.Promise.wrap(null);
}
```

Notice that the `change()` method returns an empty promise. The method just completes without returning anything special.

Handling Errors

If there is an error when inserting, removing, or changing an item then you can return an `EditError` object. You can return one of the following four values:

▶ `WinJS.UI.EditError.canceled`—Return this error when the edit operation, for whatever reason, is canceled.

▶ `WinJS.UI.EditError.noResponse`—Return this error when the edit operation times out.

▶ `WinJS.UI.EditError.notPermitted`—Return this error when writing to a read-only data source.

▶ `WinJS.UI.EditError.noLongerMeaningful`—Return this error when the item has already been changed.

For example, when creating a read-only data source, you can create the `insertAtEnd()` method like this:

```
insertAtEnd: function (unused, data) {
    return WinJS.Promise.wrapError(new WinJS.ErrorFromName(WinJS.UI.EditError.
➥notPermitted));
}
```

Implementing the `setNotificationHandler()` Method

The `setNotificationHandler()` method enables you to raise notifications when the status of a data source changes. You can call any of the following methods:

- ▶ `beginNotifications()`
- ▶ `changed()`
- ▶ `endNotifications()`
- ▶ `inserted()`
- ▶ `invalidateAll()`
- ▶ `moved()`
- ▶ `reload()`
- ▶ `removed()`

You don't need to raise these notifications when using the standard data adapter methods such as the `insertAtEnd()`, `remove()`, and `change()` methods discussed earlier. However, you will need to raise these notifications when you add a custom method to your data source.

Imagine, for example, that you want to add a `nuke()` method to your data source. When you call the `nuke()` method, all of the data is removed from your data source.

Here's how you would implement the `nuke()` method in the data adapter class:

```
setNotificationHandler: function (notificationHandler) {
    this._notificationHandler = notificationHandler;
},

nuke: function () {
    this._arrayData = [];
    this._notificationHandler.reload();
}
```

6

In the preceding code, the setNotificationHandler() method assigns the predefined notificationHandler method to a private variable named _notificationHandler. This makes this predefined notificationHandler method available to all of the methods in the data adapter.

The nuke() method, our custom method, sets the data source array to an empty array and calls the notificationHandler reload() method. If you don't call reload() then a ListView bound to the data source won't clear away its items.

Here's how you can expose the custom nuke() method from a data source:

```
var MyDataSource = WinJS.Class.derive(
    WinJS.UI.VirtualizedDataSource,
    // Constructor
    function (fileName) {
        this._adapter = new MyDataAdapter();
        this._baseDataSourceConstructor(this._adapter);
    },
    // Instance methods
    {
        nuke: function () {
            this._adapter.nuke();
        }
    }
);
```

The MyDataSource class in the code includes a nuke() method. The nuke() method simply delegates to the data adapter nuke() method.

Creating a File Data Source

In this section, I discuss how you can create a custom file data source. The file data source stores and retrieves data from the file system.

> **NOTE**
>
> The complete source code for the FileDataSource is included in the GitHub source code in a folder named file.

The FileDataSource includes implementations of the getCount(), itemsFromIndex(), insertAtEnd(), remove(), and change() methods.

When you call either the getCount() or itemsFromIndex() methods, the FileDataSource loads its data from the file system and calls JSON.parse() to parse the file data into a JavaScript array. The FileDataSource loads data in its _ensureData() method:

```
_ensureData: function () {
    var that = this;

    // Attempt to return cached data
    if (this._cachedData) {
        return WinJS.Promise.wrap(that._cachedData);
    }

    // Otherwise, load from file
    return new WinJS.Promise(function (complete, error) {
        var local = WinJS.Application.local;
        var def = '{"maxKey":-1,"items":[]}';
        local.readText(that._fileName, def).done(function(fileContents) {
            that._cachedData = JSON.parse(fileContents);
            complete(that._cachedData);
        });
    });
}
```

The `readText()` method reads a text file from the file system. If the text file does not exist then the `readText()` method returns the value of `def` instead. In either case, the results of reading the text file is converted into a JavaScript array with the help of the `JSON.parse()` method.

When you call the `insertAtEnd()`, `remove()`, or `change()` methods, the `FileDataSource` calls `JSON.stringify()` to convert the data into a string. The `FileDatasource` then saves the data to the file system. The `FileDataSource` saves the data in its `_saveData()` method:

```
_saveData: function (data) {
    this._cachedData = data;
    var local = WinJS.Application.local;
    var str = JSON.stringify(data);
    return local.writeText(this._fileName, str);
}
```

Using the File Data Source

Imagine that you want to create a simple task list app with the file data source. You want to be able to display a list of existing tasks and create new tasks (see Figure 9.1).

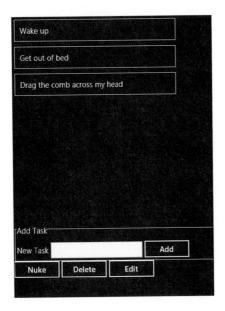

FIGURE 9.1   Task list created with a file data source

You also want to be able to delete individual tasks by right-clicking/swiping a task and clicking the Delete button (see Figure 9.2) or delete all of the tasks by clicking the Nuke button.

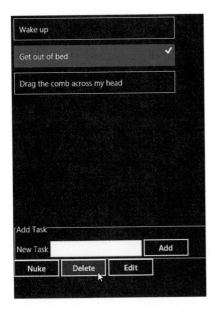

FIGURE 9.2   Deleting tasks with the file data source

The user interface for the task list app is contained in the HTML page in Listing 9.1. The HTML page includes a `ListView` control that displays the list of tasks.

LISTING 9.1   File Data Source (file\file.html)

```html
<!DOCTYPE html>
<html>
<head>
    <meta charset="utf-8" />
    <title>List Data Source</title>

    <!-- WinJS references -->
    <link href="//Microsoft.WinJS.2.0/css/ui-dark.css" rel="stylesheet" />
    <script src="//Microsoft.WinJS.2.0/js/base.js"></script>
    <script src="//Microsoft.WinJS.2.0/js/ui.js"></script>

    <!-- DataSources references -->
    <link href="file.css" rel="stylesheet" />
    <script type="text/javascript" src="fileDataSource.js"></script>
    <script src="file.js"></script>
</head>
<body>
    <div id="tmplTask" data-win-control="WinJS.Binding.Template">
        <div class="taskItem">
            <span data-win-bind="innerText:name"></span>
        </div>
    </div>

    <div id="lvTasks"
        data-win-control="WinJS.UI.ListView"
        data-win-options="{
            layout: {type: WinJS.UI.ListLayout},
            itemTemplate: select('#tmplTask'),
            selectionMode: 'single'
        }"></div>

    <form id="frmAdd">
        <fieldset>
            <legend>Add Task</legend>
            <label>New Task</label>
            <input id="inputTaskName" required />
            <button>Add</button>
        </fieldset>
    </form>
    <button id="btnNuke">Nuke</button>
    <button id="btnDelete">Delete</button>
```

```
        <button id="btnEdit">Edit</button>
</body>
</html>
```

The JavaScript file associated with the HTML page is contained in Listing 9.2. This
JavaScript code contains the code that binds the `ListView` control to the `FileDataSource`.

LISTING 9.2   File Data Source (file\file.js)

```javascript
function init() {

    WinJS.UI.processAll().done(function () {
        var lvTasks = document.getElementById("lvTasks").winControl;

        // Create data source and bind to ListView
        var tasksDataSource = new DataSources.FileDataSource("tasks.json");
        lvTasks.itemDataSource = tasksDataSource;



        // Wire-up frmAdd and Delete, Nuke buttons
        document.getElementById("frmAdd").addEventListener("submit", function (evt)
{
            evt.preventDefault();
            tasksDataSource.beginEdits();
            tasksDataSource.insertAtEnd(null, {
                name: document.getElementById("inputTaskName").value
            }).done(function (newItem) {
                tasksDataSource.endEdits();
                document.getElementById("frmAdd").reset();

                // Show last item added
                lvTasks.itemDataSource.getCount().done(function (count) {
                    lvTasks.ensureVisible(count);
                })

            });
        });

        document.getElementById("btnDelete").addEventListener("click", function () {
            if (lvTasks.selection.count() == 1) {
                lvTasks.selection.getItems().done(function (items) {
                    tasksDataSource.beginEdits();
                    tasksDataSource.remove(items[0].key).done(function () {
                        tasksDataSource.endEdits();
                    });
                });
```

```
        }
    });


    document.getElementById("btnEdit").addEventListener("click", function () {
        if (lvTasks.selection.count() == 1) {
            lvTasks.selection.getItems().done(function (items) {
                tasksDataSource.beginEdits();
                tasksDataSource.change(items[0].key, { name: "Changed!"
➡ }).done(function () {
                    tasksDataSource.endEdits();
                });
            });
        }
    });


    document.getElementById("btnNuke").addEventListener("click", function () {
        tasksDataSource.nuke();
    });


    });


}


document.addEventListener("DOMContentLoaded", init);
```

The file data source is created and bound to the `ListView` with the following two lines
of code:

```
var tasksDataSource = new DataSources.FileDataSource("tasks.json");
lvTasks.itemDataSource = tasksDataSource;
```

The name of the file to create is passed to the constructor of the `FileDataSource`. In the
preceding code, a file named tasks.json is used to store the list of tasks.

New tasks are created with the help of the following code:

```
document.getElementById("frmAdd").addEventListener("submit", function (evt) {
    evt.preventDefault();
    tasksDataSource.beginEdits();
    tasksDataSource.insertAtEnd(null, {
        name: document.getElementById("inputTaskName").value
    }).done(function (newItem) {
        tasksDataSource.endEdits();
        document.getElementById("frmAdd").reset();

        // Show last item added
```

```
    lvTasks.itemDataSource.getCount().done(function (count) {
        lvTasks.ensureVisible(count);
    })

    });
});
```

When you submit the HTML form for adding new tasks, the file data source
`insertAtEnd()` method is called to create the new task. If the new task is successfully
created then the `ListView` control's `ensureVisible()` method is called to ensure that the
new task is scrolled into view.

> **WARNING**
>
> Always call `beginEdits()` and `endEdits()` when inserting, editing, or deleting data with
> a data source. If you neglect to use `beginEdits()` and `endEdits()` then you can get null
> reference exceptions when you edit items too fast.

Creating a Web Service Data Source

In this section, I discuss how you can build a web service data source. The web service
data source enables you to bind a `ListView` control to a remote web service. You can use
the data source to both retrieve and modify data.

You can use the web service data source, for example, to retrieve a list of products from a
catalog of products stored in a database on a remote website. That way, when the catalog
of products is updated, your Windows Store app will display the latest products.

> **NOTE**
>
> When working with Ajax, I strongly recommend that you take advantage of the free
> Fiddler2 tool to help debug failed Ajax requests. You can download Fiddler2—which works
> great with Windows 8—from http://fiddler2.com.

> **NOTE**
>
> The complete source code for the `WebServiceDataSource` is included in the GitHub
> source in a folder named webService.

Creating the Data Source

The web service data source uses the `WinJS.xhr()` method to make the Ajax calls to the
remote web service. For example, the `getCount()` method looks like this:

```
getCount: function () {
    var that = this;

    return new WinJS.Promise(function (complete, error) {
        var options = {
            url: that._url + "/getCount"
        };
        return WinJS.xhr(options).then(function (xhr) {
            var count = JSON.parse(xhr.response);
            complete(count);
        },
        function (xhr) {
            console.log("Could not call getCount()");
        });
    });
}
```

The `getCount()` method invokes a remote web service action named `getCount()` by performing an HTTP GET request.

Here's another of the methods of the web service data source. The `remove()` method invokes a remote web service action named `remove()` by performing an HTTP DELETE request. The `remove()` method looks like this:

```
remove: function(key) {
    var that = this;
    return new WinJS.Promise(function (complete, error) {
        var options = {
            url: that._url + "/remove/" + key,
            type: "DELETE",
            headers: {
                authenticationToken: that._authenticationToken
            }
        };
        WinJS.xhr(options).then(
            function (xhr) {
                complete();
            },
            function (xhr) {
                console.log("Could not call remove()");
            }
        );
    });
}
```

6

In general, each method of the web service data source delegates to a remote web service action with the same name.

Creating the Web Service

There are several ways that you can create a web service. Even if you restrict yourself to Microsoft technologies, you have several options. You can create a WCF service, a WCF Data Service, an ASMX Web service, a Windows Azure Mobile Services service, or an ASP.NET Web API service.

> **NOTE**
>
> In the next chapter, you learn how to interact with web services created with Azure Mobile Services.

In this chapter, I create a web service by taking advantage of the ASP.NET Web API. You can add a Web API controller to either an ASP.NET Web Forms or an ASP.NET MVC project. I create an ASP.NET MVC 4 project. When creating the ASP.NET MVC 4 project, I used the Web API project template (see Figure 9.3).

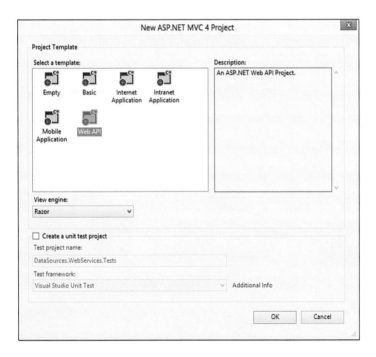

FIGURE 9.3   Creating an ASP.NET MVC 4 project using the Web API project template

To take advantage of an ASP.NET Web API service, you need to add the right routes to the App_Start\RouteConfig.cs file. These routes map incoming browser requests to the correct API controller and API controller action.

I added the following routes to the App_Start\RouteConfig.cs file:

```
routes.MapHttpRoute(
    name: "TasksGetCount",
    routeTemplate: "api/tasks/getCount",
    defaults: new { controller="tasks", action="getCount" }
);

routes.MapHttpRoute(
    name: "TasksItemsFromIndex",
    routeTemplate: "api/tasks/itemsFromIndex",
    defaults: new { controller = "tasks", action = "itemsFromIndex" }
);

routes.MapHttpRoute(
    name: "TasksInsertAtEnd",
    routeTemplate: "api/tasks/insertAtEnd",
    defaults: new { controller = "tasks", action = "insertAtEnd" }
);

routes.MapHttpRoute(
    name: "TasksRemove",
    routeTemplate: "api/tasks/remove/{key}",
    defaults: new { controller = "tasks", action = "remove" }
);

routes.MapHttpRoute(
    name: "TasksNuke",
    routeTemplate: "api/tasks/nuke",
    defaults: new { controller = "tasks", action = "nuke" }
);
```

For example, when you make an HTTP GET request for /api/tasks/getcount then the `TasksController.GetCount()` Web API controller action is invoked.

The Web API controller is named `TasksController`. It contains `GetCount()`, `ItemsFromIndex()`, `InsertAtEnd()`, `Remove()`, and `Nuke()` controller actions. The controller actions use the Microsoft Entity Framework to interact with a database table of tasks.

Here's what the `GetCount()` controller action looks like:

```
[HttpGet]
public int GetCount() {
    return _db.Tasks.Count();
}
```

The GetCount() method returns the total number of tasks stored in the Tasks database table. Notice that the GetCount() method is decorated with an [HttpGet] attribute. This attribute enables you to invoke the GetCount() method by performing an Ajax GET request.

The Remove() controller action looks like this:

```
[HttpDelete]
public bool Remove(string key)
{
    var id = int.Parse(key);
    _db.Tasks.Remove(_db.Tasks.Find(id));
    _db.SaveChanges();
    return true;
}
```

The Remove() controller action accepts a key argument that represents the item to be deleted. The key argument must be a string argument because the WinJS ListView/data source requires keys to be strings.

Notice that the Remove() method is decorated with an [HttpDelete] attribute. The Remove() action can be invoked only with an HTTP DELETE request.

There is one wrinkle when using nonstandard HTTP methods such as the HTTP DELETE or HTTP PUT methods. You must add the following section to the ASP.NET MVC application's root Web.config file:

```
<system.webServer>
  <modules runAllManagedModulesForAllRequests="true">
  </modules>
</system.webServer>
```

If you don't add the preceding section to the Web.config file then all HTTP DELETE requests return 404 status codes.

Using the Web Service Data Source

After you create and configure the remote web service, using the web service data source is straightforward. The following code illustrates how you can create an instance of the web service data source and bind it to a ListView control named lvTasks:

```
var lvTasks = document.getElementById("lvTasks").winControl;
var tasksDataSource = new DataSources.WebServiceDataSource("http://localhost:51807/
api/tasks", "id");
lvTasks.itemDataSource = tasksDataSource;
```

When you create an instance of the web service data source, you must supply two arguments to the constructor: the URL of the web service and the name of the primary key property of the data to retrieve.

The URL http://localhost:51807/api/tasks is the address of a local web service using port 51807. This port is generated randomly. You can determine the port number used by a Visual Studio project by opening the Project Properties dialog and selecting the Web tab (see Figure 9.4).

> **NOTE**
>
> In the sample code, I use a web service located at localhost instead of providing a domain name. Using localhost while developing a new Windows Store app is fine, but if you attempt to release a Windows Store app that uses localhost then the app will fail certification.

FIGURE 9.4   Determining the port number used by a Visual Studio project

Creating an `IndexedDB` **Data Source**

The Indexed Database API (`IndexedDB`) is a W3C recommendation for exposing a database in the browser. The `IndexedDB` recommendation is supported by Firefox 12+, Chrome 19+, and IE 10+. And, of course, the `IndexedDB` recommendation is supported by Windows Store apps.

Behind the scenes, different browsers use different databases behind the `IndexedDB` API. For example, Firefox uses SqlLite and IE uses SQLCE. The `IndexedDB` API provides a standard way to interact with these databases across browsers and across platforms.

If you need to store lots of data in a Windows Store app, and query subsets of the data, then `IndexedDB` is a good choice. Because `IndexedDB` supports indexes and cursors, you can work efficiently with large sets of data.

In this section, I discuss how you can create an IndexedDB data source. I discuss how you can build a simple app which enables you to filter a list of movies by category (see Figure 9.5).

9

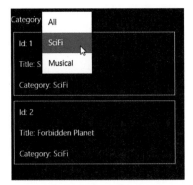

FIGURE 9.5   Using the IndexedDB data source

Overview of `IndexedDB`

An IndexedDB database might be different than the type of database that you normally use. An IndexedDB database is an object-oriented database and not a relational database. Instead of storing data in tables, you store data in object stores. An IndexedDB database contains one or more object stores that contain a collection of JavaScript objects.

The `IndexedDB` API includes both asynchronous and synchronous methods. Currently, only the asynchronous methods are widely supported by browsers. If you want to open a database connection, add an object to an object store, or get a count of items in an object store, then you need to perform these operations asynchronously.

Creating or Connecting to an IndexedDB Database

You don't create a new IndexedDB database upfront—instead, you create a new database when a user first tries to make a connection to your database. You create new IndexedDB databases by handling the `upgradeneeded` event when attempting to open a connection to an IndexedDB database.

For example, here's how you would both open a connection to an existing database named TasksDB and create the TasksDB database when it does not already exist:

```
var reqOpen = window.indexedDB.open("TasksDB", 2);
reqOpen.onupgradeneeded = function (evt) {
    var newDB = evt.target.result;
    newDB.createObjectStore("tasks", { keyPath: "id", autoIncrement: true });
};
reqOpen.onsuccess = function () {
    var db = reqOpen.result;
    // Do something with db
};
```

When you call `window.indexedDB.open()`, and the database does not already exist, then the `upgradeneeded` event is raised. In the preceding code, the `upgradeneeded` handler creates a new object store named `tasks`. The new object store has an auto-increment column named `id` that acts as the primary key column.

If the database already exists with the right version, and you call `window.indexedDB.open()`, then the success event is raised. At that point, you have an open connection to the existing database and you can start doing something useful with the database.

Adding Objects to an Object Store

You use asynchronous methods to interact with an IndexedDB database. For example, the following code illustrates how you would add a new object to the `tasks` object store:

```
var transaction = db.transaction("tasks", "readwrite");
var store = transaction.objectStore("tasks");
var reqAdd = store.add({
    name: "Feed the dog"
});
reqAdd.onsuccess = function () {
    // Task added successfully
};
```

> **NOTE**
>
> Notice that you use callbacks and not promises when interacting with `IndexedDB`. Realize that `IndexedDB` is not a Microsoft technology so it works independently of the promise pattern in WinJS.

The preceding code creates a new read-write database transaction, adds a new task to the tasks object store, and handles the success event. If the new task gets added successfully then the success event is raised.

Getting a Count of Objects in an Object Store

You can get a count of the number of objects in a particular object store by taking advantage of the `count()` method. For example, you can use the following code to determine the number of items in the `tasks` objects store:

```
var transaction = db.transaction("tasks");
var store = transaction.objectStore("tasks");
var reqCount = store.count();
reqCount.onsuccess = function (evt) {
    var count = evt.target.result;
    console.log(count);
};
```

6

The preceding code creates a new read-only database transaction and gets a count of the number of objects in the `tasks` object store by calling the `count()` method.

Notice that the call to the `count()` method is asynchronous. You get the count by handling the `success` event and reading the `target.result` property.

Retrieving Objects from an Object Store

You retrieve objects from an object store by opening a cursor and moving through the cursor one object at a time. For example, the following code opens a cursor that returns the objects from the `tasks` object store:

```
var items = [];
var transaction = db.transaction("tasks");
var store = transaction.objectStore("tasks");
var req = store.openCursor();
req.onsuccess = function (evt) {
    var cursor = evt.target.result;
    if (cursor) {
        items.push(cursor.value);
        cursor.continue();
    } else {
        // All done!
    }
}
```

When you open a cursor and nothing goes wrong, then the `success` event is raised. You can use `cursor.value` to get the current object. Calling `cursor.continue()` moves the cursor forward and raises the `success` event again.

When you reach the end of the cursor then cursor will have the value null. In that case, you know that you have retrieved all of the objects from the object store.

> **NOTE**
>
> `cursor.continue()` advances by a single object. If you need to advance by more than one object then you can use `cursor.advance()`.

Using Indexes and Key Ranges

When you create a database, you can create indexes on object properties. An index enables you to efficiently retrieve objects that match a value or range of values.

Here's how you would create a tasks object store that includes an index on its `dateCreated` property:

```
var reqOpen = window.indexedDB.open("TasksDB", 2);
reqOpen.onupgradeneeded = function (evt) {
    var newDB = evt.target.result;
```

```
      var store=newDB.createObjectStore("tasks", { keyPath: "id", autoIncrement: true
➥})};
      store.createIndex("dateCreatedIndex", "dateCreated");
};
```

After you create an index, you can retrieve objects from an object store by using the index with a key range. A key range represents the criteria that an index uses to match objects in a store.

When creating a key range, you can specify the following properties:

- ▶ `only`—Enables you to retrieve only the objects that match the supplied value

- ▶ `lowerBound`—Enables you to retrieve all objects that have a value greater than the supplied value

- ▶ `upperBound`—Enables you to retrieve all objects that have a value less than the supplied value

- ▶ `bound`—Enables you to retrieve all objects that have a value greater than or less than the supplied values

For example, here is how you would retrieve all of the tasks from the `tasks` object store that were created before 1999:

```
var items = [];
var transaction = db.transaction("tasks");
var store = transaction.objectStore("tasks");
var index = store.index("dateCreatedIndex");
var keyRange = IDBKeyRange.upperBound(new Date("1/1/1999"));
var req = index.openCursor(keyRange);
req.onsuccess = function (evt) {
    var cursor = evt.target.result;
    if (cursor) {
        items.push(cursor.value);
        cursor.continue();
    } else {
        // All done!
    }
}
```

You also can use an index when getting a count of objects that match a particular key range. For example, the following code gets a count of the number of tasks that were created before 1999:

```
var transaction = db.transaction("tasks");
var store = transaction.objectStore("tasks");
var index = store.index("dateCreatedIndex");
```

6

```
var keyRange = IDBKeyRange.upperBound(new Date("1/1/1999"));
var req = index.count(keyRange);
req.onsuccess = function (evt) {
    var count = evt.target.result;
}
```

Using the IndexedDB Data Source

The IndexedDB data source enables you to bind a `ListView` control to a collection of JavaScript objects stored in an IndexedDB database. You create an IndexedDB data source by providing three arguments:

▶ `objectStoreName`—The name of the object store to represent with the data source.

▶ `creationOptions`—The `creationOptions` determine how the IndexedDB database and object store are created.

▶ `cursorOptions`—(optional) If you supply `cursorOptions` then you can filter the objects in the object store using a key range.

For example, here is how you would create an instance of the IndexedDB data source that represents a collection of movies:

```
// Create the data source options
var createOptions = {
    databaseName: "MoviesDB",
    databaseVersion: 1,
    indexNames: ["category"]
};


// Create the IndexedDB data source
var moviesDataSource = new DataSources.IndexedDbDataSource("movies", createOptions);
```

In the code, the `creationOptions` represent the properties of an IndexedDB database, object store, and indexes. If the database does not already exist, then the IndexedDB data source creates the database.

Here are the properties of the `creationOption` object:

▶ `databaseName`—The name of the IndexedDB database

▶ `databaseVersion`—The version of the IndexedDB database

▶ `indexNames`—An index is created for each property name in this array.

When you create an instance of the IndexedDB data source, you also have the option of supplying a `cursorOptions` object. The `cursorOptions` object filters the object store. Here are the properties of the `cursorOptions` object:

▶ `indexName`—Create a key range using this index

▶ `only`—Create a key range and only return objects that match this value

▶ `lowerBound`—Create a key range and only return objects that have a value greater than this lower bound

▶ `upperBound`—Create a key range and only return objects that have a value less than this upper bound

For example, here is how you would filter tasks so that only tasks created before 1999 are returned:

```
WinJS.UI.processAll().done(function () {
    var lvTasks = document.getElementById("lvTasks").winControl;

    var createOptions = {
        indexNames: ["dateCreated"],
        databaseVersion: 3
    };

    var cursorOptions = {
        indexName: "dateCreated",
        upperBound: new Date("1/1/1999")
    };

    var tasksDataSource = new DataSources.IndexedDbDataSource("tasks",
➥createOptions, cursorOptions);
    lvTasks.itemDataSource = tasksDataSource;
});
```

In the code, the `createOptions` object causes the `tasks` object store to be created with an index on its `dateCreated` property. The `cursorOptions` object uses that index to return only those tasks that have a `dateCreated` below the upperBound 1/1/1999.

I want to show you a more complete sample of using the IndexedDB data source. The Movie app contained in Listing 9.3 and Listing 9.4 enables you to select different movie categories and display only the movies in the selected category. The app also enables you to create new movies and delete existing movies (see Figure 9.6).

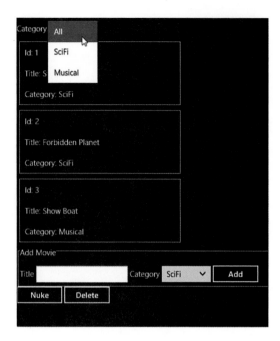

FIGURE 9.6   Using the IndexedDB data source

LISTING 9.3   Creating a Movie App with the IndexedDB Data Source (indexedDb\
indexedDb.html)

```html
<!DOCTYPE html>
<html>
<head>
    <meta charset="utf-8" />
    <title>DataSources</title>

    <!-- WinJS references -->
    <link href="//Microsoft.WinJS.2.0/css/ui-dark.css" rel="stylesheet" />
    <script src="//Microsoft.WinJS.2.0/js/base.js"></script>
    <script src="//Microsoft.WinJS.2.0/js/ui.js"></script>

    <!-- DataSources references -->
    <link href="indexedDb.css" rel="stylesheet" />
    <script type="text/javascript" src="indexedDbDataSource.js"></script>
    <script src="indexedDb.js"></script>
</head>
<body>

    <div id="tmplMovie" data-win-control="WinJS.Binding.Template">
        <div class="movieItem">
```

```
            Id: <span data-win-bind="innerText:id"></span>
            <br /><br />
            Title: <span data-win-bind="innerText:title"></span>
            <br /><br />
            Category: <span data-win-bind="innerText:category"></span>
        </div>
    </div>


    <div>
        <label>Category</label>
        <select id="selectCategory">
            <option>All</option>
            <option>SciFi</option>
            <option>Musical</option>
        </select>
    </div>


    <div id="lvMovies"
        data-win-control="WinJS.UI.ListView"
        data-win-options="{
            itemTemplate: select('#tmplMovie'),
            selectionMode: 'single'
        }"></div>


    <form id="frmAdd">
        <fieldset>
            <legend>Add Movie</legend>
            <div>
                <label>Title</label>
                <input id="inputMovieTitle" required />

                <label>Category</label>
                <select id="selectMovieCategory">
                    <option>SciFi</option>
                    <option>Musical</option>
                </select>
                <button>Add</button>
            </div>
        </fieldset>
    </form>


    <button id="btnNuke">Nuke</button>
    <button id="btnDelete">Delete</button>
```

```
</body>
</html>
```

The HTML page in Listing 9.3 contains a select list that enables you to select a movie category (All, SciFi, Musical). When you select a particular movie category, only those movies in the category are displayed in a `ListView` control.

LISTING 9.4   Creating a Movie App with the IndexedDB Data Source (indexedDb\indexedDb.js)

```
function init() {

    WinJS.UI.processAll().done(function () {
        var lvMovies = document.getElementById("lvMovies").winControl;

        // Create the data source options
        var createOptions = {
            databaseName: "MoviesDB",
            databaseVersion: 1,
            indexNames: ["category"]
        };

        // Create the IndexedDB data source
        var moviesDataSource = new DataSources.IndexedDbDataSource("movies",
➥createOptions);

        // Add seed data
        addSeedData().done(function () {

            // Bind data source to ListView
            lvMovies.itemDataSource = moviesDataSource;
        });


        function addSeedData() {
            return new WinJS.Promise(function (complete) {
                moviesDataSource.getCount().then(function (count) {
                    if (count > 0) {
                        complete();
                    } else {
                        var seedData = [
                            { title: "Star Wars", category: "SciFi" },
                            { title: "Forbidden Planet", category: "SciFi" },
                            { title: "Show Boat", category: "Musical" }
                        ];

                        var promises = [];
```

```
                        seedData.forEach(function (data) {
                            promises.push(moviesDataSource.insertAtEnd(null, data));
                        });
                        WinJS.Promise.join(promises).done(function () {
                            complete();
                        });
                    }
                });
            });
        }



        // Wire-up SelectCategory, Add, Delete, Nuke buttons
        document.getElementById("selectCategory").addEventListener("change",
➥function (evt) {
            var category = document.getElementById("selectCategory").value;
            if (category === "All") {
                moviesDataSource = new DataSources.IndexedDbDataSource("movies",
➥createOptions);
            } else {
                var cursorOptions = {
                    indexName: "category",
                    only: document.getElementById("selectCategory").value
                };
                moviesDataSource = new DataSources.IndexedDbDataSource("movies",
➥createOptions, cursorOptions);
            }
            lvMovies.itemDataSource = moviesDataSource;
        });


        document.getElementById("frmAdd").addEventListener("submit", function (evt)
{
            evt.preventDefault();
            moviesDataSource.beginEdits();
            moviesDataSource.insertAtEnd(null, {
                title: document.getElementById("inputMovieTitle").value,
                category: document.getElementById("selectMovieCategory").value
            }).done(function (newItem) {
                moviesDataSource.endEdits();
                document.getElementById("frmAdd").reset();

                // Show last item added
                lvMovies.itemDataSource.getCount().done(function (count) {
                    lvMovies.ensureVisible(count);
                })
```

```
            });
        });

        document.getElementById("btnDelete").addEventListener("click", function () {
            if (lvMovies.selection.count() == 1) {
                moviesDataSource.beginEdits();
                lvMovies.selection.getItems().done(function (items) {
                    moviesDataSource.remove(items[0].key);
                    moviesDataSource.endEdits();
                });
            }
        });

        document.getElementById("btnNuke").addEventListener("click", function () {
            moviesDataSource.nuke();
        });

    });
}


document.addEventListener("DOMContentLoaded", init);
```

Listing 9.4 contains the JavaScript code for the Movie app. When you first open the app, an IndexedDB data source is created without any `cursorOption` and all of the movies stored in the `movies` object store are displayed:

```
// Create the IndexedDB data source
var moviesDataSource = new DataSources.IndexedDbDataSource("movies", createOptions);


// Add seed data
addSeedData().done(function () {
    // Bind data source to ListView
    lvMovies.itemDataSource = moviesDataSource;
});
```

Notice that the preceding code also includes a call to a method named `addSeedData()`. This method adds initial seed data to the IndexedDB database so the database is not empty when you first run the Movie app.

If you select a particular movie category using the select list then the following code executes:

```
document.getElementById("selectCategory").addEventListener("change", function (evt)
{
    var category = document.getElementById("selectCategory").value;
```

```
    if (category === "All") {
        moviesDataSource = new DataSources.IndexedDbDataSource("movies",
➥createOptions);
    } else {
        var cursorOptions = {
            indexName: "category",
            only: document.getElementById("selectCategory").value
        };
        moviesDataSource = new DataSources.IndexedDbDataSource("movies",
➥createOptions, cursorOptions);
    }
    lvMovies.itemDataSource = moviesDataSource;
});
```

This code uses a `cursorOption` object to create a new IndexedDB data source that only represents a subset of objects from the `movies` store.

Summary

In this chapter, I focused on creating custom data sources that you can use with the controls in the WinJS library. You learned how to derive a new data source from the base `VirtualizedDataSource` class.

I discussed three custom data sources. First, I created a file data source which enables you to store and retrieve data from your computer's file system. Next, I created a web service data source that enables you to interact with a remote web service. Finally, I discussed how you can create a data source that works with IndexedDB.

CHAPTER 10

Using Windows Azure Mobile Services

The easiest way to store data in a Windows Store app is to take advantage of Windows Azure Mobile Services. Windows Azure Mobile Services enables you to store your data in a SQL Azure database hosted in the cloud.

If you take advantage of Mobile Services then you don't need to build and host your own web service on your own web server. You can let Microsoft worry all about that.

Imagine, for example, that you want to create a Task List app and be able to access the list of tasks from multiple computers and tablets. In that case, you can store the list of tasks in a database table hosted on Azure and retrieve the list of tasks from anywhere. You can even access Mobile Service from non-Microsoft clients running iOS or Android.

In this chapter, I explain how you can set up and create Azure Mobile Services. I demonstrate how you can insert, update, and delete an Azure database table from your Windows Store app. I also discuss how you can handle validating form data when you submit the data to the cloud.

> **NOTE**
>
> I discuss authorization and Windows Azure Mobile Services in Chapter 14, "Using the Live Connect API."

Creating a Mobile Service

The first step required to use Azure Mobile Services is to log in to the Windows Azure Management Portal and create a new Mobile Service. You log in to the portal by navigating to http://manage.WindowsAzure.com.

> **NOTE**
>
> I am assuming that you have subscribed to Windows Azure. If you haven't subscribed then you need to visit http://WindowsAzure.com. They provide a free trial account if you just want to play with Microsoft's multibillion dollar data centers.

After you log in to the portal, you can create a new Mobile Service by clicking the tab on the left of the page (see Figure 10.1). You create a new Mobile Service by providing a URL and creating a SQL Azure database. For example, I created a new service with the URL https://unleashed.azure-mobile.net/.

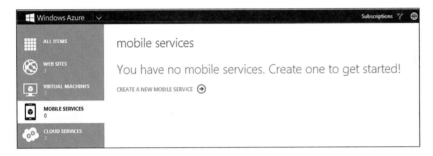

FIGURE 10.1   Creating a new Mobile Service in the Windows Azure Management Portal

As an alternative to using the web portal, you can create a new Mobile Service from directly inside Visual Studio. You first need to import your Windows Azure subscriptions into Visual Studio. Open the Server Explorer window, right-click Windows Azure Mobile Services, and select Import Subscriptions. Use the Import Subscriptions dialog to download and import your Azure subscriptions.

Next, you can create a new Mobile Service by right-clicking Windows Azure Mobile Services and selecting Create Service (see Figure 10.2). Use the Create Mobile Service dialog to select a URL and a database for your new Mobile Service.

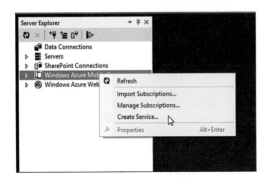

FIGURE 10.2   Creating a new Mobile Service inside Visual Studio

After you create a Mobile Service—by using the Windows Azure Management Portal or by using Visual Studio—you need to retrieve your secret application key. Navigate to the Management Portal at http://manage.WindowsAzure.com, navigate to the dashboard for your Mobile Service, and click the Manage Keys button located at the bottom of the page. Write down your key (see Figure 10.3). You will need this key to interact with your Mobile Service.

FIGURE 10.3   Retrieving your Mobile Service application key

> **NOTE**
>
> All of the code discussed in this chapter is in the Chapter10 folder. You need to change the API key in the default.js file to run the code.

> **NOTE**
>
> The difference between a master key and an application key is that you use the master key when performing operations restricted to "Scripts and Admins". You don't distribute your master key with your Windows Store app.

Creating a Database Table

In this chapter, I am going to build a Task List app that stores tasks in a database table exposed by Windows Azure Mobile Services. Therefore, the next step is to create this database table.

Again, you have a choice. You can either create the database table using the Windows Azure Management Portal or you can create the database table directly inside of Visual Studio. This is purely a matter of preference.

To create the table from within Visual Studio, right-click the Windows Azure Mobile Services node within the Server Explorer window and select New Table (see Figure 10.4). Enter the name Tasks for the new table name.

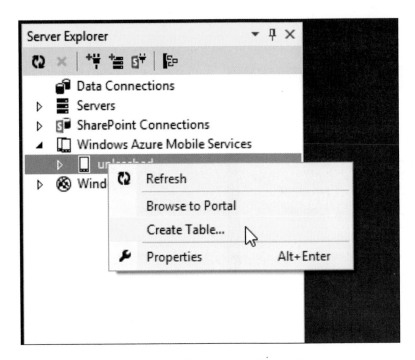

FIGURE 10.4   Creating a new SQL Azure database table

Notice that you do not specify the columns for the new table. The columns are created dynamically based on the data you insert into the table. This feature is called *Dynamic Schema*. Taking advantage of Dynamic Schema makes it easier to develop a new Mobile Service. However, Microsoft recommends that you disable Dynamic Schema for a production database. You can disable Dynamic Schema by selecting your Mobile Service and opening the Visual Studio Properties Window.

Installing the Mobile Services for WinJS Library

Okay, so now we have our Mobile Service and our database table. In order to interact with our Mobile Service from our Windows Store app, we need to install the *Mobile Services for WinJS* client library.

The fastest way to install this library is to take advantage of the NuGet Package Manager Console. After opening or starting a new project in Visual Studio, select Tools, Library Package Manager, Package Manager Console and enter the following command:

```
Install-Package WindowsAzure.MobileServices.WinJS
```

Executing this command adds a new set of Mobile Services scripts to your project's js folder. To use the Mobile Services for WinJS client library, you need to add a script reference to the MobileServices.min.js file to a page such as your default.js page like this:

```
<script src="/js/MobileServices.min.js"></script>
```

After you add this reference, you will have the full power of the Mobile Services client library at your disposal.

Performing Inserts, Updates, and Deletes

In the previous sections, I created a new Azure Mobile Service named unleashed, I created a new database table named Tasks, and I installed the Mobile Services for WinJS client library. Now it is time to write some code and actually interact with the Tasks database table from a Windows Store app. In this section, I explain how to perform basic insert, update, and delete operations against the Tasks database table.

Connecting to the Remote Database Table

Before you can perform any operation against a remote database table such as inserting or updating data, you must first connect to a Mobile Service and get a reference to the remote table.

There are two main objects included in the Mobile Services library: the MobileServiceClient object and the MobileServiceTable object. Here's how you use these two objects to get a reference to the Tasks table:

```
// Get Tasks table from Azure Mobile Services
var mobileServiceClient = new WindowsAzure.MobileServiceClient(
    "https://unleashed.azure-mobile.net/",
    "IwZcChdiEkqUvZBzPrHCNVifFpVgto72"
);
var tasksTable = mobileServiceClient.getTable('Tasks');
```

The constructor for the MobileServiceClient object accepts two parameters. You need to pass the URL and application key for the Mobile Service. After you create a MobileServiceClient, you use its getTable() method to retrieve a MobileServiceTable object that represents an Azure database table.

Inserting Database Data

You insert database data into a Mobile Service table by calling the MobileServiceTable insert() method. For example, the following code adds a new task to the Tasks database table:

```
var newTask = {
    name: "Finish writing book"
};
```

10

```
// Call insert on the mobile service
tasksTable.insert(newTask).done(
    // Success
    function (result) {},
    // Failure
    function (err) {}
);
```

The `insert()` method returns a promise. You can supply a success and an error function to handle the result of performing the insert.

Notice that the success function takes a `result` parameter. The `result` parameter represents the new task returned by the `insert()` operation. The task returned by the `insert()` method includes an `id` property that represents the primary key value of the new database record.

The error function also accepts a parameter. You can use err.request.responseText to get any error message returned while attempting to perform the insert. You might, for example, want to display the error message in a modal popup dialog.

Updating Database Data

You edit an existing database record by calling the `MobileServiceTable update()` method.

```
var taskToUpdate = {
    id: 3,
    name: "Finish writing chapter 10"
};
```

```
tasksTable.update(taskToUpdate).done(
    // Success
    function (result) {},
    // Fail
    function (err) {}
);
```

When you update a record, you must include the primary key of the record being updated in the object passed to the update method. In this case, the `taskToUpdate` object must include an `id` property that corresponds to the primary key of the record in the database being updated.

When you create a new table using Azure Mobile Services, the new table gets a primary key column named `id` automatically. The `id` column is an auto-increment column.

Deleting Database Data

You delete data from a database table by calling the `del()` method. Here is how you would delete a task from the Tasks table:

```
var taskToDelete = {
    id: 3,
    name: "Finish writing chapter 10"
};


tasksTable.del(taskToDelete).done(
    // Success
    function () {},
    // Fail
    function (err) {}
)
```

You must pass the value of the primary key of the object being deleted to the `del()` method. In the preceding code, the `taskToDelete` has both an `id` and `name` property and the task with an `id` of 3 is deleted. (This code would work fine even if I left out the name property.)

You don't get anything back when a record is deleted successfully. Therefore, there is no reason to include a parameter for the success function.

> **NOTE**
>
> Why is the method named `del()` instead of `delete()`? The problem is that delete is a JavaScript reserved word.

Performing Database Queries

In this section, I talk about the different ways in which you can use the Mobile Services for WinJS library to retrieve database records from a Mobile Service. I discuss methods for retrieving a single record and a set of records.

Looking Up a Single Database Record

If you want to retrieve a single database record from a Mobile Service then you can call the `MobileServiceTable lookup()` method like this:

```
var id = 3;
tasksTable.lookup(id).done(
    // Success
    function (result) {},
    // Fail
    function (err) {}
);
```

10

You pass the `id` of the record that you want to retrieve to the `lookup()` method. The `id` should be an integer and represent a primary key value.

If there is no matching record then an error is returned and the promise error function is executed.

Retrieving a Set of Database Records

The `MobileServiceTable` object supports the following methods for performing database queries that retrieve a set of records:

- `includeTotalCount()`—Includes the total count of matching records in the results
- `orderBy(col1, col2, ...)`—Returns the matching records sorted in ascending order
- `orderByDescending(col1, col2, ...)`—Returns the matching records sorted in descending order
- `read(query)`—Executes the database query
- `select(function)`—Returns a specific set of columns
- `skip(count)`—Skips a certain count of records
- `take(count)`—Returns a limited count of records
- `where(function | object)`—Filters the records returned

These methods are chainable. You can call the methods in succession to build a complex query.

> **NOTE**
>
> You can execute the queries discussed in this section by navigating to the queries\queries.html page.

For example, the following query returns the first three tasks from the Tasks table in order of the Tasks name column:

```
tasksTable.take(3).orderBy("name").read().done(
    // Success
    function (results) {},
    // Fail
    function (err) {}
);
```

Executing this query returns results like the following:

```
[
    {"id":4,"name":"Task A"},
    {"id":3,"name":"Task B"},
    {"id":1,"name":"Task C"}
]
```

If you call the `includeTotalCount()` method then you get the total number of matching results included in your results even when you limit the results:

```
tasksTable.includeTotalCount().take(3).orderBy("name").read().done(
    // Success
    function (results) {
        var totalCount = results.totalCount;
    },
    // Fail
    function (err) {}
);
```

Executing this query returns the same array of results as the previous query. However, the results include a property named `totalCount` that contains the total count of records in the Tasks database table (see Figure 10.5).

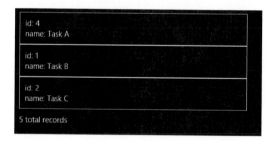

FIGURE 10.5   Displaying a total count

Finally, you can use an OData query when calling the `read()` method. For example, you can retrieve all of the tasks that have a name that starts with the letter *s* with the following query:

```
var odataQuery = "$filter=startswith(name, 's')";
tasksTable.read(odataQuery).done(
    // Success
    function (results) {},
    // Fail
    function (err) {}
);
```

Executing this query returns only those tasks which start with the letter *s* or letter *S*—the query is case-insensitive.

> **NOTE**
>
> OData has a powerful filtering vocabulary. For example, OData supports logical operators such as *greater than* and *less than* and string operators such as `startswith` and `substring`. You can learn more about OData by visiting http://odata.org.

Performing Validation

In Chapter 5, "Creating Forms," I explained how you can use HTML5 validation attributes to validate form data submitted in a Windows Store app. However, it is important to realize that any validation performed in a Windows Store app can always be bypassed when calling a remote Mobile Service. A user can interact directly with the remote service and submit any data that you can imagine.

If you want to validate the data submitted to a Mobile Service then you should create delete.js, insert.js, read.js, or update.js scripts that execute on Azure when a Mobile Service is invoked. It is worth emphasizing that these scripts execute on the Azure server (in one of Microsoft's data centers) and not within a Windows Store app. Because these scripts execute on the server, the scripts cannot be bypassed.

The easiest way to modify these server scripts is from within Visual Studio. Open the Server Explorer window and expand the node that represents a particular Mobile Service table. For example, in Figure 10.6, I've revealed the server scripts for the Tasks table.

FIGURE 10.6   Modifying the server scripts for the Tasks table

You can open the delete.js, insert.js, read.js, or update.js files in the Visual Studio code editor by double-clicking the file. When you save the file, the file is saved back on Windows Azure automatically.

Imagine, for example, that you want to prevent people from submitting tasks with empty names. In that case, you can enter the following script in Listing 10.1 for the insert.js script.

LISTING 10.1   Server insert.js Script

```
function insert(item, user, request) {
    // Cleanup data
    item.name = item.name.trim();

    // Validate
    if (item.name.length === 0) {
        request.respond(statusCodes.BAD_REQUEST, "You fool! Task name is
➥required!!!");
        return;
    }

    // Otherwise, execute request
    request.execute();
}
```

The `insert()` function in Listing 10.1 accepts three parameters:

▶ **item**—The item being inserted

▶ **user**—The authenticated user doing the inserting

▶ **request**—The current request

If there are no validation issues then the `insert()` function in Listing 10.1 calls the `request.execute()` method to perform the insert of the new task into the Tasks database table.

Before calling `request.execute()`, the `insert()` function first verifies that the `item.name` property is not empty by trimming the value of the `name` property and checking the length. If the name property is empty, then a BAD_REQUEST response (HTTP status code 400) is returned from the function.

NOTE

We discuss the `user` parameter passed to the `insert()` function when we discuss authentication in Chapter 14.

You can capture a BAD_REQUEST response in your Windows Store app by including an error handler when you call the `insert()` method like this:

```
// Call insert on the mobile service
tasksTable.insert(newTask).done(
    // Success
    function (result) {},
    // Failure
    function (err) {
```

10

```
        var errorText = err.request.responseText;
        var md = new Windows.UI.Popups.MessageDialog(errorText);
        md.showAsync();
    }
);
```

This error function displays whatever error message is returned from the Mobile Service in a popup message dialog (see Figure 10.7).

FIGURE 10.7   Attempting to insert an empty value

> **NOTE**
>
> You can use the delete.js, insert.js, read.js, and update.js scripts in scenarios beyond those for validation. For example, you can use these scripts to clean up data before inserting the data into the database. Or, you can use these scripts to add extra properties to the data such as a time stamp. You can even use server scripts to interact with Azure Table Storage or Azure Blob Storage in scenarios in which you want to store big chunks of data such as pictures.

Performing Custom Actions

By default, there are four standard scripts that you can execute in an Azure Mobile Service: delete.js, insert.js, read.js, and update.js scripts. However, you also have the option of creating a custom Mobile Service script.

Creating a custom script is useful when you need to do a more complicated database operation. For example, you might want to include a Nuke button in your Tasks app that enables you to delete all of your tasks. In that case, it would be great if you could create a nuke.js script that performs a SQL Truncate to delete all of the tasks from the Tasks table.

You can create a custom script from the Windows Azure Management Portal. Navigate to your Mobile Service at http://manage.WindowsAzure.com and click the API tab. Next, click the Create button to create a new custom API (see Figure 10.8).

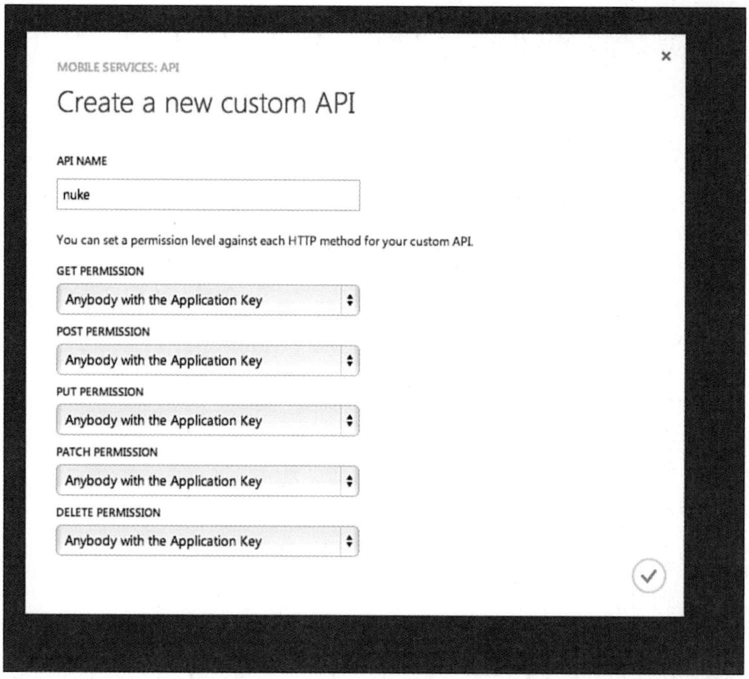

FIGURE 10.8   Creating a custom API

Enter a name for your custom script. For example, I entered the name nuke. After you submit the form, you can enter your script. I entered the script in Listing 10.2 for my nuke.js script.

LISTING 10.2   Custom API Script (nuke.js)

```
exports.post = function (request, response) {
    var mssql = request.service.mssql;
    var sql = "TRUNCATE TABLE Tasks";
    mssql.query(sql, {
        success: function () {
            response.send(200);
        }
    })
};
```

Because I want to invoke my custom script in response to an HTTP POST operation, I define my function as the value of exports.post. I could also handle other HTTP operations by defining, for example, an exports.get, exports.put, exports.delete, or an exports. patch function.

> **NOTE**
>
> Under the covers, custom API scripts are implemented on Windows Azure as NodeJS modules. The exports represent module exports and the request and response objects are NodeJS Express objects. Visit http://ExpressJS.com to learn more about Express.

Within my script, I execute a SQL TRUNCATE TABLE command by calling the `mssql.query()` method. Executing this command will delete all of the tasks in my Tasks table and reset the identity counter to the value zero.

You invoke a custom script by calling the `MobileServiceClient invokeApi()` method. For example, here is how you would invoke the nuke script from a Windows Store app:

```
mobileServiceClient.invokeApi("nuke", { method: "post" }).done(
    // Success
    function () {},
    // Failure
    function (err) {}
)
```

The `invokeApi()` method accepts two parameters. The first parameter represents the name of the remote API to invoke. The second parameter represents a set of options. In this case, the method property is used to specify the HTTP operation to perform (an HTTP POST).

> **NOTE**
>
> The complete sample code for invoking the remote nuke API method can be found in the insert/insert.js file in the Chapter 10 project.

Debugging Script Errors

The last thing that I want to mention in this chapter is how to debug errors in remote Azure Mobile Service scripts. If something goes wrong in your insert.js script, for example, then it is hard to know this from your local computer.

Fortunately, you can view a log of all error messages associated with your Mobile Service scripts in the Windows Azure Management Portal. Navigate to http://manage. WindowsAzure.com, select your Mobile Service, and click the Logs tab. All error messages are logged here (see Figure 10.9).

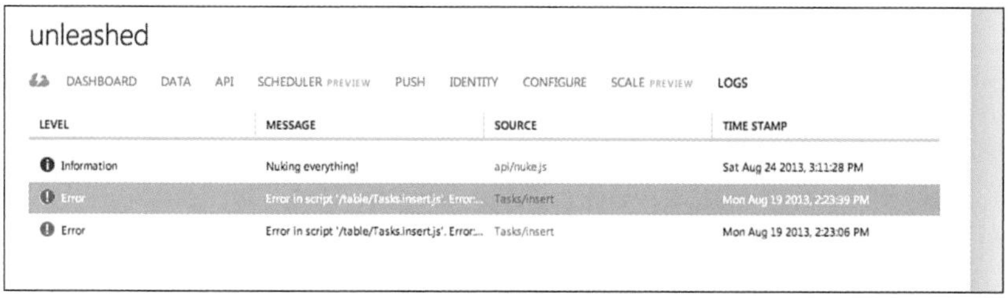

FIGURE 10.9   Viewing the Mobile Service Logs

You can even log custom messages by calling `console.log()` in your scripts. Any string that you pass to `console.log()` appears on the Logs page.

> **NOTE**
>
> A useful online tool for debugging Mobile Services is named Runscope (http://www. Runscope.com). This tool enables you to capture all requests and responses against a remote Mobile Service. For example, if nothing happens when you invoke a Mobile Service, you might want to use Runscope to figure out why.

Summary

The goal of this chapter was to explain how you can store data using Windows Azure Mobile Services. You learned how to create a Mobile Service and insert, update, delete, and query database data.

I also discussed two advanced features of Mobile Services. You learned how to validate data passed to a remote service and how to create custom API methods.

If you need to build a Windows Store app that enables you to share data across the Internet then there is no easier approach than using Windows Azure Mobile Services.

> **NOTE**
>
> In Chapter 14, I discuss how you can authenticate users—and prevent one user from reading another user's data—when using Mobile Services. In Chapter 16, "Creating a Task List App," I demonstrate how you can build an entire Windows Store App using Mobile Services.

10

CHAPTER 11

App Events and States

The goal of this chapter is to explain Windows Store app events, lifecycle, and view states. In the first part, I explain the standard sequence of events which are raised whenever you start a Windows Store app. You learn how to handle the loaded, activated, and ready events.

In the next part, I explain how you can handle application suspension, termination, and resumption. You learn how to store and retrieve the state of your application in session state so you can maintain the illusion that your app is always running.

Finally, I discuss application view states. You learn how to gracefully handle displaying your app with different screen widths by taking advantage of the window resize event and media queries.

App Events

Whenever you launch a Windows Store app, the following WinJS application events are fired in the order shown here:

▶ `WinJS.Application.loaded`—Triggered by the standard browser `DOMContentLoaded` event, right after the HTML document has finished loading

▶ `WinJS.Application.activated`—Triggered when your application is activated

▶ `WinJS.Application.ready`—Triggered after the loaded and activated events

▶ `WinJS.Application.unload`—Triggered by the standard browser `beforeunload` event, right before a page is unloaded

You also can handle these other application events that are triggered by particular events:

▶ **WinJS.Application.error**—Triggered by an unhandled error in your application

▶ **WinJS.Application.checkpoint**—Triggered when your application is being suspended

▶ **WinJS.Application.settings**—Triggered when application settings are changed

None of these events are raised unless you call WinJS.Application.start(). The events are queued and the events are not raised until the WinJS.Application.start() method is called.

The following JavaScript code illustrates how you can create a handler for each of these events and log when the event happens to the Visual Studio JavaScript console window (shown in Figure 11.1):

```
WinJS.Application.addEventListener("loaded", function (evt) {
    console.log("loaded");
});
WinJS.Application.addEventListener("activated", function (evt) {
    console.log("activated");
});
WinJS.Application.addEventListener("ready", function (evt) {
    console.log("ready");
});
```

FIGURE 11.1   Logging WinJS application events

Handling the Activated Event

The activated event is raised when a Windows Store app is activated (started). A Windows Store app can be activated in several different ways, and you can use the ActivationKind property to determine exactly how the app was activated:

```
WinJS.Application.addEventListener("activated", function (evt) {
    var activationKind = Windows.ApplicationModel.Activation.ActivationKind;
    switch (evt.detail.kind) {
        case activationKind.launch:
            console.log("Launched from a tile");
            break;
        case activationKind.search:
```

```
            console.log("Activated from a search");
            break;
        default:
            console.log("Activated for some other reason");
    }
});
```

The most common way in which a Windows Store app is activated is when a user clicks the tile for the app in the Start screen. In that case, the ActivationKind enumeration has the value Launch.

However, there are other ways that a Windows Store app can be activated. For example, an app can be activated in response to a user performing a search from the Search charm, in response to a user sharing something from the Share charm, or in response to a user clicking on a file from another app, such as an email app. In these cases, you can use the ActivationKind property to determine the exact reason that the app was activated.

Handling the Error Event

By default, when there is an unhandled error in a Windows Store app—an error that is not handled within a try...catch block—the following three things happen:

1. The error is logged by calling the WinJS.log() method.

2. The debugger statement is called to break into the debugger when the app is running in Visual Studio in Debug mode.

3. The app is terminated by calling the MSApp.terminateApp() method.

After the terminateApp() method is called, the user is thrown back to the Windows Start screen (violently, unexpectedly, and without explanation).

You can handle the application error event to provide a better user experience. For example, here's how you can display a message to the user when an unhandled error happens:

```
WinJS.Application.addEventListener("error", function (evt) {
    var message = new Windows.UI.Popups.MessageDialog(
        "There was an error."
    );
    message.showAsync();
    return true;
});


WinJS.Application.addEventListener("ready", function () {
    throw new WinJS.ErrorFromName("MyError", "Yikes! An Error!");
});


WinJS.Application.start();
```

The preceding code displays a modal dialog when there is an error with the message `There was an error.` (see Figure 11.2).

There was an error.

Close

FIGURE 11.2   Displaying an error message

Notice that the error handler returns the value true. When the error handler returns true, the error is considered handled and the app is not terminated. If you want to terminate the app after executing your custom error handler code then don't return true.

> **WARNING**
>
> If the error happens before the `WinJS.application.start()` method is called, then your custom error handler won't be invoked.

Deferring Events with Promises

`WinJS.Application` events are different than normal DOM events because they support promises. You can execute an asynchronous task during a `WinJS.Application` event and delay the next event until a promise completes.

For example, the default.js file created when you create a new Windows Store app project delays the completion of the `WinJS.Application.activated` event until the asynchronous call to `WinJS.UI.processAll()` completes. This ensures that all of the controls in the page are processed before the splash screen is torn down.

Here's what the `WinJS.Application.activated` event handler looks like in the default.js file with some code removed:

```
app.onactivated = function (args) {
    if (args.detail.kind === activation.ActivationKind.launch) {
        args.setPromise(WinJS.UI.processAll());
    }
};
```

In the preceding code, the `args.setPromise()` method is used to execute a method that returns a promise: the `processAll()` method. The `processAll()` method executes asynchronously and the `ready` event is not raised until the `processAll()` method completes.

Creating Custom Events

You can create and listen to custom application events. You can make up any type of event that you please.

For example, if you are creating a game, you might want to create a heartbeat event that is raised every second so that you can refresh the game board. The following code demonstrates how you can raise and listen to a custom heartbeat event:

```
window.setInterval(function () {
    WinJS.Application.queueEvent({ type: "heartbeat" });
}, 1000);

WinJS.Application.addEventListener("heartbeat", function (evt) {
    console.log("heartbeat");
});

WinJS.Application.start();
```

The preceding code uses the `setInterval()` method to execute code once every second. The `queueEvent()` method is called to queue up a custom heartbeat event.

The `addEventListener()` method is used to listen to the event. Every second, the message "heartbeat" is written to the Visual Studio JavaScript Console window.

You can supply additional event details by supplying a `detail` property when queuing an event like this:

```
WinJS.Application.queueEvent({
    type: "heartbeat",
    detail: { numberOfPlayers: 12 }
});
```

Suspending, Terminating, and Resuming an App

When you are building a Windows Store app, you need to maintain the illusion that the app is always running even when the user might be switching compulsively among multiple open apps. Normally, you do not explicitly close a Windows Store app—instead, you just switch to a new one.

If you switch from one app to another, Windows will suspend the app but keep the app in memory. If memory resources become low because of other running apps, Windows will quietly terminate the app in the background.

From the perspective of a user, an app should behave in the same way regardless of whether the app was suspended or terminated. You expect the app to be in the same state when you switch back to it—even if you don't switch back to the app for many hours. For example, if the user was reading a particular news story, the same story should be selected when the user switches back to the app.

Detecting When an App Is Suspended and Terminated

You can detect when an app is suspended by handling the `WinJS.Application.checkpoint` event. You should use this event to save the state of your app so you can reload the state when the app starts again.

There is no method within a Windows Store app to detect when an app is terminated. In particular, there is no app terminated event. For this reason, if you need to save the state of your app so the state can be reloaded after termination, then you should save your app state during the checkpoint event.

Here's some sample code for handling this event:

```
WinJS.Application.addEventListener("checkpoint", function () {
    // Save app state
});
```

> **NOTE**
>
> Creating an app terminated event would not make sense because Windows would need to wake your app from a suspended state to raise the terminated event. It would not make sense for Windows to wake your app at the very moment that it detects that memory resources have gotten low.

Detecting the Previous Execution State

When a Windows Store app is activated, you can use the `previousExecutionState` property to determine whether the app is being newly launched, whether it was previously closed by the user, or whether it is coming back after being suspended and terminated.

Depending on the value of `previousExecutionState`, you might want to load default values or load the previous app state. For example, if you are creating a news app, then you probably want to load the previous article that the user was reading. If, on the other hand, the user has never run the app, then you might want to load a default page such as the home page.

Here's what the code looks like for checking the previous state:

```
WinJS.Application.addEventListener("activated", function (evt) {
    var appState = Windows.ApplicationModel.Activation.ApplicationExecutionState;
    if (evt.detail.previousExecutionState == appState.notRunning) {
        // The app has not been run in the current user session
```

```
        // or it crashed.
        // Should load defaults.
    }
    if (evt.detail.previousExecutionState == appState.closedByUser) {
        // The app was closed by the user.
        // Should load defaults.
    }
    if (evt.detail.previousExecutionState == appState.terminated) {
        // The app was suspended and terminated.
        // Should restore previous state.
    }
});
```

The preceding code contains a handler for the `WinJS.Application.activated` event. The `event.previousExecutionState` property represents the previous state of the application. All of the previous states are represented by the `ApplicationExecutionState` enumeration.

Here are all of the possible values of the `ApplicationExecutionState` enumeration:

▶ `notRunning`—The user activates the app after installing the app from the Windows Store, rebooting the computer, logging in and out, ending the task, the app crashing, or closing the app and restarting it within 10 seconds of closing it.

▶ `running`—The app is already running and the user activates it through a secondary tile or through one of the activation contracts or extensions.

▶ `suspended`—The app is suspended and the app is activated through a secondary tile or through one of the activation contracts or extensions.

▶ `terminated`—The app was terminated by Windows.

▶ `closedByUser`—The app was closed by the user and not restarted for more than 10 seconds.

NOTE

You cannot detect whether an app is being activated after suspension. You can detect only when an application is activated after suspension *and termination*. The activated event is not raised for apps that get suspended without termination.

Testing Application State with Visual Studio

You can use Visual Studio to test how your Windows Store app behaves when it is suspended, terminated, or resumes. When you run an app from Visual Studio, the drop-down in Figure 11.3 appears (it is part of the Debug Location toolbar).

FIGURE 11.3   Change app state options

If you want to simulate app suspension and resumption then you can click the Suspend option to suspend your application and then click the Resume option to resume your application again. When you click the Suspend option, the checkpoint event is raised. When you click the Resume option, the activated event is *not* raised (your app does not know when it was resumed after suspension).

If you want to simulate app suspension and termination then you can click the Suspend and shutdown button. When you click the Suspend and shutdown button, the checkpoint event is raised and your app stops. When you run the app again, by actually running your app again in Visual Studio, the previous execution state property will have the value of terminated.

Storing State with Session State

If an app is suspended then the app does not lose state. However, if an app is suspended and terminated then the state of the app is lost. Any variables will lose their values and the app will start from scratch.

There is a special object, the `WinJS.Application.sessionState` object, which you can use to store state across app suspension. Anything you add to session state survives until the app is activated again.

The code in Listing 11.1 illustrates how you can use session state to store the user's current game score.

LISTING 11.1   Using Session State (sessionState/sessionState.js)

```
(function () {
    "use strict";

    var _gameScore;

    WinJS.Application.addEventListener("activated", function (evt) {
        var appState = Windows.ApplicationModel.
➡Activation.ApplicationExecutionState;
        if (evt.detail.previousExecutionState == appState.notRunning ||
            evt.detail.previousExecutionState == appState.closedByUser) {
            // Set default game score
            _gameScore = 0;
            console.log("setting default gamescore");
```

```
        }
        if (evt.detail.previousExecutionState == appState.terminated) {
            // Load game score from session state
            _gameScore = WinJS.Application.sessionState.gameScore;
            console.log("setting gamescore from session state");
        }
    });

    WinJS.Application.addEventListener("checkpoint", function () {
        // Save game score to session state
        WinJS.Application.sessionState.gameScore = _gameScore;
    });

    WinJS.Application.addEventListener("ready", function (evt) {
        // Killed alien, +1 to game score
        document.getElementById("btnKillAlien").addEventListener("click",
➡function () {
            _gameScore++;
            showGameScore();
        });

        showGameScore();
    });


    function showGameScore() {
        document.getElementById("gameScore").innerText = _gameScore;
    }


    WinJS.Application.start();
})();
```

The code in Listing 11.1 includes three event handlers:

▶ `click`—When you click the `btnKillAlien` button, the current game score goes up by 1.

▶ `checkpoint`—Called when the app is suspended. This event handler stores the current game score in session state.

▶ `activated`—Called when the app is activated. If the app is activated after termination then the current game score is loaded from session state. Otherwise, a default value for the game score is assigned.

Session state is only loaded when an app is activated after termination. Session state is not preserved, for example, when a user explicitly closes an app or reboots her machine.

> **NOTE**
>
> Behind the scenes, session state is stored in local storage in a file named
> _sessionState.json. After the checkpoint event, session state is written to this file auto-
> matically. When an app is activated after termination, session state is loaded from this
> file automatically.

Designing for Different Window Sizes

Windows 8.1 supports running up to four apps side-by-side on the same monitor. For
example, you can have your mail app open next to your music app next to your calendar app next to your solitaire app. You can even go completely crazy and attach multiple
monitors to your computer and each monitor can display multiple side-by-side apps.

> **NOTE**
>
> The number of apps that you can display side by side on a single monitor depends on
> your screen resolution. For example, you can't display more than two apps side by side on
> a 1,024 pixel by 768 pixel monitor.

You can resize a running app at any time. For example, you can stretch out the width of
your mail app while you are reading your emails and then shrink your mail app when
shifting your focus to playing solitaire. A well-designed Windows Store app will intelli-
gently adapt to the available real estate. For example, if a fat app is forced to get skinny, it
will hide extra content automatically.

If you are using a tablet computer—such as a Microsoft Surface—then you can switch
the orientation of your computer at any time from portrait to landscape. Again, a well-
designed Windows Store app will detect orientation changes and adapt automatically.

In this section, you learn how to detect when the width or the orientation of your app
changes. You learn how to gracefully adapt to different display widths and orientations.

> **NOTE**
>
> Windows 8, unlike Windows 8.1, had discrete view states. In particular, Windows 8
> supported snapped, filled, and full screen view states. Windows 8.1 no longer supports
> discrete view states. Instead, you should build your app with the expectation that a user
> might change the width of your app continuously to any size larger than the minimum.

Setting the Minimum App Width

By default, a Windows Store app has a minimum width of 500 pixels. You should design
your Windows Store app so that it looks nice at 500 pixels and any resolution greater than
500 pixels (within reason).

> **NOTE**
>
> According to Microsoft statistics, the most common screen resolution used with Windows is 1,366 x 768. But you can use very high resolution monitors with Windows 8, including 2,560 x 1600 monitors.

For certain apps, it might make sense to support a resolution lower than the default 500 pixels. You can change the default minimum width to a lower width of 320 pixels. Open the package.appxmanifest file and pick the lower resolution from the drop-down list (see Figure 11.4).

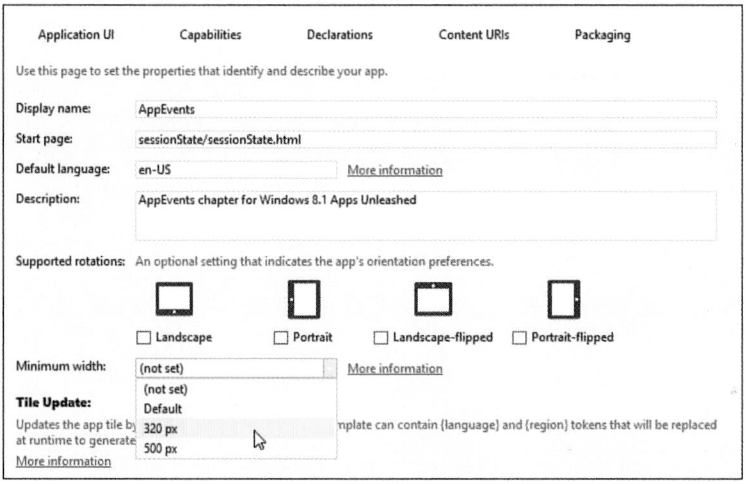

FIGURE 11.4   Setting the minimum width

Using CSS Media Queries

You can take advantage of *media queries* in conjunction with Cascading Style Sheets to adapt to different app sizes automatically. You can use media queries to detect the characteristics of a device and modify the presentation of content.

> **NOTE**
>
> Media queries is a W3C recommendation. You can use media queries not only with Windows Store apps, but also with normal websites. Media queries are supported by Google Chrome 4+, Mozilla Firefox 3.5+, Apple Safari 4+, and Microsoft Internet Explorer 9+.

Imagine, for example, that you want to display different content depending on the horizontal resolution of a device. In that case, you can group styles by using the `@media` rule.

For example, the HTML page in Listing 11.2 contains three sets of style rules. One set applies to all devices, one set applies to medium resolution devices, and one set applies to high resolution devices.

LISTING 11.2   Using CSS Media Queries (mediaQueries\mediaQueries.htm)

```html
<!DOCTYPE html>
<html>
    <head>
        <title></title>
        <style type="text/css">
            /* Default Styles */
            .displayInMedium, .displayInHigh {
                display:none;
            }

            /* Greater than or equal to 1,366px */
            @media screen and (min-width:1366px) {
                .displayInMedium {
                    display: block;
                }
            }

            /* Greater than or equal to 1,920px */
            @media screen and (min-width:1920px) {
                .displayInMedium, .displayInHigh {
                    display: block;
                }
            }

        </style>
    </head>
    <body>
        <div>
            <h1>You can see me at all resolutions.</h1>
        </div>

        <div class="displayInMedium">
            <h1>You can see me at medium resolutions.</h1>
        </div>

        <div class="displayInHigh">
            <h1>You can see me at high resolutions.</h1>
        </div>
    </body>
</html>
```

You can simulate different device sizes by running your Windows Store app using the Visual Studio simulator and selecting different resolutions (see Figure 11.5). When you switch to different resolutions, the content in different DIV elements is displayed.

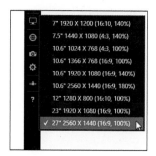

FIGURE 11.5   Changing screen resolution in the simulator

You can also use media queries to detect whether an app is being displayed with a portrait or landscape orientation. The page in Listing 11.3 defines two CSS classes named `displayInLandscape` and `displayInPortrait`, which you can use to hide and display content in the page.

LISTING 11.3   Using Media Queries to Detect Orientation (mediaQueryOrientation\mediaQueryOrientation.htm)

```html
<!DOCTYPE html>
<html>
    <head>
        <title>Media Query Orientation</title>

        <style>
            .displayInLandscape, .displayInPortrait {
                display:none;
            }

            @media screen and (orientation: landscape) {
                .displayInLandscape {
                    display:block;
                }
            }

            @media screen and (orientation: portrait) {
                .displayInPortrait {
                    display:block;
                }
            }
```

```
        </style>
    </head>
    <body>

        <div class="displayInLandscape">
            <h1>You can see me in landscape orientation!</h1>
        </div>

        <div class="displayInPortrait">
            <h1>You can see me in portrait orientation!</h1>
        </div>

    </body>
</html>
```

You can use the simulator to switch your running app into different orientations by clicking the Rotate clockwise (90 degrees) and Rotate counterclockwise (90 degrees) buttons (see Figure 11.6).

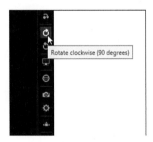

FIGURE 11.6   Testing orientations with the simulator

NOTE

In your app manifest—the package.appxmanifest file—you are given the option to specify your supported rotations. If you specify landscape then your app display won't be repainted when the orientation of your app changes to portrait. Rotating your device will be ignored.

Using the `window resize` Event

As an alternative to using media queries to detect changes in app width or orientation, you can use JavaScript to detect these changes. The `window resize` event is raised whenever the size or the orientation of your app changes.

For example, the JavaScript file in Listing 11.4 displays a DIV element named `sidebar` whenever the width of the app is greater than 600 pixels or the app is in landscape orientation.

LISTING 11.4   Handling the `window resize` Event (resize\resize.js)

```
(function () {
    "use strict";

    function resize() {
        var width = document.documentElement.offsetWidth;
        var isLandscape = window.innerWidth > window.innerHeight;

        if (isLandscape && width > 600) {
            // Show sidebar
            document.getElementById("sidebar").style.display = "";
        } else {
            // Hide sidebar
            document.getElementById("sidebar").style.display = "none";
        }
    }

    window.addEventListener("resize", resize);

})();
```

When the app is displayed with a width of greater than 600 pixels and an orientation of landscape then the extra sidebar content is displayed (see Figure 11.7).

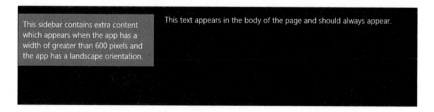

FIGURE 11.7   Display sidebar content

Notice that orientation is detected by comparing the window `innerHeight` and `innerWidth` properties. If the window is more wide than tall then the orientation is detected to be landscape.

Scaling Content to Fit Different Screen Resolutions

In the previous section, you learned how to use media queries and JavaScript to hide or display content depending on the width and orientation of an app. In this section, I discuss how you can build your Windows Store app so it will adapt gracefully to different screen resolutions.

Defining a Viewport

You can take advantage of the `@-ms-viewport` rule to scale content to fit different device resolutions—devices with different widths and heights—automatically.

The `@-ms-viewport` rule enables you to define a *viewport*. A viewport determines the width and height of the available screen real estate used to display content independent of the actual screen size.

For example, the following page displays some text and a picture of a Tesla:

```
<!DOCTYPE html>
<html>
    <head>
        <title>viewport</title>
    </head>
    <body>
        <h1>A fast, red Tesla</h1>
        <img src="../images/tesla.jpg" />
    </body>
</html>
```

When the page is displayed full screen (see Figure 11.8) then everything looks fine. When you share the screen with another app, and lose half the horizontal resolution, then the picture is cut off (see Figure 11.9).

FIGURE 11.8   Full screen Tesla

FIGURE 11.9   Partial screen Tesla

Here's how you can use the `@-ms-viewport` rule to scale the page automatically:

```
<!DOCTYPE html>
<html>
    <head>
        <title>viewport</title>
        <style type="text/css">
            @-ms-viewport {
                width: 1024px;
            }
        </style>
    </head>
    <body>
        <h1>A fast, red Tesla</h1>
        <img src="../images/tesla.jpg" />
    </body>
</html>
```

The viewport is set to 1,024px by 768px. If the page is displayed at a lower resolution than 1,204px by 768px then the content of the page is shrunk (see Figure 11.10).

FIGURE 11.10   Partial screen and shrunk

If the page is displayed at a resolution higher than 1,024px by 768px then the content of the page (including the picture) is expanded (see Figure 11.11).

A fast, red Tesla

FIGURE 11.11   Full screen and expanded

Using the `ViewBox` Control

As an alternative to defining a viewport, you can use the `ViewBox` control. The `ViewBox` control enables you to resize content to fit available screen real estate while retaining the correct aspect ratio.

Imagine, for example, that you happen to have a picture of a Tesla and the picture measures 800px by 484px. You want the picture to fill the entire available space but not get distorted.

The page in Listing 11.5 demonstrates how you can wrap the picture in a `ViewBox`.

LISTING 11.5   Using the `ViewBox` Control (viewBox\viewBox.html)

```
<div data-win-control="WinJS.UI.ViewBox">
    <img src="/images/tesla.jpg" />
</div>
```

Figure 11.12 illustrates the appearance of the picture on a device with a resolution of 1,024px by 768px. Notice that the picture has been scaled automatically to fit the available space.

FIGURE 11.12   Picture shown with 1,024px by 768px resolution

If you view the very same picture on a device with a different resolution then the picture will be scaled automatically to fit the new resolution. For example, Figure 11.13 illustrates what happens when you display the picture on a device with a resolution of 1,920px by 1,084px. Notice that you get pillars on either edge of the photo so that the photo will not be distorted.

FIGURE 11.13   Picture shown with 1,920px by 1,048px resolution

The `ViewBox` even resizes its child element automatically when you shrink the width of an app (see Figure 11.14).

FIGURE 11.14   Resized picture when app size is shrunk

The `ViewBox` control has some significant limitations. You can add only one child element to a `ViewBox`. If you want to apply the `ViewBox` to multiple elements then you must wrap the elements in a DIV (with a particular width and height).

Furthermore, the `ViewBox` does not work with text. You can use the `ViewBox` to resize a picture or an HTML5 canvas.

The main scenario in which it makes sense to use the `ViewBox` is when you want to create a game, and you want the game to look good on computers and tablets with different resolutions. You don't want your angry bird to look fat on one computer and skinny on another. We use the `ViewBox` control with the Brain Eaters game in Chapter 15, "Graphics and Games."

NOTE

Behind the scenes, the `ViewBox` control uses the Cascading Style Sheet 3 `translate` and `scale` functions.

Summary

This chapter was all about Windows Store app events and states. In the first part, I explained the standard types of events that are raised whenever you run a Windows Store app. You learned how to handle the application loaded, activated, and ready events.

Next, I discussed how Windows Store apps get suspended and terminated automatically in Windows 8. You learned how to take advantage of session state to store and retrieve app data.

Finally, you learned how to gracefully adapt to changes in the width, height, orientation, and resolution of a Windows Store app. You learned how to use media queries to hide and display content when the size of a Windows app changes. You also learned to scale a Windows Store app using the `@-ms-viewport` rule and the `ViewBox` control.

CHAPTER 12

Page Fragments and Navigation

The goal of this chapter is to explain three controls: the `HtmlControl`, the `Page` control, and the `PageControlNavigator` control. All three controls enable you to display the contents of one HTML page in another HTML page using Ajax.

The `HtmlControl` enables you to add a chunk of HTML to a page. You can use this control to reuse the same HTML markup in multiple places in your app.

Creating custom `Page` controls enables you to easily create new WinJS controls out of an HTML page, JavaScript file, and style sheet. Create a `Page` control when you want to encapsulate both markup and behavior in a new control.

Finally, the `PageControlNavigator` control enables you to build single page apps that contain multiple virtual pages. The `PageControlNavigator` enables you to load `Page` controls to simulate the experience of navigating between pages.

Using the `HtmlControl` Control

If you want to include the same chunk of HTML in multiple pages in a Windows Store app, or you want to break up an existing page into more manageable parts, then you can use the WinJS `HtmlControl` control. This control requires you to set one option: a URI. You set the URI to indicate the content that you want to load.

> **NOTE**
>
> You can find the code discussed in this section in the Chapter12\Fragments folder in the GitHub source.

Imagine, for example, that you want to display a page with includes a form for entering both a billing and shipping address. In other words, you want to display the same address form twice (see Figure 12.1).

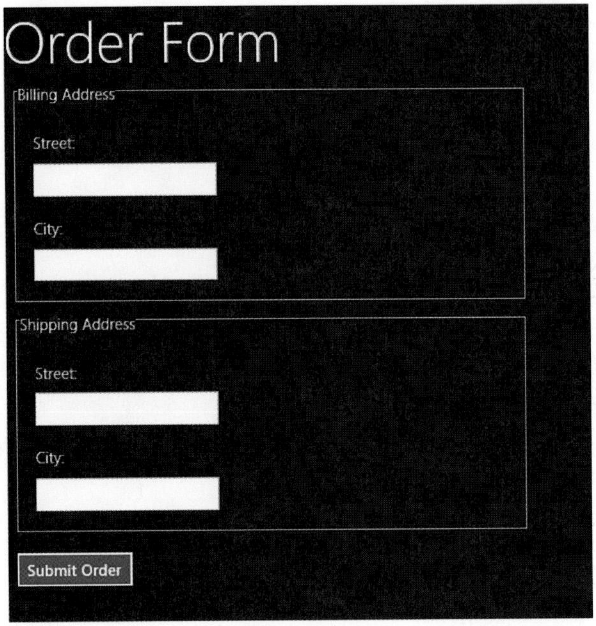

FIGURE 12.1   Using the `HtmlControl` to display address forms

In this case, you can create the Address form in a separate HTML file named address.html:

```
<div>
    <div class="label">
        <label for="inpStreet">Street:</label>
    </div>
    <div class="field">
        <input class="inpStreet" required />
    </div>
</div>
<div>
    <div class="label">
        <label for="inpCity">City:</label>
    </div>
    <div class="field">
        <input class="inpCity" required />
    </div>
</div>
```

> **NOTE**
>
> Notice that I am using class names for the form fields instead of IDs because I want to avoid creating conflicting IDs when the form is displayed twice.

Next, you can load this form into the same page twice using the `HtmlControl` control like this:

```
<h1>Order Form</h1>
<form id="frmOrder">
<fieldset>
    <legend>Billing Address</legend>
    <div id="divBillingAddress"
        data-win-control="WinJS.UI.HtmlControl"
        data-win-options="{
            uri: 'address.html'
        }"></div>
</fieldset>

<fieldset>
    <legend>Shipping Address</legend>
    <div id="divShippingAddress"
        data-win-control="WinJS.UI.HtmlControl"
        data-win-options="{
            uri: 'address.html'
        }"></div>
</fieldset>

<input type="submit" value="Submit Order" />
</form>
```

Finally, here is how you can handle the form submit event to grab the values of both the billing and shipping address forms:

```
WinJS.UI.processAll().done(function() {
    var frmOrder = document.getElementById("frmOrder");

    // Get the order
    frmOrder.addEventListener("submit", function (e) {
        e.preventDefault();
        var order = {
            billing_street: document.querySelector("#divBillingAddress .inpStreet").
value,
            billing_city: document.querySelector("#divBillingAddress .inpCity").
value,
```

```
        shipping_street: document.querySelector("#divShippingAddress
➥.inpStreet").value,
        shipping_city: document.querySelector("#divShippingAddress .inpCity").
➥value
    };


    // Save to Database
  });


});
```

In the preceding code, the `querySelector()` method is used to retrieve the values of both the billing and shipping address form fields. The values of all of the fields are assigned to an object named orders.

> **WARNING**
>
> Don't forget to call `WinJS.UI.processAll()` or the `HtmlControl` will never become a control.

> **NOTE**
>
> In a Windows Store app, you can't use a server-side `#INCLUDE` directive to include content from other files. If you want to include content then you need to use an `HtmlControl` control.

Creating a `Page` **Control**

A `Page` control, as its name suggests, enables you to create a control from a page. A `Page` control provides you with an easy method of creating custom WinJS controls. When you create a `Page` control, you create a new WinJS control out of an HTML page, JavaScript file, and CSS file.

Creating a new `Page` control makes sense when you need to do more than simply add a chunk of HTML to a page. A `Page` control enables you to encapsulate both appearance and behavior in a control.

Furthermore, a `Page` control has its own event lifecycle. For example, a `Page` Control has its own `ready` event which you can handle to initialize the control.

Imagine, for example, that you want to create an `Alert` control. When someone clicks the button rendered by the `Alert` control, a WinRT modal dialog appears that displays a message (Figure 12.2). I'll walk through each of the steps required to create the `Alert` control as a `Page` control.

FIGURE 12.2   Displaying an alert with a custom `Page` control

First, we need to create the following three files:

▶ alert.html

▶ alert.js

▶ alert.css

You can create these three files by adding an HTML page, a JavaScript file, and a style sheet to your project. I added all three of these files to a new folder named myControls.

The alert.html page contains all of the markup for our new control:

```
<!DOCTYPE html>
<html>
<head>
    <meta charset="utf-8" />
    <title>confirmButton</title>
    <link href="alert.css" rel="stylesheet" />
    <script src="alert.js"></script>
</head>
<body>
    <button class="alert"></button>
</body>
</html>
```

Notice that the alert.html page looks like a normal HTML page with both a HEAD and BODY section. The HEAD section contains all of the style sheets and JavaScript files required by the page. The body section contains all of the markup required by the `Alert` control.

> **NOTE**
>
> All of the scripts and style sheets referred to in the head of a `Page` control HTML file are removed from the HTML file and added to the parent page. In other words, all of the scripts and styles are promoted up from the control to the containing page.

The alert.css file looks like this (not super exciting):

```css
.alert {
    background-color: red
}
```

The CSS file changes the background color of the Alert button to the color red.

Finally, the alert.js file looks like this:

```javascript
(function () {
    "use strict";

    var Alert = WinJS.UI.Pages.define("myControls/alert.html", {

        ready: function (element, options) {
            var btn = WinJS.Utilities.query("button", element);

            // Set option defaults
            options.buttonLabel = options.buttonLabel || "Show Alert";
            options.message = options.message || "Alert!!!";

            // Update button label text
            btn[0].innerText = options.buttonLabel;

            // Setup click handler
            btn.listen("click", function () {
                var md = new Windows.UI.Popups.MessageDialog(
                    options.message
                );
                md.showAsync();
            });
        }
    });

    WinJS.Namespace.define("MyControls", {
        Alert: Alert
    });
})();
```

The alert.js JavaScript file creates the `Alert` control. The `Alert` control is created by calling the `WinJS.Pages.define()` method with the path to the alert.html file.

When you create a `Page` control, you can create an event handler for the `Page` control ready event. This event is raised after the control has been rendered so you can access any elements in the alert.html file. The ready event has an options parameter that allows the consuming script to pass options just like a standard control using the `data-win-options` attributes.

In the preceding code, the `ready` handler configures a `click` handler for the button. When you click the button, a `Windows.UI.Popups.MessageDialog` is displayed.

There is one other important section in the alert.js file. The following code exposes the `Alert` control in the global namespace so that the control can be used declaratively in other HTML pages:

```
WinJS.Namespace.define("MyControls", {
    Alert: Alert
});
```

Now that I have created the `Alert` control, I can use it in a page. The following page displays a button with the label `Click Here!` When you click the button, the alert `You Clicked the Button!` is displayed:

```
<!DOCTYPE html>
<html>
<head>
    <meta charset="utf-8" />
    <title>Fragments</title>

    <!-- WinJS references -->
    <link href="//Microsoft.WinJS.2.0/css/ui-dark.css" rel="stylesheet" />
    <script src="//Microsoft.WinJS.2.0/js/base.js"></script>
    <script src="//Microsoft.WinJS.2.0/js/ui.js"></script>

    <script type="text/javascript" src="pageControl.js"></script>
    <script type="text/javascript" src="/pageControl/alert.js"></script>
</head>
<body>

    <div id="btnDelete"
        data-win-control="MyControls.Alert"
        data-win-options="{
            buttonLabel: 'Click Here!',
            message: 'You clicked the button!'
        }"></div>

</body>
</html>
```

Notice that the page includes a refererence to the alert.js JavaScript file. You must include a reference to your custom `Page` control in any page that uses the control declaratively.

The `Alert Page` control is created declaratively in the body of the page just like any other standard WinJS control such as the `ListView` or `DatePicker` control.

> **WARNING**
>
> Remember to call `WinJS.UI.processAll()` or your `Page` controls, just like any other WinJS control, won't get processed and turned into a control.

Creating Multi-Page Apps

You can create a Windows Store app that contains multiple HTML pages and create links between the pages. However, Microsoft strongly discourages you from doing this. Instead, you are encouraged to create a single page app and dynamically load different `Page` controls that represent individual pages.

Why does Microsoft make this recommendation? When you are building a Windows Store app, you are not building a website (even though you are using many of the same technologies). Instead, you are building a Windows application.

Users have different expectations when using a Windows application than a web application. In a web application, it is normal to click a link and wait (and wait, and wait) for another page to load. While you are waiting, the application freezes. When the new page loads, you start over in a completely new context—the context of the new page.

In a Windows application, this experience would be unacceptable. Microsoft Word, for example, never freezes when you click a button (well, hardly ever). You don't navigate between pages in a Windows application. Instead, you navigate content by opening dialogs and switching between tabs.

To create this same type of Windows application experience in a Windows Store app, you are encouraged to create a single-page app.

Creating a Navigation App

The easiest way to create a single-page app that contains multiple pages is to take advantage of the Visual Studio Navigation App project template (see Figure 12.3). There are several differences between this template and the Blank App template.

FIGURE 12.3   Creating a navigation app

First, the Navigation App template contains a pages folder. The pages folder contains all of the `Page` controls that represent the pages in your application. Each `Page` control is contained in a separate subfolder of the pages folder.

The Navigation App template includes a pages/home folder that contains a `Page` control that represents the home page. This `Page` control is loaded by default when you start a Navigation App template.

The Navigation App template, like the Blank App template, does include a default.html file. However, this file mainly acts as a shell for loading up different `Page` controls from the pages folder. When you navigate from page to page, the content in the body of the default.html file is loaded with new content.

Finally, the Navigation App template includes a WinJS control that is not included in the Blank App template named the `PageControlNavigator` control. This control is located in a file named js/navigator.js. The `PageControlNavigator` control handles all of the details of loading the `Page` controls into the default.html page.

Let me dig into how all of this works a little deeper.

Understanding the Navigation App `default.html` Page

As I mentioned previously, the default.html page in a navigation app is mainly a shell for the content contained in the `Page` controls. The entire contents of the default.html page is contained in Listing 12.1.

LISTING 12.1   The default.html Page

```
<!DOCTYPE html>
<html>
<head>
    <meta charset="utf-8" />
    <title>MultiPage</title>

    <!-- WinJS references -->
    <link href="//Microsoft.WinJS.2.0/css/ui-dark.css" rel="stylesheet" />
    <script src="//Microsoft.WinJS.2.0/js/base.js"></script>
    <script src="//Microsoft.WinJS.2.0/js/ui.js"></script>

    <!-- MultiPage references -->
    <link href="/css/default.css" rel="stylesheet" />
    <script src="/js/default.js"></script>
    <script src="/js/navigator.js"></script>
</head>
<body>
    <div id="contenthost" data-win-control="Application.PageControlNavigator" data-
win-options="{home: '/pages/home/home.html'}"></div>
    <!-- <div id="appbar" data-win-control="WinJS.UI.AppBar">
        <button data-win-control="WinJS.UI.AppBarCommand" data-win-
options="{id:'cmd', label:'Command', icon:'placeholder'}"></button>
    </div> -->
</body>
</html>
```

The body of the page in Listing 12.1 contains two controls. The first control is the PageControlNavigator control. This control has the ID contenthost and it acts as the host for the content loaded up from the Page controls. I'll discuss the PageControlNavigator control in more depth shortly.

The second control (which is commented out) is an AppBar control. Any content that you place in the default.html page will be displayed for every page in the application. Because an AppBar should be the same across all of the pages in a Windows Store app, the default. html page is a good place to declare it.

> **NOTE**
>
> I discussed the AppBar control in Chapter 6, "Menus and Flyouts."

Any other content that you add to the default.html page will also be displayed for all pages in a navigation app. For example, if you want to create a standard header, footer, or sidebar then it makes sense to add this standard content to the default.html page.

Adding New Page Controls to a Navigation App

A single page app that contained only a single `Page` control—the home page—would not be worth the effort. So let me show you how to add a second page.

The easiest way to add a new `Page` control to your project is to take advantage of the Visual Studio Page Control item template. Create a new subfolder named anotherPage located at pages\anotherPage. Select the menu item Project, Add New Item, and select the Page Control template (see Figure 12.4). Name your new `Page` control with the name **anotherPage.html**.

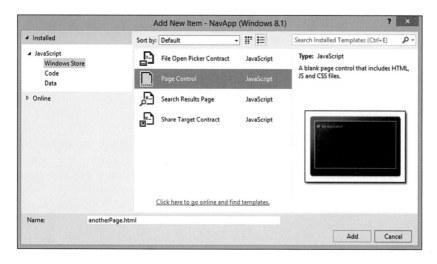

FIGURE 12.4   Creating a new `Page` control with Visual Studio

When you add a `Page` control named anotherPage.html to a project, you get the following three files:

▶ anotherPage.html

▶ anotherPage.js

▶ anotherPage.cs

Of course, you could create these exact same three files by hand, but using the Visual Studio item template saves you a little time.

The entire contents of anotherPage.html is contained in Listing 12.2. Notice that the body of the page contains an HTML5 HEADER tag (not to be confused with the HEAD tag). The HEADER tag contains a WinJS `BackButton` control and the page title (see Figure 12.5).

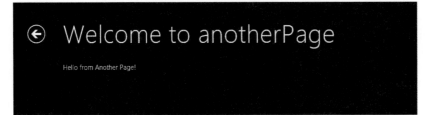

FIGURE 12.5   The header of a `Page` control

LISTING 12.2   The Contents of anotherPage.html

```html
<!DOCTYPE html>
<html>
<head>
    <meta charset="utf-8" />
    <title>anotherPage</title>

    <!-- WinJS references -->
    <link href="//Microsoft.WinJS.2.0/css/ui-dark.css" rel="stylesheet" />
    <script src="//Microsoft.WinJS.2.0/js/base.js"></script>
    <script src="//Microsoft.WinJS.2.0/js/ui.js"></script>

    <link href="anotherPage.css" rel="stylesheet" />
    <script src="anotherPage.js"></script>
</head>
<body>
    <div class="anotherPage fragment">
        <header aria-label="Header content" role="banner">
            <button data-win-control="WinJS.UI.BackButton"></button>
            <h1 class="titlearea win-type-ellipsis">
                <span class="pagetitle">Welcome to anotherPage</span>
            </h1>
        </header>
        <section aria-label="Main content" role="main">
            <p>Content goes here.</p>
        </section>
    </div>
</body>
</html>
```

So that we can tell when we have navigated to anotherPage.html, I am going to modify the body of the page by replacing the text `Content goes here` with the text `Hello from Another Page!`.

The contents of the anotherPage.js JavaScript are contained in Listing 12.3.

LISTING 12.3   The Contents of anotherPage.js

```
(function () {
    "use strict";

    WinJS.UI.Pages.define("/pages/anotherPage/anotherPage.html", {
        // This function is called whenever a user navigates to this page. It
        // populates the page elements with the app's data.
        ready: function (element, options) {
            // TODO: Initialize the page here.
        },

        unload: function () {
            // TODO: Respond to navigations away from this page.
        },

        updateLayout: function (element) {
            /// <param name="element" domElement="true" />

            // TODO: Respond to changes in layout.
        }
    });
})();
```

Notice that the JavaScript file in Listing 12.3 contains the code to define a new `Page` control. The `Page` control has three event handlers: `ready`, `updateLayout`, and `unload`. I modify the `ready` event handler to support page navigation in the next section.

Navigating to Another Page

I now have a page named home and a page named anotherPage in my app, how do I navigate between these two pages? You navigate between pages by using the `WinJS.Navigate.navigate()` method.

Let me modify the home page so we can navigate from the home page to anotherPage. Add a hyperlink to the main section of the home page that looks like this:

```
<section aria-label="Main content" role="main">
    <p>Content goes here.</p>
    <a id="lnkAnotherPage">Visit Another Page</a>
</section>
```

This hyperlink has an ID attribute but no HREF attribute.

> **NOTE**
>
> You can find the code discussed in this section in the Chapter12\Multipage folder in the GitHub source.

Next, I'll modify the code in the home.js file so it sets up a `click` handler for the hyperlink in its `ready` handler:

```
WinJS.UI.Pages.define("/pages/home/home.html", {
    ready: function (element, options) {
        var lnkAnotherPage = document.getElementById("lnkAnotherPage");
        lnkAnotherPage.addEventListener("click", function (evt) {
            evt.preventDefault();
            WinJS.Navigation.navigate("/pages/anotherPage/anotherPage.html");
        });
    }
});
```

The `click` event handler first calls `preventDefault()` to prevent normal link navigation from happening. Remember that we are fake navigating here.

Next, the `WinJS.Navigation.navigate()` method is called to navigate to the anotherPage. html page.

When you click the link in the home page then you navigate to the anotherPage page (see Figure 12.6). What's even cooler, on the anotherPage page, the back button works. If you click the back button, you return to the home page.

FIGURE 12.6   Navigating between pages

Understanding the Navigation API

The `WinJS.Navigatation.navigate()` method is just one method of the WinJS Navigation API. You can use all of the following methods to control user navigation:

▶ `back()`—Enables you to navigate back in history. If you supply an integer parameter then you can go back in history a certain number of entries.

▶ `forward()`—Enables you to navigate forward in history. If you supply an integer parameter then you can go forward in history a certain number of entries.

▶ `navigate()`—Enables you to navigate to a particular page (`Page` control). You can also supply a custom object which represents the initial state of the page.

And, you can use the following properties with navigation:

▶ `canGoBack`—Returns true when you can navigate back.

▶ `canGoForward`—Returns true when you can navigate forward.

▶ `history`—Returns an object that represents all of the history entries. The history object has a `current`, `backStack`, and `forwardState` property.

▶ `location`—Return the URL associated with the current page.

▶ `state`—Returns the state associated with the current page.

Finally, the Navigation API supports the following three navigation events:

▶ `beforenavigate`

▶ `navigating`

▶ `navigated`

For each of these three events, you can use the event `detail` property to read the `location` and `state` properties.

Understanding the `PageControlNavigator` Control

The `PageControlNavigator` control is included with the Navigation App, Grid App, Split App, and Hub App Visual Studio project templates—but it is not included with the Blank App template.

The `PageControlNavigator` control handles the navigated event and takes care of loading the right `Page` control in response to this event. For example, if you call `WinJS.Navigation.navigate("/pages/somePage/somePage.html")` then the `PageControlNavigator` control loads the somePage.html `Page` control into the default. html page.

Understanding Navigation State

When building a multi-page app with the Navigation API, you can take advantage of Navigation state to preserve state as you navigate back and forth between pages. Each entry in history has a `state` property associated with it. You can assign whatever value that you want to this `state` property.

Imagine, for example, that you are building a simple product catalog. The app consists of only two pages: a home page, which displays a list of categories, and a details page, which displays a list of matching products (see Figures 12.7 and 12.8). When you click a category on the home page then you see a list of matching products on the details page.

FIGURE 12.7   The store app home page

FIGURE 12.8   The store app details page

After you select a category on the home page, and you navigate to the details page and back again, then you want the same category to be selected. That way, the customer knows which category was just selected. The customer does not lose his place in the list of categories (see Figure 12.9).

FIGURE 12.9   Preserving state in the store app

NOTE

You can find the code discussed in this section in the Chapter12\NavigationState folder in the GitHub source.

Let me build this app, starting with the home page. The home page contains a `ListView` that displays a list of product categories:

```
<div id="tmplCategory"
    data-win-control="WinJS.Binding.Template">
    <div class="categoryItem">
        <span data-win-bind="textContent:categoryName"></span>
    </div>
</div>

<div id="lvCategories"
    data-win-control="WinJS.UI.ListView"
    data-win-options="{
        itemTemplate: select('#tmplCategory'),
        selectionMode: 'single',
        tapBehavior: 'directSelect',
        swipBehavior: 'select'
    }"></div>
```

The `ListView` is initialized in the home `Page` control's `ready` event handler:

```
(function () {
    "use strict";
```

```
WinJS.UI.Pages.define("/pages/home/home.html", {
    ready: function (element, options) {
        var lvCategories = document.getElementById("lvCategories").winControl;

        // Bind the categories to the ListView
        var dsCategories = new WinJS.Binding.List(MyApp.categoriesAndProducts);
        lvCategories.itemDataSource = dsCategories.dataSource;

        // Retrieve selected category index from state
        WinJS.Navigation.state = WinJS.Navigation.state || {};
        var selectedCategoryIndex = WinJS.Navigation.
➥state.selectedCategoryIndex;
        if (selectedCategoryIndex > -1) {
            lvCategories.selection.set(selectedCategoryIndex);
        }

        // Navigate when item invoked
        lvCategories.addEventListener("iteminvoked", function (e) {
            // Store index of invoked category in history
            WinJS.Navigation.state = { selectedCategoryIndex: e.detail.itemIndex
};

            // Navigate with invoked category name
            e.detail.itemPromise.done(function (item) {
                WinJS.Navigation.navigate(
                    "/pages/details/details.html",
                    { selectedCategoryName: item.data.categoryName }
                );

            });
        });
    }
});
})();
```

Actually, there are several things happening in the code. The first couple of lines in the ready event handler are used to bind the ListView control to the categoriesAndProducts data.

NOTE

Notice that you do not need to call WinJS.UI.processAll() to initialize the ListView control when working with Page controls. The Page control handles calling this method for you.

Next, if a selected category index has been stored in Navigation state, then the selected category index is retrieved and assigned to the `ListView` control.

The next section of code contains a listener for the `ListView` `iteminvoked` event. When a new category is selected in the `ListView`, the index of the selected category is stored in navigation state.

The `iteminvoked` handler also handles navigating to the details page. When the `WinJS.Navigation.navigate()` method is called, the selected category name is passed to the details page.

Let me switch to the details page. The details page also contains a `ListView` that is used to display the list of products that match the selected category. The details `ready` event handler takes care of binding the products to the `ListView`:

```
WinJS.UI.Pages.define("/pages/details/details.html", {
    ready: function (element, options) {
        var lvProducts = document.getElementById("lvProducts").winControl;

        // Get selected category
        var selectedCategoryName = options.selectedCategoryName;

        // Filter products by category
        var selectedCategory = MyApp.categoriesAndProducts.filter(function
➡(category) {
            return category.categoryName == selectedCategoryName;
        });

        // Bind products to ListView
        var dsProducts = new WinJS.Binding.List(selectedCategory[0].products);
        lvProducts.itemDataSource = dsProducts.dataSource;
    }

});
```

The selected category name is retrieved from the options passed to the `ready` event handler. The matching category and products are retrieved and assigned to the `ListView` control's `itemDataSource` property.

Summary

This chapter focused on two topics: how to reuse the same fragment of HTML across multiple pages and how to build apps with multiple pages. In the first part of this chapter, I discussed the `HtmlControl`, which enables you to include one HTML page in another HTML page.

Next, I discussed how you can create `Page` controls. `Page` controls provide you with an easy way of creating new WinJS controls out of an HTML page, JavaScript file, and style sheet.

Finally, I explained how you can create a single-page app that contains multiple pages. You learned how to use the `PageControlNavigator` control—in conjunction with the Navigation API—to load `Page` controls dynamically and simulate the experience of navigating to separate pages.

CHAPTER 13

Creating Share and Search Contracts

The focus of this chapter is the two topics of share and search. Enabling sharing for your app enables your app to participate in the ecosystem of other apps living on your machine. For example, you can share a winning score in a game app, or pictures from a camera app, or appointments from a calendar.

Adding support for search enables users of your app to quickly find content in your app. For example, users might search for an appointment in a Calendar app, a picture in a Photo Gallery app, or an article in a News app.

In this chapter, I discuss two ways to implement search: you learn how to implement search both using the Search charm and using the new `SearchBox` control. I also explain how you can index content using the new Windows 8.1 Content Indexer.

Throughout this chapter, I demonstrate how to implement share and search in the context of a single sample app. I demonstrate how you can build a note gathering app, named My Notes, which enables you to share and search notes (see Figure 13.1).

> **NOTE**
>
> You can find the full source code for this chapter in the Chapter 13 folder in the repository that accompanies this book on GitHub.

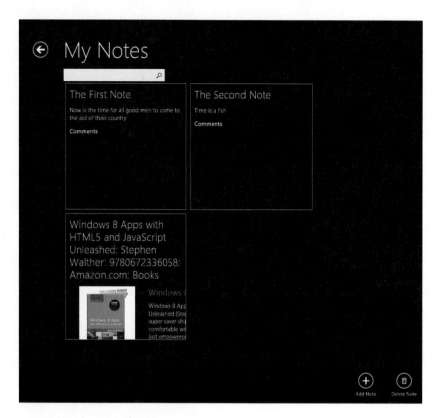

FIGURE 13.1   The My Notes app

Supporting Sharing

When you build a Windows Store app, you can decide whether you want your app to act as a share source, a share target, or both. Let me explain the difference between being a share source and a share target.

When your app acts as a share source, you can share information from your app with other Windows apps. Every app acts as a share source automatically. You share from an app by opening the Windows Charm bar and clicking the Share charm.

NOTE

At a minimum, every Windows Store app enables you to share a screenshot of the app.

If you click the Share charm in the Internet Explorer app, for example, then you can share a web page with other apps installed on your machine such as the Mail app, the Reader app, and the Twitter app (see Figure 13.2). If you share a web page with the Mail app then a link with a summary of the web page is opened in a new mail message.

> **NOTE**
>
> You can open the Windows Charm bar by swiping from the right edge of the screen or mousing to either of the right corners or pressing the keyboard combination Win+C.

FIGURE 13.2   Using Internet Explorer and a share source

If you want your app to act as a share source then you can decide on the information that you want to share. For example, in the case of a game app, you might want players of your game to be able to share a winning score on Twitter or Facebook. Or, if you are building a Calendar app, you might want to be able to share appointments by email.

Your app can act not only as a share source, your app can also act a share target. When your app acts as a share target then it appears in the list of apps in the Share charm as a target for sharing information.

You can register your app as a share target for different types of content. In that case, your app appears in the Share charm only when a particular type of content is being shared.

For example, if you are building a photo gallery app, then it would make sense to make your app a share target for pictures. Or, if you are building an app for taking notes then you would want to make your app a share target for all sorts of content such as HTML and plain text. Again, it is up to you to decide what types of content you want to accept for your app.

Let me show you how all of this works in the context of the My Notes app.

Creating a Share Source

The My Notes app acts a share source by enabling you to share notes with other apps. For example, you might want to share notes by email or (don't ask me why) Facebook or Twitter.

Here's how it works. You select a note from the list of notes, click the Share charm, and select the app that you want to share the note with (Figure 13.3). If you select the Mail app then a new email message is created with the note (Figure 13.4).

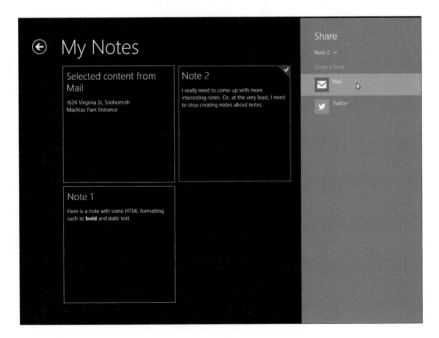

FIGURE 13.3   Sharing a note with the My Notes app

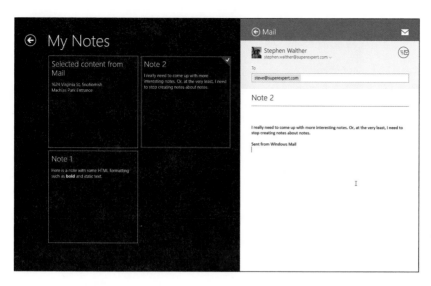

FIGURE 13.4   Sharing a note with the Mail app

To get this to work, you need to handle the `DataTransferManager datarequested` event with an event handler that looks like this:

```
var share = Windows.ApplicationModel.DataTransfer.DataTransferManager.
➥getForCurrentView();
share.addEventListener("datarequested", function (e) {
});
```

The `datarequested` event is raised whenever you open the Share charm. You handle this event to select the information that you want to offer to share from your app.

For the My Notes app, I added the code in Listing 13.1 to the default.js JavaScript file.

LISTING 13.1   Acting as a Share Source (ShareSource\js\default.js)

```
var share = Windows.ApplicationModel.DataTransfer.DataTransferManager.
➥getForCurrentView();
share.addEventListener("datarequested", function (e) {
    var lvNotes = document.getElementById("lvNotes").winControl;

    if (lvNotes.selection.count() == 1) {
        lvNotes.selection.getItems().done(function (items) {
            var itemToShare = items[0].data;
            e.request.data.properties.title = itemToShare.title;
            e.request.data.properties.description = "Share a Note";
```

```
                // Share plain text version
                e.request.data.setText( convertToText(itemToShare.contents));

                // Share HTML version
                var htmlFormatHelper = Windows.ApplicationModel.DataTransfer.
➥HtmlFormatHelper;
                e.request.data.setHtmlFormat(htmlFormatHelper.
➥createHtmlFormat(itemToShare.contents));
            });
      } else {
          e.request.failWithDisplayText("Please select a note to share.");
      }

});
```

The `datarequested` handler in Listing 13.1 first checks whether any notes are selected in the `ListView` used to display the list of notes. If there are no notes selected then the `failWithDisplayText()` method is called with the message `"Please select a note to share."`. There is no sense in sharing when the user has not selected anything to share.

Next, the selected `ListView` item is retrieved and a `DataPackage` is created. A `DataPackage` represents all of the data that you want to share with other apps. This class supports the following properties and methods (this is not a complete list):

▶ `properties`—A property that represents a `DataPackagePropertySet`

▶ `setApplicationLink()`—A method that enables you to share a link to an app

▶ `setBitmap(value)`—A method that enables you to share an image

▶ `setData(formatId, value)`—A method that enables you to share custom data

▶ `setHtmlFormat(value)`—A method that enables you to share HTML

▶ `setRtf(value)`—A method that enables you to share Rich Text Format (RTF) content

▶ `setStorageItems([IIterable(IStorageItem)])`—A method that enables you to share one or more files or folders

▶ `setText()`—A method that enables you to share plain text

▶ `setWebLink()`—A method that enables you to share an HTTP or HTTPS link

The `DataPackage` properties property represents a `DataPackagePropertySet`. Here is a partial list of the properties that you can set:

▶ `applicationListingUri`—The URI of the app in the Windows Store

▶ `applicationName`—The name of the app which created the DataPackage

▶ `contentSourceApplicationLink`—The link to the content being shared in the app

- ▶ **contentSourceWebLink**—The link to the content being shared in the app (HTTP/ HTTPS version)

- ▶ **description**—The description of the content being shared

- ▶ **logoBackgroundColor**—The background color used with the square30x30Logo image

- ▶ **square30x30Logo**—The source app's logo image

- ▶ **thumbnail**—The thumbnail image associated with the content being shared

- ▶ **title**—The title of the DataPackage being shared

You also have the option of creating custom properties if you need to pass custom information with your DataPackage.

The basic idea is that you create a DataPackage by setting properties such as the title and description. In Listing 13.1, the title property is set to the title of the note and the description property is set to the string value "Share a Note".

Next, you call one of the set() methods such as setBitmap() or setHtmlFormat() to assign the data that you want to share with the DataPackage. In Listing 13.1, both the setText() and the setHtmlFormat() methods are called to share both a text and HTML representation of a note.

Notice that there is nothing wrong with sharing the same information using multiple data formats such as text or HTML. Different share targets support different data formats. Offering as many formats as possible opens up more possibilities for sharing.

The setText() method assigns a plain text version of a note to the DataPackage. The note is converted into plain text with the help of the following JavaScript utility method:

```
// Converts HTML string to plain text string
function convertToText(html) {
    var div = document.createElement("DIV");
    div.innerHTML = html;
    return div.innerText;
}
```

This method creates a temporary DIV element and reads the innerText property to get a plain text representation of an HTML fragment.

The setHtmlFormat() method also takes advantage of a utility method. It calls the WinRT createHtmlFormat() method to convert the HTML being shared into an appropriate format for sharing.

NOTE

You can find all of the code discussed in this section in the Chapter13\ShareSource project in the GitHub source.

Creating a Share Target

The other half of sharing is being a share target. A share target appears in the list of apps when you open the Share charm. For example, if you are creating a photo gallery app then you might want to make the app a share target for pictures.

The My Notes app acts as a share target for text or HTML content. For example, if you are in the standard Windows Mail app, you can click the Share charm to create a new note that contains the email message. Or, if you are viewing a web page in Internet Explorer then you can click the Share charm to create a note that contains a summary of the web page (see Figure 13.5 and Figure 13.6).

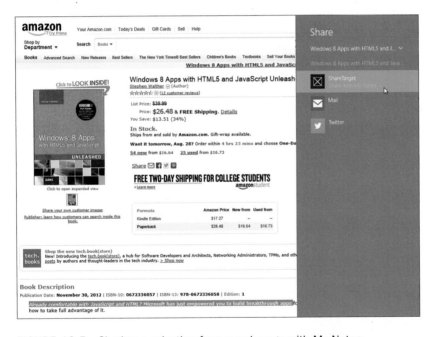

FIGURE 13.5   Sharing a selection from a web page with My Notes

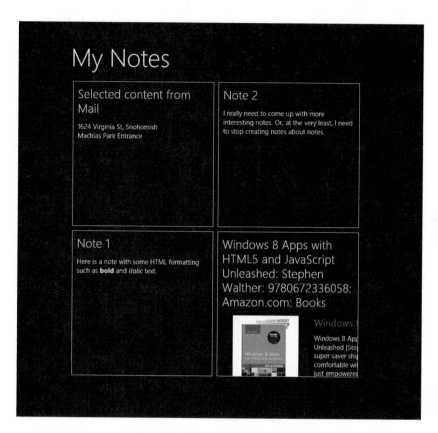

FIGURE 13.6   A note with HTML

Making your app into a share target consists of two steps: You need to declare your app as a share target, and you need to create a share page. Let me demonstrate both steps with the My Notes app.

Declaring Your App as a Share Target
You declare your app as a share target in your app manifest file (package.appxmanifest). Open your app manifest and select the Declarations tab (see Figure 13.7).

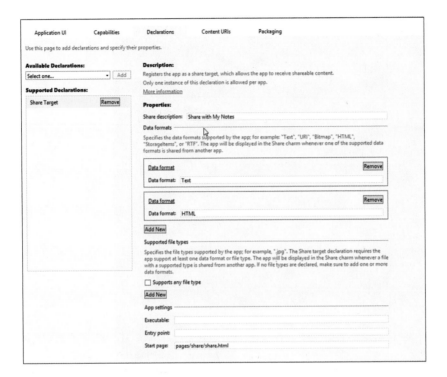

FIGURE 13.7   Declaring an app as a share target

Under Available Declarations, select Share Target. When you declare your app as a share target, you must indicate the type of content that can be shared with your app. You can provide one or more supported data formats or you can provide one or more supported file types.

In the case of the My Notes app, the app supports two data formats: You can pass either Text or HTML to the app. In Figure 13.7, notice that Text and HTML are listed under Data formats.

The last thing that you should set is the Start page. Enter the Start page path pages/share/share.html under App settings. This is the page that will be opened in your app when it is selected by the user as the target for sharing. In the next section, I'm going to show you how to build this start page.

Creating a Share Page

Typically, when you share content with an app, you open a page other than the app's usual home page. In other words, when you make an app a share target, you typically provide the app with a dedicated share page that opens when a user shares content with your app.

The My Notes app has a dedicated share page (see Figure 13.8). The page includes a form for adding comments to a note. This page also contains the logic necessary for creating a new note for the content being shared.

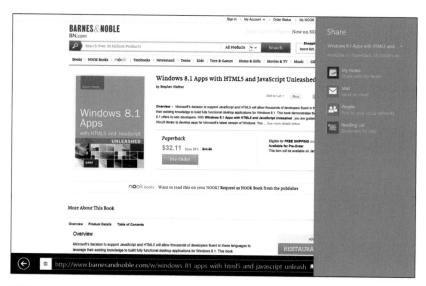

FIGURE 13.8   The My Notes Share page

NOTE

Because we created our My Notes app using the Navigation App project template (see Chapter 12, "Page Fragments and Navigation"), our pages are inside a /pages folder.

The easiest way to create the share page is to take advantage of the Share Target Contract item template included with Visual Studio. Create a new folder in your pages folder named *share* and select the menu option Project, Add New Item, and pick the Share Target Contract item template (see Figure 13.9).

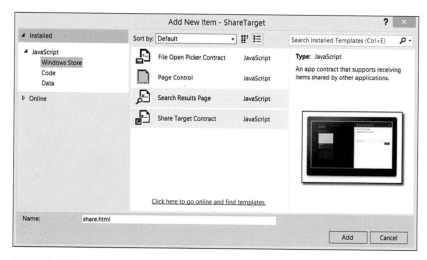

FIGURE 13.9   Adding a share page

After you add the Share Target Contract item, you get an HTML page, a JavaScript file, and a CSS file. You can customize these files to change the appearance of the share landing page.

The file in Listing 13.2 contains the default content of the Share Contract Target JavaScript file.

LISTING 13.2   The Share Target Contract JavaScript File

```javascript
(function () {
    "use strict";

    var app = WinJS.Application;
    var share;

    function onShareSubmit() {
        document.querySelector(".progressindicators").style.visibility = "visible";
        document.querySelector(".commentbox").disabled = true;
        document.querySelector(".submitbutton").disabled = true;

        // TODO: Do something with the shared data stored in the 'share' var.

        share.reportCompleted();
    }

    // This function responds to all application activations.
    app.onactivated = function (args) {
        var thumbnail;

        if (args.detail.kind === Windows.ApplicationModel.Activation.ActivationKind.
➥shareTarget) {
            document.querySelector(".submitbutton").onclick = onShareSubmit;
            share = args.detail.shareOperation;

            document.querySelector(".shared-title").textContent = share.data.
➥properties.title;
            document.querySelector(".shared-description").textContent = share.data.
➥properties.description;

            thumbnail = share.data.properties.thumbnail;
            if (thumbnail) {
                // If the share data includes a thumbnail, display it.
                args.setPromise(thumbnail.openReadAsync().done(function
➥displayThumbnail(stream) {
                    document.querySelector(".shared-thumbnail").src = window.URL.
➥createObjectURL(stream);
                }));
```

```
            } else {
                // If no thumbnail is present, expand the description  and
                // title elements to fill the unused space.
                document.querySelector("section[role=main] header").style.
➥setProperty("-ms-grid-columns", "0px 0px 1fr");
                document.querySelector(".shared-thumbnail").style.visibility =
➥"hidden";
            }
        }
    };

    app.start();
})();
```

Notice that the code in Listing 13.2 includes an event handler for the WinJS application
activated event. The activated event is raised whenever a Windows Store app is first
activated. In this case, the handler checks whether the app has been activated in response
to a sharing operation (ActivationKind.shareTarget).

The code in Listing 13.2 sets up a submit handler for the HTML form displayed by the
Share Target Contract HTML file. When you submit the form, the onShareSubmit()
method is invoked.

You need to place your custom logic for doing something with the item being shared in
the OnShareSubmit() method. In the case of the My Notes app, I want to create a new
note from the text or HTML content being shared.

Listing 13.3 contains an updated version of the onShareSubmit() method.

LISTING 13.3   Updated onShareSubmit Method (pages\share\share.js)

```
function onShareSubmit() {
    document.querySelector(".progressindicators").style.visibility = "visible";
    document.querySelector(".commentbox").disabled = true;
    document.querySelector(".submitbutton").disabled = true;


    // TODO: Do something with the shared data stored in the 'share' var.
    var StandardDataFormats = Windows.ApplicationModel.DataTransfer.
➥StandardDataFormats;

    // Process HTML
    if (share.data.contains(StandardDataFormats.html)) {
        share.data.getHtmlFormatAsync().done(function (html) {
            // Retrieve sanitized HTML fragment
            var htmlFormatHelper = Windows.ApplicationModel.DataTransfer.
➥HtmlFormatHelper;
            var htmlFragment = htmlFormatHelper.getStaticFragment(html);
```

```
            // Save shared note to data source
            saveNote(share.data.properties.title, htmlFragment);
        });
    } else {
        // Process Text
        if (share.data.contains(StandardDataFormats.text)) {
            share.data.getTextAsync().done(function (text) {
                saveNote(share.data.properties.title, text);
            });
        }
    }
}


// Save note to database
function saveNote(title, contents) {
    // Save shared note to data source
    var notesDataSource = new DataSources.FileDataSource("notes.json");
    notesDataSource.insertAtEnd(null, {
        title: title,
        contents: contents,
        comments: document.querySelector(".commentbox").value
    }).done(function () {
        // Let everyone know that the notes have been updated
        Windows.Storage.ApplicationData.current.signalDataChanged();

        // All done
        share.reportCompleted();
    });
}
```

NOTE

You can find all of the code discussed in this section in the Chapter13\ShareTarget project in the GitHub repository that accompanies this book.

The code in Listing 13.3 first checks whether there is an HTML version of the content being shared. If there is an HTML version then a new note is created with the HTML version and the note is saved to the file data source. Otherwise, if there is not an HTML version of the content, a text version of the note is created instead.

The shared content is retrieved by calling methods of the DataPackageView class. This class has the following properties and methods (this is not a complete list):

▶ **availableFormats**—This property represents a list of all of the data formats being shared with the DataPackage.

▶ **properties**—This property represents a `DataPackagePropertySetView` that is a read-only representation of all of the properties associated with the `DataPackage` (like title and description).

▶ **contains(formatId)**—This method returns true if the `DataPackage` includes the data format.

▶ **getApplicationLinkAsync()**—This method returns a promise that contains the application link shared in the `DataPackage`.

▶ **getBitmapAsync()**—This method returns a promise that contains the bitmap shared in the `DataPackage`.

▶ **getDataAsync(formatId)**—This method returns a promise that contains the custom data shared in the `DataPackage`.

▶ **getHtmlFormatAsync()**—This method returns a promise that contains the HTML shared in the `DataPackage`.

▶ **getRtfAsync()**—This method returns a promise that contains the Rich Text Format content shared in the `DataPackage`.

▶ **getStorageItemsAsync()**—This method returns a promise that contains the collection of files or folders shared in the `DataPackage`.

▶ **getTextAsync()**—This method returns a promise that contains the text shared in the `DataPackage`.

▶ **getWebLinkAsync()**—This method returns a promise that contains the web link shared in the `DataPackage`.

So you share a `DataPackage` and receive a `DataPackageView`. The `DataPackage` class has all of the properties and methods for including data and the `DataPackageView` class has all of the properties and methods for retrieving the data. The code in Listing 13.3 uses the methods of the `DataPackageView` class to retrieve the HTML or text content and call the `saveNote()` method.

When the `saveNote()` method finishes saving the new note, the method raises two signals. First, it calls the `signalDataChanged()` method to signal to any open My Notes apps that the underlying notes data has changed. Calling `signalDataChanged()` raises the `datachanged` event. The My Notes app listens to the `datachanged` event in the home.js file so it can reload the notes displayed by its `ListView` when a new note is added:

```
// Listen for changes to notes
Windows.Storage.ApplicationData.current.addEventListener("datachanged", function ()
{
    lvNotes.itemDataSource.reload();
});
```

The `SaveNote()` method raises a second signal when the `reportCompleted()` method is called. The `reportCompleted()` method signals that the share operation is complete. If you neglect to call this method then the share page opened by clicking the Share charm never closes, and the progress indicator continues to spin forever.

Using the Search Charm

There are two ways to implement search for a Windows Store app: You can implement search using the Search charm or you can implement search with the new WinJS 2.0 `SearchBox` control. In this section, you learn how to implement search with the Search charm.

Users expect to be able to perform a search by using the Search charm. The Search charm is one of the standard charms that appear when you open the Charms bar (see Figure 13.10).

FIGURE 13.10   The Search charm in the Windows Charm bar

> **NOTE**
>
> You can open the Windows Charm bar by swiping from the right edge of the screen or mousing to either of the right corners or pressing the keyboard combination Win+C.

When you perform a search using the Search charm, you pick the area in which you want to search. For example, you can search Everywhere, Settings, Files, Web Images, or Web Videos. If the current app is registered as a search provider then you can also search the current app.

Figure 13.11 illustrates the search areas displayed when you open the Search charm in Internet Explorer. Notice that you can pick the Internet Explorer app as one of the search areas. If you pick Internet Explorer and your search area then you get search results from Internet Explorer.

FIGURE 13.11   Using the Search charm in Internet Explorer

In this section, I explain how you can set up your Windows Store app as a search provider and wire up your app to work with the Search charm.

> **NOTE**
>
> Search in Windows 8.1 is very different than search in Windows 8. The user interface has changed significantly. By default, search in Windows 8.1 is powered by Bing.

Declaring Your App as a Search Provider

Before you do anything else, you need to declare your app as a search provider. You declare your app as a search provider in your app manifest file. Open the package.appxmanifest file in Visual Studio and select the Declarations tab (see Figure 13.12).

Application UI	Capabilities	Declarations	Content URIs	Packaging

Use this page to add declarations and specify their properties.

Available Declarations:

Select one...   ▼   Add

Supported Declarations:

Search   Remove

Share Target

Description:

Registers the app as a search provider. The app's indexed content can appear as search results in the global search experience launched via the Search charm.

Only one instance of this declaration is allowed per app.

More information

Properties:

App settings

Executable:

Entry point:

Start page:

FIGURE 13.12   Declaring your app as a search provider

Under Available Declarations, pick Search. You can leave the properties with their default empty values. You don't need to set anything else.

Providing Search Suggestions

Now that you have registered your app as a search provider, you can provide search suggestions as a user types in the Search pane. In the case of the My Notes app, I want to display matching notes as the user types (see Figure 13.13).

To open the Search pane and view the search suggestions, you need to run the app, select My Notes from the drop-down list, and start typing. You should see suggestions that match the titles of the notes.

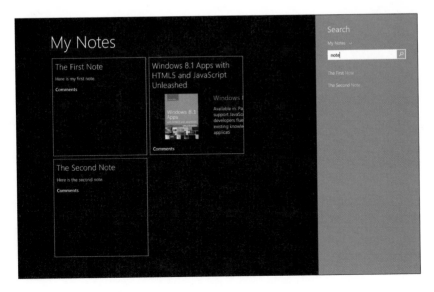

FIGURE 13.13   Providing search suggestions

You provide search suggestions from your app by handling the `suggestionsrequested` event. Listing 13.4 contains the `suggestionsrequested` handler located in default.js used by the My Notes app.

LISTING 13.4   Providing Search Suggestions (js\default.js)

```
// Handle requests for search suggestions
Windows.ApplicationModel.Search.SearchPane.getForCurrentView().
➡onsuggestionsrequested = function (e) {
    var queryText = e.queryText;
    var searchSuggestions = e.request.searchSuggestionCollection;

    // Needed because we are async
    var deferral = e.request.getDeferral();

    // Get all of the notes
    notesDataSource.getAll().then(function (notes) {
        // Get matching results
        var MAX_RESULTS = 3;
        for (var i = 0; i < notes.length; i++) {
            var note = notes[i].data;
            if (note.title.toLowerCase().indexOf(queryText.toLowerCase()) >= 0) {
                searchSuggestions.appendQuerySuggestion(note.title);
            }
            if (searchSuggestions.size >= MAX_RESULTS) {
                break;
            }
        }

        // All done
        deferral.complete();
    });
};
```

The basic idea is that you get the text that the user has typed into the search box by using `e.queryText`. You populate a set of suggestions to display to the user while the user is typing by adding items to `e.request.searchSuggestionCollection` collection.

In Listing 13.4, all of the notes are retrieved from the file system by calling the `getAll()` method. Next, the notes are filtered to match the query text by checking whether the note title matches the query text:

```
if (note.title.toLowerCase().indexOf(queryText.toLowerCase()) >= 0) {
}
```

A maximum of five matching notes are added to the search suggestions. This is the maximum number of suggestions that the Search pane will display.

Retrieving the list of notes from the file system is an asynchronous operation. For that reason, a deferral object is retrieved before the asynchronous operations start with this line of code:

```
var deferral = e.request.getDeferral();
```

When the asynchronous operation completes, you call the `complete()` method like this:

```
deferral.complete();
```

> **NOTE**
>
> You can find all of the code discussed in this section in the Chapter13\Search project in the GitHub repository that accompanies this book.

Handling Search Activation

After a user enters query text in the Search pane and submits their query then you need to display search results from your app. You can detect when your app is activated in response to a search by listening for the activated event and checking whether the `ActivationKind` property has the value search.

The My Notes app uses the code in Listing 13.5 to detect search activation. This code is contained in the default.js file.

LISTING 13.5   Handling Search Activation (js\default.js)

```
app.addEventListener("activated", function (args) {

    // Navigate to search results on search
    if (args.detail.kind === Windows.ApplicationModel.Activation.ActivationKind.
➡search) {
        return WinJS.Navigation.navigate(
            "/pages/searchResults/searchResults.html",
            { searchDetails: args.detail }
        );
    }
}
```

If the My Notes app is activated by a search query then the user is navigated to a page located at /pages/searchResults.searchResults.html. I discuss the searchResults.html page in the next section.

NOTE

This is a matter of preference. As an alternative to listening to the activated event to detect when a query has been submitted, you can handle the `querysubmitted` event like this:

```
Windows.ApplicationModel.Search.SearchPane.getForCurrentView().onquerysubmitted
=function (eventObject) {
    // Respond to query and perform search
};
```

The `querysubmitted` event handler takes precedence over `activated`.

13

Adding a Search Results Page

The final step in getting the Search charm to work is to add a search results page. The purpose of this page is to display the matching results for the search query.

One way to add the search results page is to use the built-in Visual Studio template. Select Project, Add New Item, and choose Search Results Page (see Figure 13.14).

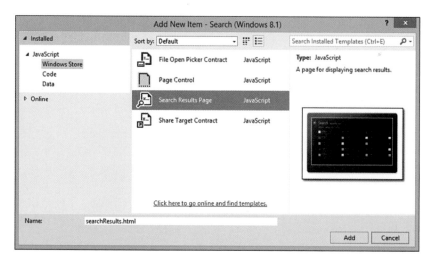

FIGURE 13.14   Adding a Search Results Page

I don't recommend taking this approach. The problem is that search results are very dependent on the data in your app. You need to customize both the appearance and the logic of the search page to match the data in your app.

For the My Notes app, I added a new subfolder named searchResults to the /pages folder. Next, I added a standard `Page` control named searchResults.html to this folder. I ended up with the HTML, JavaScript, and CSS file depicted in Figure 13.15.

FIGURE 13.15   Adding a Search Results Page with a `Page` control

The searchResults.js contains all of the logic for displaying the search results. The
searchResults.js JavaScript file is included in Listing 13.6.

LISTING 13.6   The Search Results JavaScript File (\pages\searchResults\searchResults.js)

```javascript
(function () {
    "use strict";

    WinJS.UI.Pages.define("/pages/searchResults/searchResults.html", {
        _lastSearch: "",

        // This function is called whenever a user navigates to this page. It
        // populates the page elements with the app's data.
        ready: function (element, options) {

            // highlight matched title text
            WinJS.Namespace.define("searchResults", {
                markText: WinJS.Binding.converter(this._markText.bind(this))
            });

            // Get the ListView
            var lvSearchResults = document.getElementById("lvSearchResults")
.winControl;

            // Get the search query
            var queryText = options.searchDetails.queryText;
            this._lastSearch = queryText;

            // Get all of the notes
            MyApp.notesDataSource.getAll().then(function(notes) {
```

```
                // Filter the results
                var filteredResults = [];
                for (var i = 0; i < notes.length; i++) {
                    var note = notes[i].data;
                    if (note.title.toLowerCase().indexOf(queryText.toLowerCase()) >=
➥0) {

                        filteredResults.push(note);
                    }
                }

                if (filteredResults.length) {
                    // Show results
                    document.getElementById("divNoResults").style.display = "none";

                    // Convert to List Data Source
                    var listResults = new WinJS.Binding.List(filteredResults);

                    // Bind to ListView
                    lvSearchResults.itemDataSource = listResults.dataSource;
                } else {
                    // Report no results
                    document.getElementById("divNoResults").style.display = "block";
                    var emptyList = new WinJS.Binding.List();
                    lvSearchResults.itemDataSource = emptyList.dataSource;
                }
            });
        },

        // This function colors the search term.
        _markText: function (text) {
            var regex = new RegExp("(" + this._lastSearch + ")", "i");
            return text.replace(regex, "<mark>$1</mark>");
        }

    });
})();
```

When the searchResults.html page is opened, the `ready()` event handler is invoked. This options argument for this handler includes the search query text. The `ready()` handler retrieves all of the notes from the file system and filters the notes to match the search query text. Finally, the matching notes are displayed in a `ListView` control.

The searchResults.js file includes a binding converter named `markText` that highlights matching text in the search results. The `markText` binding converter uses a regular expression to wrap text that matches the search query text in a `<mark></mark>` element. A little bit of CSS is used to display the highlighted text (see Figure 13.16).

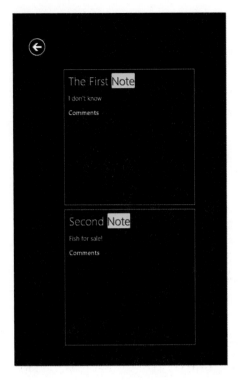

The First Note

I don't know

Comments

Second Note

Fish for sale!

Comments

FIGURE 13.16   Displaying search results with highlighted text

NOTE

We discussed binding converters all the way back in Chapter 3, "Observables, Bindings, and Templates."

Using the `SearchBox` Control

When building Windows 8 apps, you were encouraged to use the Search charm for implementing search in your app. There was a problem, however. Users had difficulty finding the Search charm. They had difficulty discovering that your app even supported search.

Windows 8.1 introduces an alternative. Instead of implementing search with the Search charm, you can implement search with the new WinJS `SearchBox` control. This control appears right on your page (right in your face). Therefore, it is much more discoverable than the Search charm.

In this section, you learn how to add a `SearchBox` control to the My Notes app.

> **NOTE**
>
> You can find all of the code discussed in this section in the Chapter13\SearchBox project in the GitHub repository that accompanies this book.

Adding the `SearchBox` Control to a Page

Adding a `SearchBox` control to a page is straightforward. You can declare a new `SearchBox` with the following markup:

```
<div id="search"
    data-win-control="WinJS.UI.SearchBox"
    data-win-options="{focusOnKeyboardInput:true}"></div>
```

I added a `SearchBox` control to the home.html page in the My Notes app (see Figure 13.17).

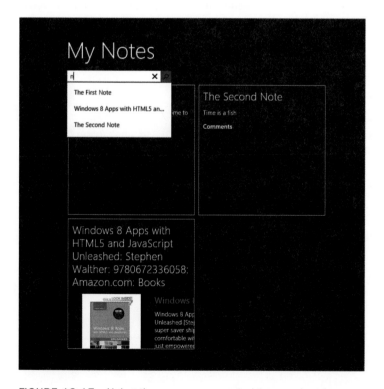

FIGURE 13.17   Using the `SearchBox` control to search notes

Notice that the `SearchBox` control includes a `focusOnKeyboardInput` property. When you assign the value true to this property then the `SearchBox` gets focus whenever you start typing anywhere on a page that contains the control.

I've enabled the `focusOnKeyboardInput` property in the My Notes app so that you can start searching from the home page simply by starting to type. There is no need for the user to find and click on the `SearchBox` before the user starts to perform a search query.

If you want to get extra fancy then you can hide the `SearchBox` until the user starts typing with the following code:

```
// Display SearchBox when a user starts typing
search.element.style.display = "none";
search.addEventListener("receivingfocusonkeyboardinput", function (e) {
    search.element.style.display = "block";
});
```

The `receivingfocusonkeyboardinput` event is raised right before the `SearchBox` gets focus when a user starts typing. The preceding code hides the `SearchBox` until this event is raised.

You should only handle the `receivingfocusonkeyboardinput` event when you have set the `focusOnKeyboardInput` property to the value true.

Providing Search Suggestions

You can provide search suggestions as the user types by handling the `SearchBox` control's `suggestionsrequested` event. The My Notes app uses the event handler in Listing 13.7.

LISTING 13.7   Handling the `suggestionsrequested` Event (\pages\home\home.js)

```
// Handle requests for search suggestions
var search = document.getElementById("search").winControl;
search.addEventListener("suggestionsrequested",  function (e) {
    var queryText = e.detail.queryText;
    var searchSuggestions = e.detail.searchSuggestionCollection;

    // Needed because we are async
    e.detail.setPromise(
        // Get all of the notes
        MyApp.notesDataSource.getAll().then(function (notes) {
            // Get matching results
            var MAX_RESULTS = 3;
            for (var i = 0; i < notes.length; i++) {
                var note = notes[i].data;
                if (note.title.toLowerCase().indexOf(queryText.toLowerCase()) >= 0){
                    searchSuggestions.appendQuerySuggestion(note.title);
                }
```

```
                  if (searchSuggestions.size >= MAX_RESULTS) {
                      break;
                  }
              }
          })
      );
});
```

In Listing 13.7, the search query text is retrieved from the `e.detail.queryText` property. The list of suggestions is added to the `e.detail.searchSuggestionCollection` collection. These are the search suggestions that are displayed to the user.

The notes are retrieved from the file system asynchronously using the `getAll()` method. The title of each note is matched against the query text. If the title includes the query text then the note is added to the search suggestions.

Because the notes are retrieved from the file system asynchronously, the `e.detail.setPromise()` method is used to execute the code that matches the search query text. The `setPromise()` method enables you to return the matching suggestions in a promise instead of returning the matching suggestions immediately.

Displaying Search Results

The final step is to display the matching search results in the Search Results page. I already created the Search Results Page in the previous section when I discussed using the Search charm. I will use the very same Search Results page with the `SearchBox` control.

When a user submits a search query from the `SearchBox` control then the `querysubmitted` event is raised. The My Notes app handles the `querysubmitted` event with the code in Listing 13.8.

LISTING 13.8   Handling the querysubmitted Event (\pages\home\home.js)

```
// Listen for search queries
var search = document.getElementById("search").winControl;
search.addEventListener("querysubmitted", function (e) {
    WinJS.Navigation.navigate("/pages/searchResults/searchResults.html", {
➡searchDetails: e.detail })
});
```

When a search query is submitted, the user is redirected to the searchResults.html page with a call to the `navigate()` method. The searchResults.html page displays the search results in a `ListView` control (see Figure 13.18).

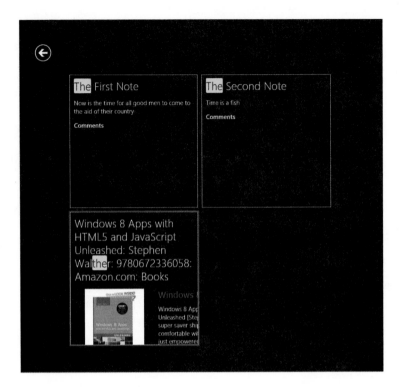

FIGURE 13.18   Showing the results of a search query

Using the Windows Content Indexer

In previous sections, I used a very simple method to determine whether a note matches a search query. If the title of the note contains the search query then that counts as a match. I did not even try to match the contents of the notes because the contents of the notes might contain HTML markup.

In order to perform more sophisticated searches, you can take advantage of the Windows Index. The Windows Index, for example, enables you to perform Boolean queries that include OR and NOT operators. You can also perform exact phrase queries by wrapping your search terms in quotation marks. Finally, the Windows Index supports different types of content including HTML content.

> **NOTE**
>
> When performing OR or NOT Boolean queries, you must enter OR and NOT in uppercase.

In this section, I show you how to take advantage of a new API that was introduced with Windows 8.1 for interacting with the Windows Index. This new API enables you to index content from an app without creating new files in the file system. Instead, you can add, update, and delete content in the Windows Index directly from your app.

Understanding the Windows Content Indexer API

To use the Windows Index from a Windows Store app, you need to know how to work with the following three WinRT classes:

▶ `ContentIndexer`—This class contains methods for adding, updating, and deleting content in an index. It also enables you to create a new index query.

▶ `IndexableContent`—This class represents content that can be added to the index.

▶ `ContentIndexerQuery`—This class represents a particular query that you can perform against the index.

So you use the `ContentIndexer` class to interact with the Windows Index that corresponds to your app. The `ContentIndexer` class enables you to add new content to the index by creating an instance of the `IndexableContent` class. The `ContentIndexer` also enables you to query the index by creating an instance of the `ContentIndexerQuery` class.

Creating an Indexer Helper

To make it easier to work with the Windows Index, I created a JavaScript Indexer helper object. This helper has methods for inserting new content in the index, deleting content from the index, and querying the index.

> **NOTE**
>
> You can find all of the code discussed in this section in the Chapter13\SearchIndex solution in the GitHub repository that accompanies this book.

The complete code for this helper object is contained in Listing 13.9.

LISTING 13.9   The IndexerHelper Object (js\indexerHelper.js)

```
(function () {
    "use strict";
    var props = Windows.Storage.SystemProperties;

    // Add new content to the index
    function add(id, value, itemNameDisplay, keywords, comment) {
        // Get the indexer
        var indexer = Windows.Storage.Search.ContentIndexer.getIndexer();

        // Create content for the indexer
        var content = new Windows.Storage.Search.IndexableContent();
        var contentStream = new Windows.Storage.Streams.
➡InMemoryRandomAccessStream();
        var contentWriter = new Windows.Storage.Streams.DataWriter(contentStream);
        contentWriter.writeString(value);

        return contentWriter.storeAsync().then(function () {
```

```
                content.id = id;
                content.properties.insert(props.itemNameDisplay, itemNameDisplay);
                content.properties.insert(props.keywords, keywords);
                content.properties.insert(props.comment, comment);
                contentStream.seek(0);
                content.stream = contentStream;
                content.streamContentType = "text/html";
                return indexer.addAsync(content);
            }).then(function () {
                contentStream.close();
                contentWriter.close();
            })
        }


        // Returns id of matching items from query
        function query(queryText) {
            var indexer = Windows.Storage.Search.ContentIndexer.getIndexer();
            var query = indexer.createQuery(queryText, []);
            return query.getAsync().then(function(queryResults) {
                var searchResults = [];
                for (var i = 0; i < queryResults.length; i++) {
                    searchResults.push(queryResults[i].id);
                }
                return searchResults;
            });
        }


        // Delete entire index
        function nuke() {
            var indexer = Windows.Storage.Search.ContentIndexer.getIndexer();
            indexer.deleteAllAsync();
        }


        WinJS.Namespace.define("Indexer", {
            add: add,
            query: query,
            nuke: nuke
        });
})();
```

In the next section, I show you how to use the `IndexerHelper` object with the My Notes app.

Using the Indexer Helper

When you add a new note to the My Notes app, you also must update the Windows Index so that it can index the new note. I've modified the code used to handle adding a new note so the note also gets added to the index (see Listing 13.10).

LISTING 13.10   Adding a Note to the Index (\pages\add\add.js)

```
document.getElementById("frmAdd").addEventListener("submit", function (e) {
    e.preventDefault();

    // Save new note and navigate home
    MyApp.notesDataSource.insertAtEnd(null, {
        title: document.getElementById("inpTitle").value,
        contents: toStaticHTML(document.getElementById("inpContents").innerHTML),
        comments: ""
    }).then(function (newItem) {
        return Indexer.add(newItem.key, newItem.data.contents, newItem.data.title);
    }).done(function () {
        WinJS.Navigation.navigate("/pages/home/home.html");
    });
});
```

The form submit handler in Listing 13.10 calls the `Indexer.add()` method to add the new note to the Windows Index before navigating to the home.html page.

The Indexer Helper is also used to get the search results in the Search Results Page (see Listing 13.11). The Indexer `query()` method is called with the search query text to get matching items from the index.

LISTING 13.11   Querying the Windows Index (\pages\searchResults\searchResults.js)

```
Indexer.query(queryText).done(function (queryResults) {
    if (queryResults.length) {
        // Show results
        document.getElementById("divNoResults").style.display = "none";

        // Get all of the notes and filter against search results
        var filteredNotes = [];
        MyApp.notesDataSource.getAll().done(function (notes) {
            for (var i = 0; i < notes.length; i++) {
                var note = notes[i];
                if (queryResults.indexOf(note.key) >= 0) {
                    filteredNotes.push(note.data);
                }
            }
            // Convert to List Data Source
            var listResults = new WinJS.Binding.List(filteredNotes);

            // Bind to ListView
            lvSearchResults.itemDataSource = listResults.dataSource;
        });
    } else {
```

```
            // Report no results
            document.getElementById("divNoResults").style.display = "block";
            var emptyList = new WinJS.Binding.List();
            lvSearchResults.itemDataSource = emptyList.dataSource;
    }
});
```

The Indexer `query()` method returns a set of query results. The query results are an array of IDs that correspond to the unique keys of notes that match the search query.

All of the notes are retrieved from the file system by calling the `getAll()` method. Any note not included in the search query results is discarded. The remaining notes are displayed in the `ListView` control.

Let me show you how all of this works. Imagine that you have the three notes displayed in Figure 13.19. If you enter the search query **note NOT second** then you get the first and third notes but not the second (see Figure 13.20). You do not get the second note because of the NOT operator.

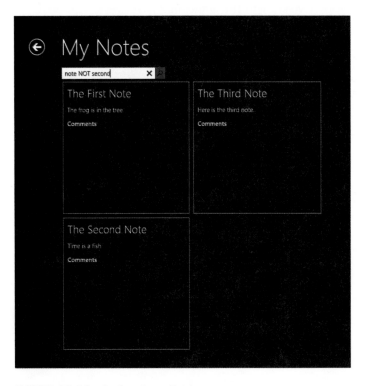

FIGURE 13.19   Performing a Boolean query

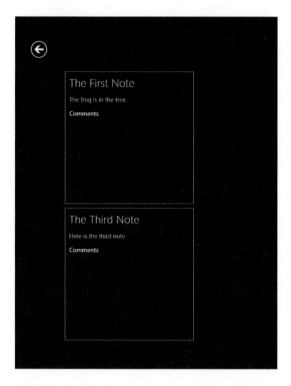

FIGURE 13.20   Getting search results from the Windows Index

Summary

The goal of this chapter was to explain how to implement share and search in a Windows Store app. I discussed share and search in the context of the My Notes sample app.

In the first part of this chapter, I showed you how you can make your app a share source or a share target. You learned how you can share notes from the My Notes app and how you can accept HTML and text content shared from another app.

Next, I demonstrated how you can support search in the My Notes app by using the Search charm or by using the SearchBox control. Finally, I explained how you can support advanced search queries, such as Boolean queries, by taking advantage of the Windows Index.

CHAPTER 14

Using the Live Connect API

The Live Connect API enables you to connect to Live Services from your Windows Store apps. Live Services provides you with services for authenticating users, retrieving user information (including a user's calendars and contacts), and interacting with a user's SkyDrive.

In the first part of this chapter, I explain the steps required to install and set up the Live SDK. For example, you learn how to register your Windows Store app at the Live Connect website.

Next, I discuss how you can take advantage of a feature called *zero-click single sign-on*. This feature enables you to authenticate the users of your Windows Store app without requiring the users to enter their usernames and passwords.

I also explain how you can take advantage of authentication when your Windows Store app interacts with Windows Azure Mobile Services. You learn how to restrict access to Mobile Services to authenticated users.

You also learn how you can retrieve user information from Live Services. For example, I show you how you can retrieve the current user's first and last name, birthday, and profile picture.

Finally, I discuss SkyDrive. You learn how you can upload and download files from your Windows Store app to the hard drive in the sky which is SkyDrive.

Installing the Live SDK

Before you can use the Live Connect API, you need to download the latest version of the
Live SDK for Windows, Windows Phone, and .NET from the Microsoft website. You can
download the SDK from the Dev Center for Windows Store apps at http://msdn.microsoft.
com/en-us/windows/apps/.

Adding a Reference to the Live SDK

After you download the Live SDK, you need to add a reference to the Live SDK JavaScript
library to your Visual Studio Windows Store app project. Select the menu option Project,
Add Reference. After picking Windows, Extensions, check the checkbox next to Live SDK
(see Figure 14.1).

> **WARNING**
>
> After downloading the Live SDK, you need to stop and start Visual Studio for the Live SDK
> to appear in the Reference Manager.

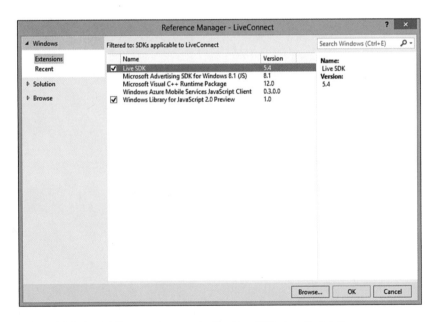

FIGURE 14.1   Adding a reference to the Live SDK JavaScript library

Next, expand your References, Live SDK, JS folder and drag the wl.js file onto your default.
html page. This will add the following JavaScript reference:

```
<script src="/LiveSDKHTML/js/wl.js"></script>
```

Registering Your App

Before you can start using the Live Connect API, you must first associate your app with the Windows Store and register your app with Live Connect.

If you haven't already then you need to associate your app with the Windows Store. Follow these steps:

1. Within Visual Studio, select the menu option Project, Store, Associate App with the Store. (In Visual Studio Express, use Store, Associate App with the Store.) This will open the Associate Your App with the Windows Store Wizard (see Figure 14.2).

2. You need to select an app name that you want to associate with your Visual Studio project. I entered the app name UnleashedLiveConnectSample.

3. Finally, when you click associate, your Visual Studio project app manifest file will be updated with the information from the Windows Store.

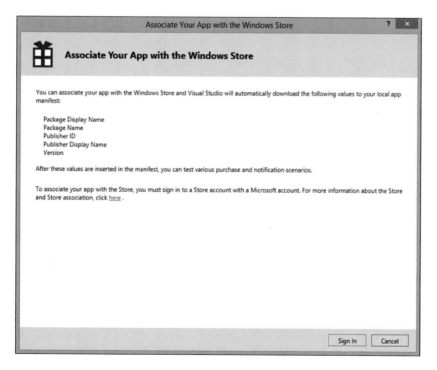

FIGURE 14.2   Associating your app with the Windows Store

After you finish associating your app with the store then you next need to register your app with Live Connect. Follow these steps.

1. In your web browser, navigate to the Windows Store Dashboard located at https://appdev.microsoft.com/StorePortals.

2. Select your Windows Store app from the dashboard and click the Services tile (see Figure 14.3).

3. Click the link to the Live Services site.

FIGURE 14.3   Editing Windows Store app services

Navigating to the Live Services site will launch one last wizard. You must complete the following three steps:

1. Identifying your app—You already completed this step when you associated your Visual Studio project with the Windows Store.

2. Authenticating your service—You should record the client secret that you see in this step (see Figure 14.4). Later in this chapter, when I discuss Azure Mobile Services, you will need this client secret to connect to Live Services.

3. Representing your app to Live Connect users—You need to provide several pieces of information in this step. In particular, you need to provide a URL where you host your Terms of Service and a Privacy Policy. You also must enter a Redirect URI.

The Redirect URI can be any valid URL that you like—the only requirement is that the URI cannot be in use by anyone else. For the sample project discussed in this chapter, I entered the Redirect URI http://liveSDKDemo.Superexpert.com.

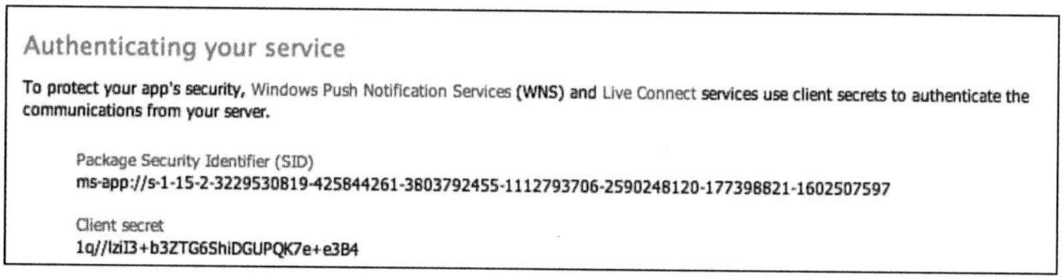

Authenticating your service

To protect your app's security, Windows Push Notification Services (WNS) and Live Connect services use client secrets to authenticate the communications from your server.

Package Security Identifier (SID)
ms-app://s-1-15-2-3229530819-425844261-3803792455-1112793706-2590248120-177398821-1602507597

Client secret
1q//lziI3+b3ZTG6ShiDGUPQK7e+e3B4

FIGURE 14.4   Getting the client secret

NOTE

I hope this goes without saying, but keep your client secret. I regenerated the one that you see in the screenshot.

Initializing the Live Connect SDK

Before you can call any of the services available from the Live Connect API, you must first initialize your connection. You initialize your connection by calling the `WL.init()` method as illustrated in Listing 14.1.

LISTING 14.1   Initializing Your Connection

```
var REDIRECT_DOMAIN = "http://liveSDKDemo.Superexpert.com";
var scopes = ["wl.signin"];
WL.init({
    scope: scopes,
    redirect_uri: REDIRECT_DOMAIN
});
```

The `WL.init()` method in Listing 14.1 is called with two arguments: a `redirect_uri` and an array of scopes. The `redirect_uri` must match (exactly) the Redirect Domain that you configured in the previous section. I discuss the array of scopes in the next section.

Specifying Different Scopes

The array of scopes that you pass to the `WL.init()` method determines the information that you have permission to access. There is all sorts of fun and scary information that you can extract from a Windows Live user account including the user birthday, email addresses, mailing address, photos, and contacts.

Here's a partial list of scopes:

▶ `wl.signin`—Single sign-in behavior

▶ `wl.basic`—Read access to basic profile information and contacts

▶ `wl.offline_access`—Ability to read and update user information even when a user is not signed in and using your app

▶ `wl.birthday`—Read access to user birthday

▶ `wl.calendars`—Read access to user calendars and events

▶ `wl.calendars_update`—Read and write access to user calendars and events

▶ `wl.contacts_birthday`—Read access to user birthday and user contacts birthdays

▶ `wl.contacts_create`—Write access to user contacts

▶ `wl.contacts_calendars`—Read access to user calendars and events and contacts calendars and events

▶ `wl.contacts_photos`—Read access to user media and media shared by other users

▶ `wl.contacts_skydrive`—Read access to user SkyDrive and files shared by other users

▶ `wl.emails`—Read access to user email addresses

▶ `wl.events_create`—Write access for creating events

▶ `wl.messenger`—Enables you to sign in to the user messenger service

▶ `wl.phone_numbers`—Read access to user phone numbers

▶ `wl.photos`—Read access to user media

▶ `wl.postal_addresses`—Read access to user mailing addresses

▶ `wl.share`—Enables you to update a user's status message

▶ `wl.skydrive`—Read access to user files in SkyDrive

▶ `wl.skydrive_update`—Read and write access to user files in SkyDrive

▶ `wl.work_profile`—Read access to a user's work and employment information

---

NOTE

For a complete listing of scopes, see http://msdn.microsoft.com/en-us/library/live/hh243646.aspx.

Obviously, not all users of a Windows Store app will want to share all information about themselves. Your Windows Store app, therefore, must get consent to access the information.

When you first run a Windows Store app that requires a particular scope, a modal dialog appears asking the user to provide permission. For example, the form in Figure 14.5 is displayed when you call `WL.init()` with the `wl.signin` scope.

FIGURE 14.5   Windows Store app asking permission to sign you in

Even if you give a Windows Store app permission to access your Windows Live user information, you can revoke this information at a later date. To revoke a permission, log into your account at the Live.com website, pick the app, and remove the permissions (see Figure 14.6).

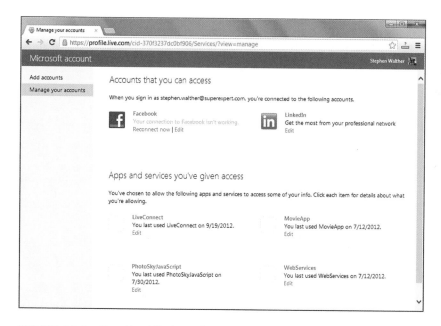

FIGURE 14.6   Revoking Windows Store app permissions

Authenticating a User

The most valuable service that Live Connect provides you is authentication. There are two different authentication experiences depending on how you log in to your Windows 8.1 machine.

If you have a connected Microsoft account—in other words, your Windows 8 account is associated with a Windows Live account—then you can take advantage of something called *zero-click single sign-on*. This feature enables you to avoid ever entering your user name or password when running a Windows store app.

When you log in to a Windows Store app then your connected Microsoft account is used automatically. Furthermore, you never log out of an app in this scenario. Whenever you run the app in the future, the app knows your identity automatically.

You also have the option of using a local account with Windows 8.1. In that case, you have not connected a Windows Live account with your Windows 8.1 local account. When using a Windows local account, a user can sign in and sign out of your app using his Windows Live account. They can even switch accounts.

> **NOTE**
>
> Microsoft strongly encourages you to use a connected account when using Windows 8.1. They keep throwing dialogs at you requesting you to associate your Windows account with a Windows Live account.

Logging a User into Live Connect

If you want to log in a user using Live Connect then you simply call the `WL.login` method as demonstrated in Listing 14.2.

LISTING 14.2   Logging in a User (login\login.js)

```
(function () {
    "use strict";

    function init() {
        var REDIRECT_DOMAIN = "http://liveSDKDemo.Superexpert.com";
        var spanResults = document.getElementById("spanResults");

        var scopes = ["wl.signin"];
        WL.init({
            scope: scopes,
            redirect_uri: REDIRECT_DOMAIN
        });

        WL.login().then(
            function (loginResults) {
```

```
            spanResults.innerText = "Connected";
        },
        function (loginResponse) {
            spanResults.innerText = "Error when calling WL.login";
        }
    );


    }

    document.addEventListener("DOMContentLoaded", init);
})();
```

Notice that the scope passed to the `WL.init()` method is the `wl.signin` scope. This scope indicates that the user does not need to enter their email and password when they are using a connected Windows account.

If you are using a connected Windows account then when you first call the `WL.login()` method then you get the warning dialog in Figure 14.7. This dialog appears only once when you run the app for the very first time. You are logged in automatically whenever you run the app in the future.

Notice that you do not enter your Windows Live email and password. If you have a connected Windows Live account, you are logged into your connected account automatically.

NOTE

The only way to log out of an app when using a connected account is to go to http://live.com, Permissions, Apps and Services and revoke the app's permissions.

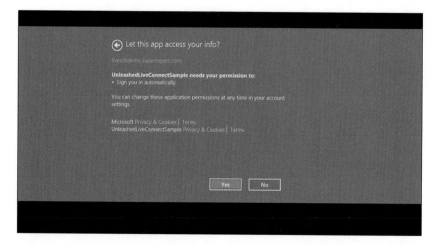

FIGURE 14.7   Logging in when using a connected Windows account

If, on the other hand, you are not using a connected Windows account, and you are using a local Windows account instead, then you get the dialog for entering your Windows Live email and password in Figure 14.8. After you enter your email and password once then you do not need to enter your email and password ever again.

FIGURE 14.8   Logging in when using a local Windows account

Creating Account Settings

Instead of logging in a user immediately when the user opens your app, you might want to make authentication optional. If someone authenticates then the person gets a better experience (for example, you can show her name).

In this scenario, you might want to provide the user with the option of logging in to your app from the Settings charm. Let me show you how you can extend the Settings charm with Account settings that enable a user to sign in and out (see Figure 14.9).

The JavaScript file in Listing 14.3 sets up two settings flyouts: one flyout for Account Settings and one flyout for Privacy Settings. The JavaScript file also displays the user's current login status by subscribing to the `auth.login` and `auth.logout` events.

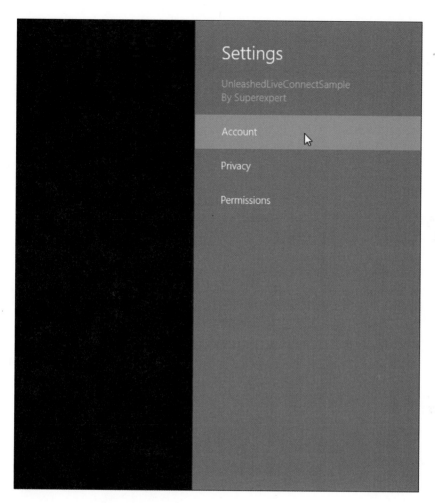

FIGURE 14.9   Selecting account settings

I talked about the `SettingsFlyout` control in Chapter 6, "Menus and Flyouts."

Notice that the page in Listing 14.3 also displays a Privacy Settings flyout. Displaying a Privacy Policy is a requirement because you are accessing a user's private data when signing in the user with the Account Settings flyout.

LISTING 14.3   Creating Account Settings (accountSettings\page.js)

```
(function () {
    "use strict";

    // Update display when login status changes
    function init() {
        var spanResults = document.getElementById("spanResults");

        WL.Event.subscribe("auth.login", function () {
            spanResults.innerText = "Signed In";
        });

        WL.Event.subscribe("auth.logout", function () {
            spanResults.innerText = "Signed Out";
        });

        var REDIRECT_DOMAIN = "http://liveSDKDemo.Superexpert.com";
        var scopes = ["wl.basic"];
        WL.init({
            scope: scopes,
            redirect_uri: REDIRECT_DOMAIN
        });
    }

    // Create Account Settings and Privacy Settings Flyouts
    function settings(e) {
        e.detail.applicationcommands = {
            "divAccount": { href: "accountSettings.html", title: "Account" },
            "divPrivacy": { href: "privacySettings.html", title: "Privacy" },
        };
        WinJS.UI.SettingsFlyout.populateSettings(e);
    }

    document.addEventListener("DOMContentLoaded", init);
    WinJS.Application.addEventListener("settings", settings);

    WinJS.Application.start();
})();
```

The code for the Account Settings flyout is contained in the JavaScript file in Listing 14.4. This code hides or displays a Sign In and Sign Out button depending on the current user's login status.

LISTING 14.4   The Account Settings Flyout (\accountSettings\accountSettings.js)

```
(function () {
    'use strict';

    WinJS.UI.Pages.define("accountSettings.html",
    {
        ready: function (element, options) {
            var btnSignIn = document.getElementById("btnSignIn");
            var btnSignOut = document.getElementById("btnSignOut");
            var divMessage = document.getElementById("divMessage");

            // Show/Hide buttons
            btnSignIn.style.display = "none";
            btnSignOut.style.display = "none";

            WL.api({
                path: "me",
                method: "GET"
            }).then(
                // Already logged in
                function (results) {
                    if (WL.canLogout()) {
                        btnSignOut.style.display = "";
                    } else {
                        divMessage.innerText = "Sign out of this app "
                            + "from your Windows Live account."
                    }
                },
                // Not logged in
                function (results) {
                    btnSignIn.style.display = "";
                }
            );

            btnSignIn.addEventListener("click", function (e) {
                e.preventDefault();

                WL.login({
                    scope: ["wl.basic"]
                }).then(function (response) {
                    WinJS.UI.SettingsFlyout.show();
                });
            });

            btnSignOut.addEventListener("click", function (e) {
```

14

```
                    e.preventDefault();

                    WL.logout().then(function (response) {
                        WinJS.UI.SettingsFlyout.show();
                    });
                });

            }
        });
    }());
```

The call to `WL.api()` is used to detect whether the current user is already logged in or not. If the user is already logged in then the first function is executed, which hides the Sign In button. If the user is not logged in then the second function executes and the Sign In button is displayed.

Notice that the `WL.canLogout()` method is used to display the Sign Out button only when a user can actually sign out. If the user is logged into Windows using a connected account then the user cannot log out. In that case, a message is displayed to the user suggesting that the user go to their Windows Live account to remove permissions for the app (see Figure 14.10).

FIGURE 14.10   You cannot log out with a connected Windows account

If, on the other hand, the user is logged in with a local Windows account then the user gets a Sign Out button. In this case, the user can actually log out. The user can even log out and then log in with a different account.

Authentication and Windows Azure Mobile Services

In Chapter 10, "Using Windows Azure Mobile Services," I demonstrated how you can use Windows Azure Mobile Services to store app data in the cloud. In particular, I showed you how you can create a Tasks database table hosted on Azure and execute inserts, updates, deletes, and queries from a Windows Store app using Mobile Services.

However, in that chapter, I avoided the whole issue of authentication. Anyone could read any data and make any changes to the Tasks table. Anyone could do anything, which is very dangerous.

In this section, I want to explain how you can use Live Connect authentication—which we discussed in the previous section—to control access to Mobile Services. I demonstrate how you can require users to authenticate before accessing the Tasks Mobile Service and how you can prevent users from accessing each other's tasks.

Configuring Your Mobile Service

Before you can use Live Connect with Azure Mobile Services, you must first provide Mobile Services with your app's client ID and client secret from Live Connect. Follow these steps:

1. Navigate to the My Applications page at the Live Connect Developers Center located at https://account.live.com/developers/applications. Select your application from the list of applications.

2. Record the client ID and client secret for your app.

3. Navigate to the Windows Azure Management portal at http://manage. WindowsAzure.com. Navigate to your Mobile Service and click the Identify tab (see Figure 14.11).

4. Enter your client ID and client secret under Microsoft Account Settings.

FIGURE 14.11   Entering your Live Connect client ID and client secret at Azure

Setting Permissions for Your Mobile Service

Next, I want to restrict access to my Mobile Service for the Tasks table so that only authenticated users can insert, update, delete, and read the tasks from the table. You can set Mobile Service permissions from within Visual Studio or you can set the permissions from the Windows Azure Management Portal (purely a matter of preference).

Here are the steps for setting permissions for the Tasks table within Visual Studio:

1. Open the Server Explorer window by selecting the menu option View, Server Explorer.

2. Expand Windows Azure Mobile Services, expand the Mobile Service, and right-click the Tasks table and select the menu option Edit Permissions (see Figure 14.12).

3. Enable only Authenticated Users to insert, update, delete, and read.

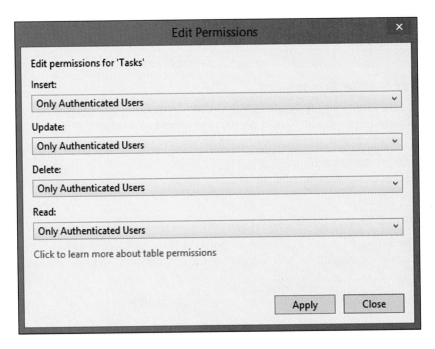

FIGURE 14.12   Setting mobile service permissions

Updating the Mobile Server Scripts

I don't want anyone else in the world to read my tasks. If I need to change the water in the goldfish bowl today then that is nobody's business except mine.

To stop people from being able to read each other's tasks, I need to update the insert.js and read.js scripts associated with the Tasks table. You can modify these scripts from within Visual Studio or from the Windows Azure Management portal (again, purely a matter of preference).

Within Visual Studio, you can view and modify the insert.js and read.js scripts by expanding the node for the Tasks table in the Server Explorer window (see Figure 14.13).

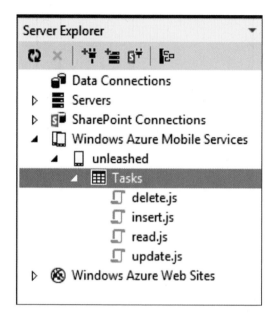

FIGURE 14.13   Modifying the insert.js and read.js scripts

The updated insert.js script is contained in Listing 14.5. Notice that I am getting the authenticated user ID from the user parameter passed to the insert function. I store the user ID in the database with the task (see Figure 14.14).

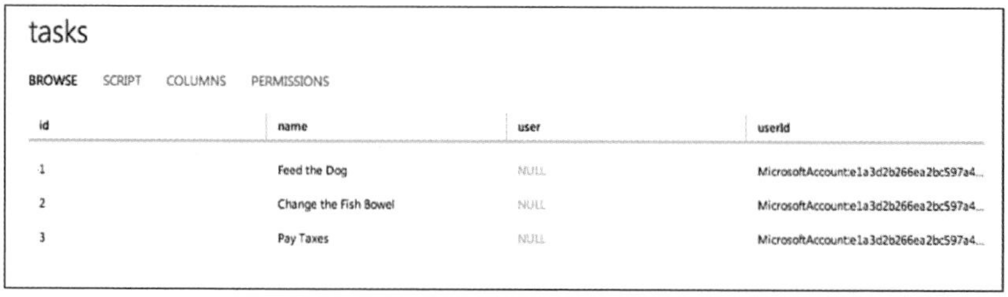

id	name	user	userId
1	Feed the Dog	NULL	MicrosoftAccount:e1a3d2b266ea2bc597a4...
2	Change the Fish Bowel	NULL	MicrosoftAccount:e1a3d2b266ea2bc597a4...
3	Pay Taxes	NULL	MicrosoftAccount:e1a3d2b266ea2bc597a4...

tasks

BROWSE   SCRIPT   COLUMNS   PERMISSIONS

FIGURE 14.14   User ID stored in SQL Azure Tasks table

LISTING 14.5   Inserting with the User ID (insert.js)

```
function insert(item, user, request) {
    // Cleanup data
    item.name = item.name.trim();

    // Validate
    if (item.name.length === 0) {
        request.respond(statusCodes.BAD_REQUEST, "You fool! Task name is
➥required!!!");
        return;
    }

    // Add user to task
    item.userId = user.userId;

    // Otherwise, execute request
    request.execute();
}
```

NOTE

The user ID is a really ugly looking identity string that looks something like "Microsoft-Account:e5a3d2b266fa2bc597a4bda73cddc25e".

When a user reads tasks from the Tasks table, I want to ensure that the user is reading their own tasks and not some other person's tasks. The updated read.js file in Listing 14.6 restricts the tasks returned to the tasks for the current authenticated user.

LISTING 14.6   Reading with the User ID (read.js)

```
function read(query, user, request) {
    query.where({ userId: user.userId });
    request.execute();
}
```

The read function in Listing 14.6 prevents anyone except me from reading my tasks.

Logging Into Azure Mobile Services

Now that I have done all of this tedious configuration and setup, I am finally in a position to do something useful. I can log in to Azure Mobile Services using my Live Connect account and insert and retrieve my tasks. I want to

1. Log in to Live Connect

2. Log in to Windows Azure Mobile Services

3. Get my tasks

The code for performing all three of these steps is contained in Listing 14.7.

LISTING 14.7   Authenticating with Mobile Services (mobileServices\mobileServices.js)

```javascript
// Login and Bind tasks to ListView
var REDIRECT_DOMAIN = "http://liveSDKDemo.Superexpert.com";
var mobileServicesClient, tasksTable;

var scopes = ["wl.signin"];
WL.init({
    scope: scopes,
    redirect_uri: REDIRECT_DOMAIN
});

WL.login().then(
    // Success
    function (wlLoginResults) {
        // Ready mobile service client
        mobileServiceClient = new WindowsAzure.MobileServiceClient(
            "https://unleashed.azure-mobile.net/",
            "TzXsPHIiLhFwtBEUpoDPDZcvwVoold62"
        );

        // Login to Windows Azure
        mobileServiceClient.login(wlLoginResults.session.authentication_token).done(
            // Success
            function(azureLoginResults) {
                // Get tasks table
                tasksTable = mobileServiceClient.getTable('Tasks');

                // Go grab the tasks
                bindTasks();
            },
            // Fail
            function (azureLoginResults) {
                var md = new Windows.UI.Popups.MessageDialog("Could not login to
➥Azure!");

                md.showAsync();
            }
        );
    },
```

```
    // Fail
    function (loginResponse) {
        var md = new Windows.UI.Popups.MessageDialog("Could not login to Live
➥Connect!");
        md.showAsync();
    }
);
```

Let me walk through the code in Listing 14.7. First, I log into Live Connect by calling `WL.login()`. This method returns a promise. If you login successfully, you get an `authentication_token` back from Live Connect.

I use the `authentication_token` when logging into Mobile Services with the `MobileServiceClient login()` method. This method also returns a promise. If you login successfully then the `bindTasks()` method is called and the tasks are retrieved from the Mobile Service and displayed in a `ListView`.

Retrieving Basic User Information

There is a wealth of user information that you can retrieve from Live Connect including the user's name, birthday, email addresses, and list of friends. In this section, I demonstrate how you can retrieve this information by taking advantage of the `WL.api()` method.

The `WL.api()` method enables you to interact with the Live Connect REST API. When you call the `WL.api()` method, you can supply the following four options:

▶ `path`—A path to a REST object

▶ `method`—An HTTP method such as GET, POST, MOVE, COPY

▶ `body`—The body of the request (serialized to JSON)

▶ `type`—Used only when creating folders or albums

The path object is the most important option because it determines the object that you are interacting with. For example, if you want to get the user's photo then you need to supply the path "me/picture". If you want to set a user's status message then you would use the path "me/share" (me refers to the current user).

> **NOTE**
>
> The documentation for all of the REST object supported by Live Connect is located at
> http://msdn.microsoft.com/en-us/library/live/hh243648.aspx.

Let me show you how this works by creating a page that displays several bits of user information (see Figure 14.15). The JavaScript source is contained in Listing 14.8.

FIGURE 14.15   Displaying user info from Live Connect

LISTING 14.8   Retrieving Basic User Information from Live Connect

```
(function () {
    "use strict";
    var REDIRECT_DOMAIN = "http://liveSDKDemo.Superexpert.com";

    function init() {
        var spanFirstName = document.getElementById("spanFirstName");
        var spanLastName = document.getElementById("spanLastName");
        var spanBirthday = document.getElementById("spanBirthday");
        var spanStatus = document.getElementById("spanStatus");
        var imgPhoto = document.getElementById("imgPhoto");

        // Initialize Windows Live
        var scopes = ["wl.signin", "wl.basic", "wl.birthday"];
        WL.init({
            scope: scopes,
            redirect_uri: REDIRECT_DOMAIN
        });

        // Log in to Windows Live
        WL.login().then(function (loginResults) {
            // Show basic info
            callLiveConnect("me", "GET").then(function (results) {
                spanFirstName.innerText = results.first_name;
                spanLastName.innerText = results.last_name;
                spanBirthday.innerText = results.birth_month
                    + "/" + results.birth_day;
            });

            // Show profile picture
            callLiveConnect("me/picture", "GET").then(function (results) {
                imgPhoto.src = results.location;
            });
```

```
            });

            // Call Live
            function callLiveConnect(path, method) {
                return new WinJS.Promise(function (complete, error) {
                    WL.api({
                        path: path,
                        method: method
                    }).then(
                        function(results) {
                            complete(results);
                        },
                        function(results) {
                            // Error calling WL.api()
                            debugger;
                        }
                    );
                });
            }

        }

    document.addEventListener("DOMContentLoaded", init);
})();
```

In Listing 14.8, all of the heavy lifting is being performed by the `callLiveConnect()` method. This method uses the `WL.api()` method to call a REST service.

The `callLiveConnect()` method is called twice: the first time to get basic user information and the second time to get the user photo.

Uploading and Downloading Files from SkyDrive

Microsoft SkyDrive enables you to store files in the cloud so the files can be easily shared across devices. Everybody on earth gets 7 gigabytes of free SkyDrive storage to play with. You can add photos, documents, or any other type of file that you please to SkyDrive.

You can take advantage of the Live Connect API to interact with a user's SkyDrive. For example, you can use the API to upload, download, copy, move, and delete files on SkyDrive.

Imagine, for example, that you want to create a Windows Store app for displaying photos. You want a user to be able to view their photo gallery anywhere from any computer. In that case, it makes sense to store the photos on SkyDrive.

In this section, I explain how you can list files and folders from a user's SkyDrive, how you can download files, and how you can upload new files.

> **NOTE**
>
> You can access your SkyDrive through a web browser by navigating to http://SkyDrive.Live.com. You also can manage your SkyDrive account directly from within Windows 8.1 from PC Settings (you can even buy more storage space right inside Windows).

> **NOTE**
>
> SkyDrive is much more tightly integrated with Windows 8.1 than Windows 8. For example, SkyDrive is now the default storage location for documents, pictures, and videos. The file save picker, discussed in the next section, opens the SkyDrive Documents folder by default.

Listing SkyDrive Folders and Files

Let me start with the basics; let me explain how you can get a list of the files and the folders on a user's SkyDrive (see Figure 14.16).

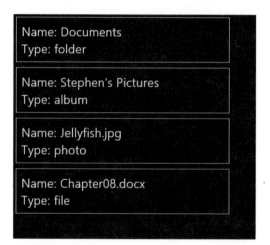

FIGURE 14.16   Displaying a list of SkyDrive files and folders

I'll display the list of SkyDrive folders and files with a `ListView` control. The HTML page in Listing 14.9 contains a `Template` and a `ListView` control. The template displays the name and type of each item retrieved from SkyDrive.

LISTING 14.9   HTML for Displaying Files from SkyDrive

```
<div id="tmplFile" data-win-control="WinJS.Binding.Template">
    <div class="fileItem">
        Name: <span data-win-bind="innerText:name"></span>
        <br />
        Type: <span data-win-bind="innerText:type"></span>
```

```
    </div>
</div>


<div id="lvFiles"
    data-win-control="WinJS.UI.ListView"
    data-win-options="{
        itemTemplate: select('#tmplFile'),
        selectionMode: 'none'
    }"></div>
```

The JavaScript file in Listing 14.10 retrieves the list of files and folders from the current user's root SkyDrive folder.

LISTING 14.10   JavaScript for Retrieving a List of Files from SkyDrive

```
(function () {
    "use strict";
    var REDIRECT_DOMAIN = "http://liveSDKDemo.Superexpert.com";

    function init() {
        WinJS.UI.processAll().done(function () {
            var lvFiles = document.getElementById("lvFiles").winControl;

            // Initialize Live Connect
            var scopes = ["wl.signin", "wl.skydrive"];
            WL.init({
                scope: scopes,
                redirect_uri: REDIRECT_DOMAIN
            });

            // Log in to Live Connect
            WL.login().then(function (loginResults) {
                // Get List of top-level SkyDrive files
                callLiveConnect("me/skydrive/files", "GET").then(function (results)
{
var dsItems = new WinJS.Binding.List(results.data);
                    lvFiles.itemDataSource = dsItems.dataSource;
                });
            });

        });

        // Call Live Connect
        function callLiveConnect(path, method) {
            return new WinJS.Promise(function (complete, error) {
```

```
                        WL.api({
                            path: path,
                            method: method
                        }).then(
                            function (results) {
                                complete(results);
                            },
                            function (results) {
                                // Error calling WL.api()
                                debugger;
                            }
                        );
                    });
                }

            }

        document.addEventListener("DOMContentLoaded", init);
        })();
```

The first section in the code initializes the connection to Live Connect by calling the `wl.init()` method with the `wl.skydrive` scope. To read files and folders from SkyDrive, the user must consent to the `wl.skydrive` permission. To update files and folders in SkyDrive, the user must consent to the `wl.skydrive_update` permission.

Next, the user is logged in by calling `wl.login()`. After the user is logged in, the list of files and folders from the user's SkyDrive is retrieved by invoking the `callLiveConnect()` method with the path "me/skydrive/files". This call retrieves the items (both files and folders) from the user's root SkyDrive folder.

The list of files and folders is returned in the data property as a JavaScript array. This array is converted into a List data source and bound to the `ListView` and the list of files and folders is displayed.

Downloading Files from SkyDrive

You can use the `WL.backgroundDownload()` method to download files from a user's SkyDrive. When you call this method, you supply the path to the file on the user's SkyDrive and the `StorageFile` where the file is saved.

Let me modify the `ListView` which we discussed in the previous section so it supports downloading files. I'll modify the `ListView` so that when you click a file in the `ListView`, a save file screen will appear, which enables you to save the file from the SkyDrive to your local hard drive (see Figure 14.17).

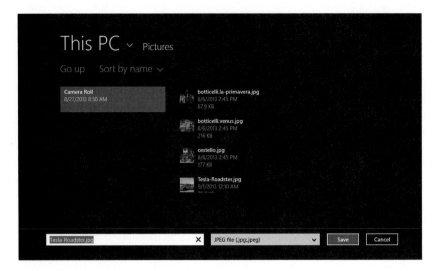

FIGURE 14.17   Saving a file from SkyDrive

First, I need to modify the options for the `ListView` so it supports raising the `iteminvoked` event when you click/tap a ListView item:

```
<div id="lvFiles"
    data-win-control="WinJS.UI.ListView"
    data-win-options="{
        itemTemplate: select('#tmplFile'),
        tapBehavior: 'invokeOnly'
    }"></div>
```

Next, I need to implement a handler for the `iteminvoked` event that saves the clicked/tapped item to the hard drive (see Listing 14.11).

LISTING 14.11   The `iteminvoked` Event Handler

```
// Set up invoke handler
lvFiles.addEventListener("iteminvoked", function (evt) {
    evt.detail.itemPromise.done(function (invokedItem) {
        var itemData = invokedItem.data;

        // Don't download folders and albums
        if (itemData.type == "folder" || itemData.type == "album") {
            return;
        }

        // Create save picker
        var savePicker = new Windows.Storage.Pickers.FileSavePicker();
```

```
        savePicker.suggestedStartLocation = Windows.Storage.Pickers.
➡PickerLocationId.documentsLibrary;
        savePicker.suggestedFileName = itemData.name;
        savePicker.fileTypeChoices.insert("PNG file", [".png"]);
        savePicker.fileTypeChoices.insert("JPEG file", [".jpg", ".jpeg"]);
        savePicker.fileTypeChoices.insert("Microsoft Word Document", [".docx",
➡".doc"]);


        // Display picker
        savePicker.pickSaveFileAsync().then(function (file) {
            if (file) {
                WL.backgroundDownload({
                    path: itemData.id + "/content",
                    file_output: file
                });
            }
        });
    })
});
```

When the `iteminvoked` event is raised, the code in Listing 14.11 retrieves the `ListView` item that was clicked/tapped with the help of the `itemPromise()` method.

Next, a `FileSavePicker` is created for saving the selected file. The `FileSavePicker` is configured to handle PNG, JPEG, and Microsoft Word Documents. If you want to handle downloading other types of files, then you need to add the new file types to the `FileSavePicker`'s `fileTypeChoices` collection.

The file save screen is displayed by calling the `pickSaveFileAsync()` method. When the user clicks the Save button, the Live Connect `WL.backgroundDownload()` method is called. This method downloads the file contents from SkyDrive and saves the file to the location that the user selected with the save file picker.

Notice the path used to save the file: `itemData.id + "/content"`. You retrieve the contents of a file (instead of a description of the file) by using the ID of the file followed by `"/content"`.

Uploading Files to SkyDrive

So how do you upload files to SkyDrive?

Before you can upload files to SkyDrive, you must get the user's consent to a stronger permission request. You need to initialize your connection to the Live API with `wl.skydrive_update` scope like this:

```
// Initialize Live Connect
var scopes = ["wl.signin", "wl.skydrive_update"];
WL.init({
```

```
    scope: scopes,
    redirect_uri: REDIRECT_DOMAIN
});
```

To enable users to upload files, I'll modify the app from the previous section so that it includes an app bar with an Upload command (see Figure 14.18). The app bar is declared like this:

```
<div data-win-control="WinJS.UI.AppBar">
    <button data-win-control="WinJS.UI.AppBarCommand"
        data-win-options="{
            id:'cmdUpload',
            label:'Upload',
            icon:'upload',
            tooltip:'Upload File'
        }">
    </button>
</div>
```

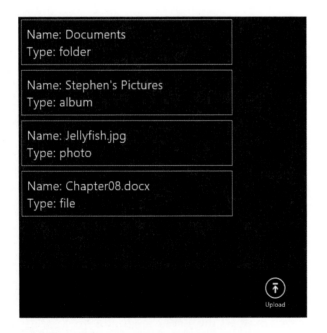

FIGURE 14.18   The Upload app bar command

Finally, I need to write the code that handles invoking the Upload command. The code for handling the Upload command, and uploading a file to SkyDrive, is contained in Listing 14.12.

LISTING 14.12   Handling the Upload Command

```
// Set up upload handler
var cmdUpload = document.getElementById("cmdUpload");
cmdUpload.addEventListener("click", function () {
    var openPicker = new Windows.Storage.Pickers.FileOpenPicker();
    openPicker.fileTypeFilter.replaceAll(["*"]);
    openPicker.pickSingleFileAsync().then(function (file) {
        WL.backgroundUpload({
            path: "me/skydrive",
            file_name: file.name,
            file_input: file
        }).then(function () {
            getFileList();
        });
    });
});
```

The code in Listing 14.12 displays a file open picker that enables you to pick a file from your hard drive. When you pick a file then the Live Connect `WL.backgroundUpload()` method is called with three parameters:

- ▶ `path`—The path on SkyDrive where you want to upload the file

- ▶ `file_name`—The name of the new file to create on SkyDrive

- ▶ `file_input`—The storage file picked from the open file picker

After the file is uploaded, the `getFileList()` method is called to refresh the list of files displayed by the `ListView` control so the `ListView` control will display the newly uploaded file.

Summary

This chapter focused on the subject of the Live Connect API. You learned how to use the Live Connect API to support zero-click single sign-on to authenticate users without requiring users to enter their usernames and passwords. You also learned how to pass an authentication token from a Windows Store app to a Windows Azure Mobile Service.

Next, you learned how you can extract a treasure trove of information about the current user from Live Services. For example, I demonstrated how you can retrieve the current user's first and last name, birthday, and profile picture from Live Services.

Finally, I explained how you can interact with SkyDrive from a Windows Store app. You learned how to list, download, and upload files to a user's SkyDrive account.

CHAPTER 15

Graphics and Games

In this chapter, you learn how to create a simple game using a Windows Store app. You learn how to create a game named Brain Eaters.

The goal of the Brain Eaters game is to avoid getting eaten by zombies while eating food pellets. If you eat all five food pellets then you win the game. If your character gets eaten by a zombie then you lose (see Figure 15.1).

The game works with keyboard, mouse, touch, and stylus. You can move your character using the arrow keys on your keyboard. Alternatively, if you are using a slate, then you can touch the screen to indicate the direction that your character should move.

The game also works at different display resolutions. The game board resizes automatically to fit the available screen size so you can play the game on both low-resolution and high-resolution screens.

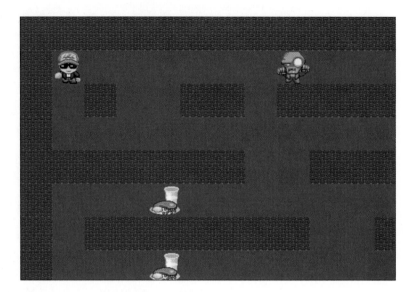

FIGURE 15.1   Brain Eaters game

Overview of the Game

I created the Brain Eaters game with the Visual Studio Navigation App template. The game includes the following four pages:

▶ `home`—The home page contains an introduction screen that explains the rules for the game. You click the Start Game button to navigate to the play page.

▶ `play`—The play page contains the actual game. Here is where you need to run away from the zombies.

▶ `lose`—If the zombies catch you then you lose the game and end up on the lose page. You can click the Play Again? button to return the play page.

▶ **win**—If you eat all of the food pellets then you win the game and you are navigated to the win page.

The home, lose, and win pages are boring—they are simple HTML pages that link to the play page (see Figure 15.2). The play page is where the game is actually played.

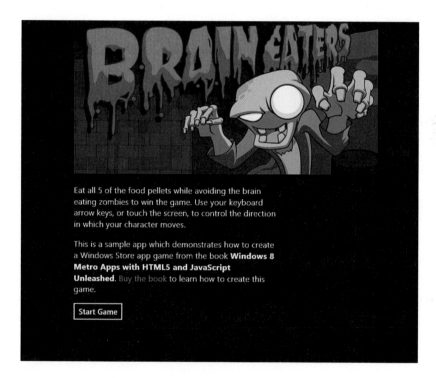

FIGURE 15.2   The Brain Eaters home page

Almost all of the code for the game is included in a JavaScript file named game.js, which contains the JavaScript Game class. This class contains the code for starting the game, stopping the game, updating the positions of the zombies, and rendering the game.

Creating the Game Tiles

The Brain Eaters game is rendered out of a set of image tiles. An image tile is simply a 50px by 50px image. The game board is rendered from background and wall tiles. The game also includes tiles for the zombies, player, and food.

All of the game tiles are created in a JavaScript file named tiles.js (see Listing 15.1).

LISTING 15.1   The tiles.js File

```
(function () {
    "use strict";

    function Tile(url) {
        this.image = new Image();
        this.image.src = url;
    }


    var tiles = {};
    tiles.background = new Tile("/images/background.jpg");
    tiles.wall = new Tile("/images/brick.jpg");
    tiles.player = new Tile("/images/hero.png");
    tiles.zombie = new Tile("/images/zombie.jpg");
    tiles.hamburger = new Tile("/images/hamburger.gif");

    WinJS.Namespace.define("Unleashed", {
        Tiles: tiles
    });

})();
```

Each tile represents an image loaded from the images folder. For example, the wall tile represents an image named brick.jpg.

Notice that the game includes PNG, GIF, and JPG images. You can create tiles using any type of image supported by a modern browser.

The set of tiles is exposed as properties from the `Unleashed.Tiles` object. For example, you can refer to the wall tile with the `Unleashed.Tiles.wall` property.

Playing the Game Sounds

When you get eaten by a zombie, you get to die a noisy death. And, when you eat a food pellet, your character says "Yum!"

The game sounds are contained in a file named sounds.js (see Listing 15.2).

LISTING 15.2   The sounds.js File

```
(function () {
    "use strict";

    WinJS.Namespace.define("Unleashed", {
        Sounds: {
            yum: new Audio("/sounds/yum.wav"),
            eaten: new Audio("/sounds/eaten.wav"),
            cheer: new Audio("/sounds/cheer.wav")
        }
    });

})();
```

Notice that the game sounds are WAV sound files. I recorded the sound files using a program named Audacity, which is a free, open-source sound recorder and editor.

The sounds are exposed as properties of the `Unleashed.Sounds` object. For example, the Yum sound is played with the following code:

```
Unleashed.Sounds.yum.play();
```

> **NOTE**
>
> I created the sound files by recording my children Jon, Ada, and Athena making zombie noises. This will most likely scar them all for life.

Creating the Game Canvas

The game graphics are rendered using an HTML5 `Canvas` element. The `Canvas` element is created in the play.html page like this:

```
<div
    data-win-control="WinJS.UI.ViewBox">
    <canvas id="canvas" width="1000" height="750"></canvas>
</div>
```

Notice that the `Canvas` element is contained in a WinJS `ViewBox` control. The `ViewBox` control scales the `Canvas` to fit the resolution of the screen automatically. You can play the game on a 1,024px by 768px screen in portrait mode (see Figure 15.3) and a 2,560px by 1,440px screen in landscape mode (see Figure 15.4). The `ViewBox` scales the `Canvas` to fit the available screen automatically.

FIGURE 15.3   Game scaled to 1,024px by 768px screen in portrait mode

The Canvas element is declared with a width of 1,000 pixels and a height of 750 pixels. All of the game tiles—such as the zombie and wall tiles—are painted on this Canvas element.

When the Game class is initialized in the game.js file, a 2-D context is retrieved from the Canvas element with the following code:

```
// Setup Canvas
this._canvas = document.getElementById("canvas");
this._ctx = this._canvas.getContext("2d");
```

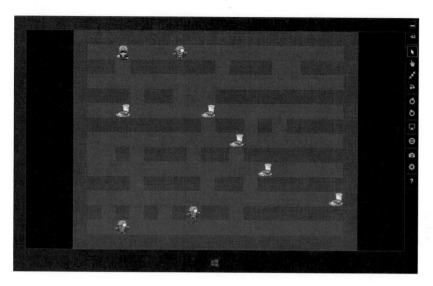

FIGURE 15.4   Game scaled to 2,560px by 1,440px screen in landscape mode

The 2-D context contains the graphics API for drawing on the `Canvas`. For example, the graphics API includes methods such as `lineTo()`, `rect()`, and `arc()` for drawing lines, rectangles, and arcs.

The Brain Eaters game only takes advantage of a single method of the Canvas API: the `drawImage()` method. The `drawImage()` method paints an image on the canvas at a particular location.

For example, the player tile is rendered with the following code:

```
renderPlayer: function () {
    this.drawImage(this._player.tile.image, this._player.x, this._player.y);
},

drawImage: function (image, x, y) {
    this._ctx.drawImage(image, x * TILE_WIDTH, y * TILE_HEIGHT);
}
```

The `renderPlayer()` method calls the `drawImage()` method passing an image and x and y coordinates. The `drawImage()` method draws the image on the `Canvas` by calling the 2-D context `drawImage()` method.

NOTE

Unfortunately, you cannot use animated GIFs with the `Canvas drawImage()` method. According to the HTML5 spec, "When the `drawImage()` method is passed an animated image as its image argument, the user agent must use the poster frame of the animation, or, if there is no poster frame, the first frame of the animation." Bummer.

15

Capturing User Interaction

The Brain Eaters game supports keyboard, mouse, touch, and stylus interaction. If you are using the keyboard then you can move your character by using the arrow keys.

The following code is used to capture keyboard interaction:

```
document.addEventListener("keydown", this.movePlayerKeyboard.bind(this));
```

When you press a key down, the `movePlayerKeyboard()` method is called. This method detects the arrow key that was pressed and changes the direction of the player:

```
movePlayerKeyboard: function (e) {
    switch (e.keyCode) {
        case WinJS.Utilities.Key.upArrow:
            this._player.direction = Unleashed.Direction.up;
            break;
        case WinJS.Utilities.Key.downArrow:
            this._player.direction = Unleashed.Direction.down;
            break;
        case WinJS.Utilities.Key.leftArrow:
            this._player.direction = Unleashed.Direction.left;
            break;
        case WinJS.Utilities.Key.rightArrow:
            this._player.direction = Unleashed.Direction.right;
            break;
        case WinJS.Utilities.Key.space:
            this._player.direction = Unleashed.Direction.none;
            break;
    }
},
```

The `movePlayerKeyboard()` method takes advantage of the `WinJS.Utilities.Key` enumeration to detect which keyboard key was pressed. This enumeration contains a list of human-friendly names for the key codes so you can use `WinJS.Utilities.Key.upArrow` instead of 38.

If you are using a tablet device then you want to use touch instead of a keyboard. In that case you can touch the screen to indicate the direction in which you want your character to move.

The following code is used to capture the MSPointerDown event. This event is raised when you press down on your mouse button, touch the screen with your finger, or touch the screen with a stylus:

```
this._canvas.addEventListener("MSPointerDown", this.movePlayerTouch.bind(this));
```

When the `MSPointerDown` event is raised, the `movePlayerTouch()` method is called. This method takes care of changing the direction in which your character moves:

```
movePlayerTouch: function(e) {
    var playerX = this._player.x * TILE_WIDTH;
    var playerY = this._player.y * TILE_HEIGHT;
    var absX = Math.abs(e.offsetX - playerX);
    var absY = Math.abs(e.offsetY - playerY);

    if (absX > absY) {
        if (e.offsetX > playerX) {
            this._player.direction = Unleashed.Direction.right;
        } else {
            this._player.direction = Unleashed.Direction.left;
        }
    } else {
        if (e.offsetY > playerY) {
            this._player.direction = Unleashed.Direction.down;
        } else {
            this._player.direction = Unleashed.Direction.up;
        }
    }
},
```

Depending on where you touch the screen, your character moves in different directions. For example, if you touch the screen below your character then your character changes direction to move down. If you touch to the right of your character then your character moves to the right (see Figure 15.5).

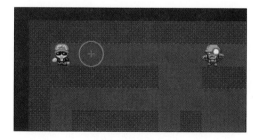

FIGURE 15.5   Touching the screen to change direction

Creating the Update Loop

The Brain Eater game uses two loops during game play. The game executes an *update loop* to update the positions of the player and the zombies. The game also executes a *render loop* to render the game.

The update loop executes every 250 milliseconds. The `executeUpdateLoop()` method is triggered with the following call to the `window.setInterval()` method when you start a game:

```
this._updateLoopId = window.setInterval(this.executeUpdateLoop.bind(this),
UPDATE_LOOP_RATE);
```

> **NOTE**
>
> The `bind()` method called on the `executeUpdateLoop()` method is used to bind the current instance of the `Game` object to the `executeUpdateLoop()` method when the `executeUpdateLoop()` method is called. In other words, it ensures that the `this` variable will refer to the current instance of the `Game` object within the `executeUpdateLoop()` method.

The `UPDATE_LOOP_RATE` constant has the value 250 milliseconds. If you want the zombies to chase you faster then you can reduce this value (the game definitely gets harder the lower that you make this number).

The `executeUpdateLoop()` method looks like this:

```
executeUpdateLoop: function () {
    this.updateMonsterPositions();
    this.updatePlayerPosition();
},
```

This method updates the positions of the zombies and the player. For example, the `updateMonsterPositions()` method moves all of the zombies in the direction of the player.

While updating the positions of the zombies and the player, the update loop also checks for collisions. The update loop must check whether there is a collision between the player and a zombie or between the player and a food pellet.

For example, the `updatePlayerPosition()` method calls the following `collideWithFood()` method to detect whether the player has walked into a food pellet:

```
collideWithFood: function () {
    for (var i = 0; i < this._food.length; i++) {
        var food = this._food[i];
        if (this._player.x === food.x && this._player.y === food.y) {
            Unleashed.Sounds.yum.play();
            this._food.splice(i, 1);
        }
    }

    // If no more food then player wins!
```

```
    if (this._food.length === 0) {
        this.win();
    }
},
```

The `collideWithFood()` method loops through the JavaScript `_food` array and checks whether the x and y position of any food pellet corresponds to the x and y position of the player. If there is a match then a "Yum!" sound is played and the food pellet is removed from the food array using `_food.splice()`. If all of the food is eaten then the player wins.

The update loop does not render anything to the screen. The update loop is responsible only for the state of the game. Rendering the game is the responsibility of the render loop.

Creating the Render Loop

The render loop is responsible for rendering the game board. Unlike the update loop, which is triggered by the `window.setInterval()` method, the render loop is executed by calling the `requestAnimationFrame()` method.

The `requestAnimationFrame()` method is defined as part of the W3C Timing Control for Script-Based Animation standard. This method was introduced specifically for the purpose of creating animated games.

When you use the `requestAnimationFrame()` method, you don't specify how often the screen should be rendered. Instead, you let the browser determine the best frame rate.

The idea is that the browser can do a better job than you in determining the best frame rate. The browser can take into account all of the animations being rendered and, therefore, render all of the animations more smoothly. If the page is not currently visible then the browser can throttle the animations and conserve CPU power.

In the Brain Eaters game, the render loop is started with the following code:

```
this._animationLoopId = window.requestAnimationFrame(this.executeRenderLoop.
➥bind(this));
```

The `executeRenderLoop()` method is passed to the `requestAnimationFrame()` method. The `executeRenderLoop()` method looks like this:

```
executeRenderLoop: function () {
    this.render();
    this._animationLoopId = window.requestAnimationFrame(this.executeRenderLoop.
➥bind(this));
},
```

The `executeRenderLoop()` method calls the `render()` method and then immediately calls the `window.requestAnimationFrame()` method again. It is up to the `window.requestAnimationFrame()` method to decide how quickly the `executeRenderLoop()` method gets called again.

The `render()` method is responsible for drawing the screen and it looks like this:

```
render: function () {
    this.renderBoard();
    this.renderFood();
    this.renderMonsters();
    this.renderPlayer();
},
```

The `render()` method draws the game board, the food pellets, the monsters, and the player.

The `renderBoard()` method draws the 20 by 15 tile game board by calling the `drawImage()` method for each tile in the game board. Here's what the `renderBoard()` method looks like:

```
renderBoard: function () {
    for (var y = 0; y < VERTICAL_TILES; y++) {
        for (var x = 0; x < HORIZONTAL_TILES; x++) {
            var tile = this.getTile(x, y);
            if (tile) {
                this.drawImage(tile.image, x, y);
            } else {
                this.drawImage(Unleashed.Tiles.background.image, x, y);
            }
        }
    }
},
```

The `renderFood()` and `renderMonsters()` methods are very similar; both methods loop through an array and render each element in the array to the screen. Here's what the `renderMonsters()` method looks like:

```
renderMonsters: function () {
    for (var i = 0; i < this._monsters.length; i++) {
        var monster = this._monsters[i];
        this.drawImage(monster.tile.image, monster.x, monster.y);
    }
},
```

In the code, the `_monsters array` contains an array of monster objects. The `drawImage()` method is used to draw each monster to the `Canvas` element.

Finally, the `renderPlayer()` method renders the player (the hero of the game) to the screen like this:

```
renderPlayer: function () {
    this.drawImage(this._player.tile.image, this._player.x, this._player.y);
},
```

> **NOTE**
>
> The `requestAnimationFrame()` method is defined in the Timing Control for Script-Based Animation standard located at http://dvcs.w3.org/hg/webperf/raw-file/tip/specs/RequestAnimationFrame/Overview.html.

Summary

The goal of this chapter was to create a simple game by creating a Windows Store app. I showed you how to create image and sound files for the game and I showed you how to render the images using the HTML5 `Canvas` element.

You also learned how to create both an update loop and a render loop. The update loop is used to update the positions of the monsters and player on the game board. The render loop is used to render the game board by calling the `requestAnimationFrame()` method to draw the image tiles.

Good luck winning the game! If you win the game, you get to hear my children cheer.

15

Creating a Task List App

In this final chapter, I walk through creating a productivity app. I demonstrate how you can create a basic tasks list app named MyTasks.

My goal in this chapter is to tackle building a more complete app: An app that can be submitted to the Windows Store, an app that includes robust error handling and all of the features that are required by a real-world app.

This app weaves together several of the technologies discussed in earlier chapters of this book:

- ▶ The MyTasks app uses Live Connect zero-click single sign-on to authenticate users. I discussed Live Connect authentication in Chapter 14, "Using the Live Connect API."

- ▶ The MyTasks app uses Windows Azure Mobile Services to save tasks to the cloud so the tasks can be accessed from multiple computers and devices. I discussed Azure Mobile Services in Chapter 10, "Using Windows Azure Mobile Services."

- ▶ The MyTasks app adapts to different screen widths automatically by using CSS Media Queries and JavaScript. I discussed how you can build apps that adapt to different view states in Chapter 11, "App Events and States."

- ▶ The MyTasks app uses a `ListView` control to display the lists of tasks. I discussed the `ListView` control in detail in Chapter 8, "Using the `ListView` Control."

- ▶ The MyTasks app uses a Binding Converter to display completed tasks with a line-through them. I discussed Binding Converters in Chapter 3, "Observables, Bindings, and Templates."

▶ The MyTasks app uses an `AppBar` to display application commands for deleting a task, marking a task as complete, and creating a new task. I discussed the `AppBar` control in Chapter 6, "Menus and Flyouts."

▶ The MyTasks app uses a `NavBar` to display a navigation menu that enables you to navigate to different days of the week. I discussed the new `NavBar` control in Chapter 6.

▶ The MyTasks app includes a custom setting that displays a Privacy Policy. I discussed creating custom settings in Chapter 6.

When building the MyTasks app, I also took advantage of a new API introduced with Windows 8.1. The MyTasks app uses the Windows 8.1 Text-To-Speech `SpeechSynthesizer` class to read tasks out loud. You know, like the computer voice in Star Trek.

> **NOTE**
>
> I submitted the MyTasks app to the Windows Store. If you would like to play with the MyTasks app while reading this chapter then you can install the app from the Windows Store.

Overview of the App

The MyTasks app is a basic task list application. It enables you to create new tasks, mark tasks as complete, and delete existing tasks.

When you first open the MyTasks app, you see a list of tasks for the current date. If you right-click the screen then you can see both the app bar and the nav bar (see Figure 16.1).

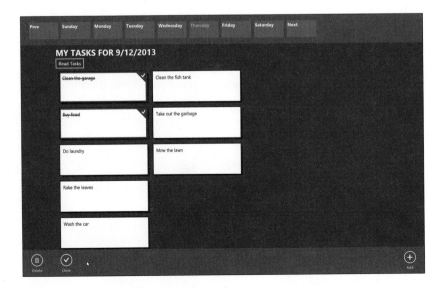

FIGURE 16.1   The MyTasks app

The app bar contains the commands for creating tasks, deleting tasks, and marking tasks as complete. Notice that the first and second tasks in Figure 16.1 have been marked as complete. Both tasks appear with a line through them.

The nav bar enables you to navigate to another date and see the tasks for that date. In Figure 16.1, Thursday is highlighted because it represents the selected date.

The MyTasks app was created by using the Visual Studio Navigation App project template. The app contains a single page named home that is located at the path \pages\home\home.html. The home page displays the content that you see in Figure 16.1.

The MyTasks app uses three custom JavaScript libraries:

▶ `live.js`—Contains methods for interacting with Live Connect services

▶ `services.js`—Contains methods for interacting with Windows Azure Mobile Services

▶ `speech.js`—Contains methods for using the Windows 8.1 Text-To-Speech speech synthesizer

All three of these libraries can be found in the Visual Studio project \js folder.

Setting Up the App

> **NOTE**
>
> If you want to avoid performing the setup steps described in this section but you still want to play with the MyTasks app then I recommend that you install the MyTasks app from the Windows Store.

All of the source code for the MyTasks app is included in the GitHub repository associated with this book. Because the MyTasks app relies on external services—Live Connect and Windows Azure Mobile Services—you must perform some setup before the app will run.

Setup is tedious and painful—but I guarantee that you can get everything to work with a strong cup of coffee and some patience in less than 15 minutes. You need to bounce back and forth between three websites:

▶ Windows Store Dashboard—https://appdev.microsoft.com/StorePortals

▶ Windows Azure Management Portal—http://manage.WindowsAzure.com

▶ Live Connect Developers Center—https://account.live.com/developers/applications

You can find detailed instructions for creating a Windows Azure Mobile Service in Chapter 10. Detailed instructions for getting an app to work with Live Connect and Windows Azure Mobile Services are in Chapter 14.

To summarize, you need to complete the following steps:

1. Within Visual Studio—from the Project, Store menu—reserve an app name and associate the MyTasks project with your app.

2. At the Windows Store Dashboard, click Services and register your app with Live Connect. You need to enter a Redirect URL in this step.

3. At the Windows Azure Management Portal, you need to create a new Mobile Service.

4. Get your Live Connect client ID and client secret from the Live Connect Developers center and associate the client ID and client secret with your Mobile Service at the Windows Azure Management Portal. You need to enter your client ID and secret under your Mobile Service's Identity tab.

5. In your Visual Studio project, update the \js\live.js file with the Redirect URL that you created in step 2.

6. In your Visual Studio project, update the \js\services.js file with your Mobile Service application key that you can retrieve from the Windows Azure Management Portal.

After you get Live Connect and Windows Azure configured, there is one more step that you must complete before the MyTasks app will work. To use the MyTasks app, you also need to create the insert.js, update.js, delete.js, and read.js server scripts hosted in your Windows Azure Mobile Service. All four of these scripts are in the \serverScripts folder.

You can add the server scripts to your Mobile Service in either of two ways. You can add the scripts through the Windows Azure Management Portal (see Figure 16.2) or you can add these scripts from within the Server Explorer window in Visual Studio. For detailed instructions see Chapter 10.

FIGURE 16.2   Updating server scripts at the Windows Azure Management Portal

Connecting to External Services

The MyTasks app cannot even get off the ground unless it can connect to Live Connect and Windows Azure Mobile Services. If the MyTasks app cannot authenticate you with Live Connect and get your tasks from Azure Mobile Services then the app has nothing useful to do. So the very first thing that the MyTasks app does is to connect to these services.

Listing 16.1 contains the startup code that is responsible for connecting to Live Connect and Azure.

LISTING 16.1   MyTasks Startup Code (/js/default.js)

```javascript
// The startup method ensures that you are
// connected to Live and Azure before
// doing anything else.
function startup() {
    return new WinJS.Promise(function (complete) {
        function login() {
            // Login to Live
            Live.login().done(
                // Success
                function () {
                    // Login to Azure Mobile Services
                    Services.login(Live.getAuthenticationToken()).done(
                        // Success
                        function () {
                            complete();
                        },
                        // Fail
                        function (errorMessage) {
                            // If first we don't succeed, try again ad nauseum
                            var message = "Could not connect to Windows Azure. " +
➥errorMessage;
                            var md = new Windows.UI.Popups.MessageDialog(message);
                            md.commands.append(new Windows.UI.Popups.
➥UICommand("&Retry"));
                            md.showAsync().done(login);
                        }
                    );
                },
                // Fail
                function () {
                    // If first we don't succeed, try again ad nauseum
                    var md = new Windows.UI.Popups.MessageDialog("Could not connect
➥to the Internet.");
                    md.commands.append(new Windows.UI.Popups.UICommand("&Retry"));
```

```
                    md.showAsync().done(login);
                }
            );
        }

        // Start recursing until complete
        login();
    });
}


app.addEventListener("activated", function (args) {
    if (args.detail.kind === activation.ActivationKind.launch) {
        // This might take a while
        args.setPromise(WinJS.UI.processAll().then(function () {
            // Login to both Live and Azure
            startup().done(function () {
                // After logging in, navigate to page
                if (app.sessionState.history) {
                    nav.history = app.sessionState.history;
                }
                if (nav.location) {
                    nav.history.current.initialPlaceholder = true;
                    return nav.navigate(nav.location, nav.state);
                } else {
                    return nav.navigate(Application.navigator.home);
                }
            });

        }));
    }
});
```

In Listing 16.1, the handler for the activated event calls the `startup()` method immediately after the MyTasks app is activated. The `startup()` method returns a promise that contains a recursive function named `login()`. The `login()` method recursively calls itself until the user is logged into both Live Connect and Windows Azure.

If the user successfully logs into both services then the `startup()` promise completes and the `navigate()` method is called to send the user to the home page. The home page displays the list of tasks for the user.

NOTE

The `Live.login()` method is implemented in the /js/live.js library and the `Services.` `login()` method is implemented in the /js/services.js library.

Both the `Live.login()` method and the `Services.login()` method return promises. If there is an error logging into either Live Connect or Windows Azure then the error message is displayed in a Message Dialog (see Figure 16.3).

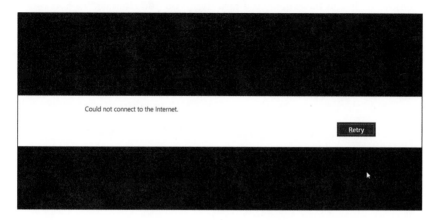

FIGURE 16.3   Error caused by no Internet connection

If you click the Retry button in the Message dialog, then the `login()` method calls itself. In other words, the `startup()` method will keep attempting to connect to the services over and over again every time you click Retry. Because the MyTasks app won't work unless you connect to these services, the app won't let you do anything else.

> **NOTE**
>
> Instead of throwing a user into an infinite loop, wouldn't it make more sense to just close the app when there is no Internet connection? Nope, definitely not. It violates Windows 8 app certification requirements to programmatically close an app: "Your app must neither programmatically close nor offer UI affordances to close it."

Optimistic Inserts, Updates, and Deletes

Always be optimistic because users are impatient.

The MyTasks app uses *optimistic* inserts, update, and deletes when calling Windows Azure Mobile Services. For example, when a user creates a new task, the new task is added to the `WinJS.Binding.List` displayed by the `ListView` immediately and the new task appears immediately. Behind the scenes, the task is inserted in the Windows Azure database *after* the task already appears in the `ListView`.

Being optimistic is important for perceived performance. When users interact with your Windows Store app, they don't want to wait for things to happen. They don't care that their tasks need to be stored in a remote database. Everything should appear to happen instantly.

But what happens if things go wrong? What happens if your Internet connection goes down and the task cannot be inserted into the remote Azure database?

In the rare cases when things go wrong, you simply revert. If you have inserted a task in the List then you remove it. If you have deleted a task then you add the task back again. If you have updated a task then you revert it. And, you throw an error message at the user so the user knows that something has gone wrong.

Listing 16.2 contains the code, from the \js\services.js library, for creating a new task.

LISTING 16.2   Optimistic Insert (/js/services.js)

```
function addMyTask(newTask) {
    return new WinJS.Promise(function (complete, error) {
        // Be optimistic
        _myTasksList.dataSource.insertAtStart(null, newTask).done(function
➡(newListItem) {
            // Actually do the insert
            _myTasksTable.insert(newTask).done(
                // Success
                function (newDBItem) {
                    // Update the list item with the DB item
                    _myTasksList.dataSource.change(newListItem.key, newDBItem).
➡done(function () {
                        complete();
                    });
                },
                // fail
                function (err) {
                    // Remove the item
                    _myTasksList.dataSource.remove(newListItem.key).done(function ()
{
                        error(err);
                    });
                }
            );
        });
    });
}
```

Let me explain what is going on in the addMyTask() method in Listing 16.2. First, let me describe what happens when everything goes right:

1. The new task is added to the local WinJS.Binding.List with the insertAtStart() method. Because the WinJS.Binding.List is bound to the ListView, the new task appears immediately in the ListView.

2. The new task is inserted in the remote MyTasks Azure database table by calling the `_myTasks.insert()` method.

3. After the new task is successfully inserted into the remote database then the task in the local `WinJS.Binding.List` is updated with the correct ID from the remote database.

So, if everything works right, when a user creates a new task then the user can see the task immediately. The user does not need to wait for the remote database to be updated.

If things don't go right, then the following steps happen:

1. The new task is added to the local `WinJS.Binding.List` and the user sees the new task in the `ListView`.

2. For whatever reason, the new task cannot be inserted into the remote Azure database table (for example, the Internet is broken).

3. The new task is removed from the local `WinJS.Binding.List` and the user sees that the task has been removed from the `ListView`.

So, if things go wrong, the user sees the new task appear and then disappear. Because the `addMyTask()` method calls the `error()` function, the user also sees the error message in Figure 16.4.

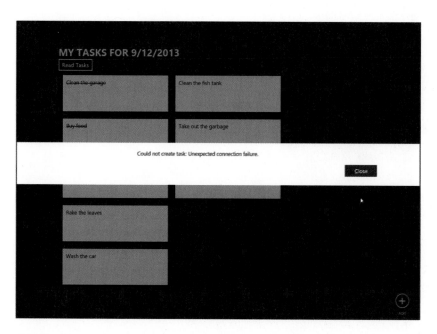

16

FIGURE 16.4   When things go wrong with an optimistic insert

Adapting to Screen Changes

Wide, thin, then wide again. The MyTasks app is designed to gracefully adapt to different screen widths. As I discussed in Chapter 11, multiple Windows 8.1 apps can be run side by side. A user can change the size of a Windows 8.1 app at any moment.

A standard Widows 8.1 app should be designed to work at any width between 500 pixels and higher. By default, 500 pixels is the minimum horizontal width for a Windows 8.1 app.

However, I wanted to be able to use the MyTasks app at widths lower than 500 pixels. In particular, I wanted to be able to open the MyTasks app side by side with other applications such as Visual Studio. That way, I can quickly add a new task to the MyTasks app while working within Visual Studio (see Figure 16.5).

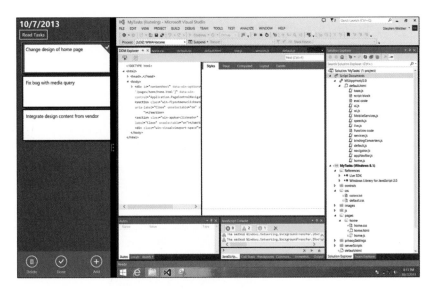

FIGURE 16.5   Using MyTasks at 320 pixels

If you want your Windows Store app to support a minimum width less than 500 pixels then you need to modify your app manifest (package.appxmanifest). I changed the minimum width for MyTasks to be 320 pixels (see Figure 16.6).

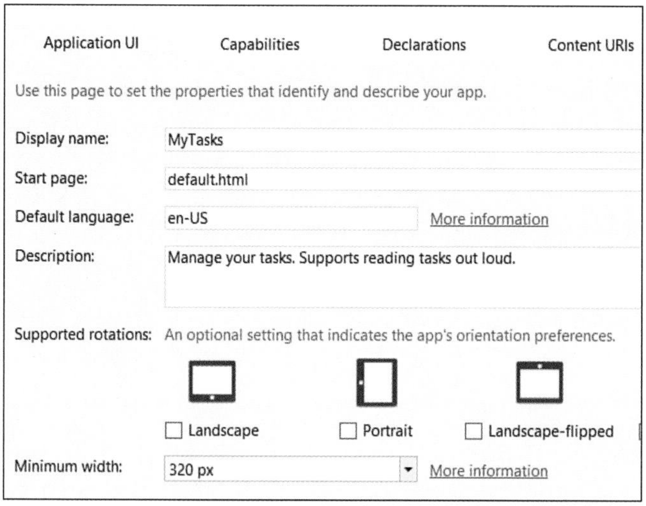

FIGURE 16.6   Setting the minimum width to 320 pixels

However, going below 500 pixels does not provide you with a lot of room. Therefore, when the MyTasks app width gets below 500 pixels then I make some changes to the app.

First, when the app is shrunk below 500 pixels, I change the margins around the page content to remove any unnecessary whitespace. I change the margins with the CSS Media Query in Listing 16.3.

LISTING 16.3   CSS Media Query (/pages/home.css)

```
@media screen and (min-width:500px) {
    .homepage #content {
        margin-left: 120px;
        margin-right: 120px;
        margin-top: 100px;
    }
}


@media screen and (max-width:500px) {
    .homepage #content {
        margin-left: 10px;
    }
}
```

The CSS in Listing 16.3 changes the left margin to 10px when the app is shrunk below 500 pixels. The right and top margins are completely removed.

Normally, the tasks are displayed by the `ListView` in a grid. When you shrink the MyTasks app below 500 pixels then I use the code in Listing 16.4 to switch the `ListView` from Grid layout to List layout.

LISTING 16.4   Handling Window Resize (/pages/home.js)

```
updateLayout: function (element) {
    this._performLayout();
},


// We show the ListView in a list when
// the screen gets too small
_performLayout: function (element) {
    var width = document.documentElement.offsetWidth;
    var height = document.documentElement.offsetHeight;
    var lvMyTasks = document.getElementById("lvMyTasks").winControl;
    var spanMyTasks = document.getElementById("spanMyTasks");

    // The height of the ListView is 80% of the screen
    lvMyTasks.element.style.height = (height * 0.80) + "px";

    // When the width of the screen is less than 500px then show as List
    if (width < 500) {
        lvMyTasks.layout = new WinJS.UI.ListLayout();
        lvMyTasks.forceLayout();
        spanMyTasks.style.display = "none";
    } else {
        lvMyTasks.layout = new WinJS.UI.GridLayout();
        lvMyTasks.forceLayout();
        spanMyTasks.style.display = "";
    }
}
```

The `updateLayout()` method in Listing 16.6 is called automatically when the size of the app changes. The `updateLayout()` method changes the `ListView` to either Grid or List layout depending on the current app width.

The `updateLayout()` method also hides or displays the `<span>` that displays the title text "My Tasks For". This extra text only appears in wide mode.

Figure 16.7 and Figure 16.8 illustrate how the MyTasks app changes its appearance when displayed with different widths.

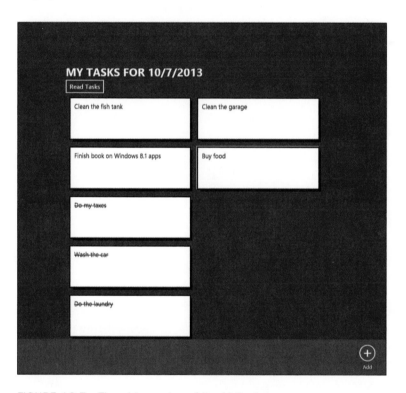

FIGURE 16.7   The wide version of the MyTasks app

FIGURE 16.8   The narrow version of the MyTasks app

Creating a Custom Control

When an app starts getting too complex, it is a good idea to start encapsulating things. For example, if you are building a complicated user interface then it helps to break the user interface into separate WinJS controls.

The nav bar used in the MyTasks app changes appearance when displayed at different screen widths. Normally, the nav bar enables you to navigate to different days by clicking the names of different days of the week (see Figure 16.9). However, when the app gets too narrow, the days of the week no longer fit in the nav bar. When the width gets below 500 pixels then I display a date picker instead (see Figure 16.10).

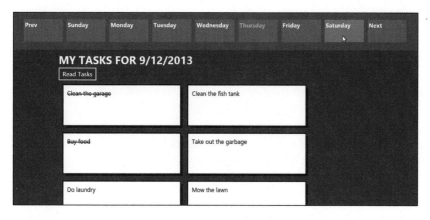

FIGURE 16.9   The days of the week version of the nav bar

FIGURE 16.10   The date picker version of the nav bar

Instead of throwing all of the WinJS controls and JavaScript logic into the home page, I encapsulated everything required by the nav bar into a separate custom WinJS control named `AppNavBar`. That way, the home page can be kept simple.

I created the `AppNavBar` control by creating a `Page` control—select the Visual Studio menu option Project, Add New Item, `Page` control. Creating a new `Page` control results in three new files named appNavBar.css, appNavBar.html, and appNavBar.js.

> **NOTE**
>
> The code for the `AppNavBar` control is located in the \controls\appNavBar folder.

After you create a custom `Page` control then you can use it in your pages just like any standard WinJS control. First, you need to add a reference to the JavaScript file for the `AppNavBar` control to the home.html page like this:

```
<script src="/controls/appNavBar/appNavBar.js"></script>
```

Now, you can add the `AppNavBar` control to the home.html page just like any other standard WinJS control like this:

```
<div id="appNavBar" data-win-control="MyControls.AppNavBar"></div>
```

Using Text to Speech

I keep waiting for the day when computers get as smart and easy to use as the computers in Star Trek. In particular, I can't wait until the day when all of my computer apps talk to me out loud.

Fortunately, that day has arrived. Windows 8.1 includes a new Text-To-Speech API that makes it easy to add speech to a Windows Store app. The Text-To-Speech API even supports different voices with different genders.

The MyTasks app includes a button, labeled Read Tasks, that reads all of the tasks on the current page out loud. Here's what the click handler for the button looks like:

```
// Read tasks out loud
btnRead.addEventListener("click", function (e) {
    e.preventDefault();

    // Build soliloquy
    var soliliquy = "Hello " + Live.getFirstName();
    if (Services.myTasksList.length == 0) {
        soliliquy += ", you do not have any tasks for this day."
    } else {
        soliliquy += ", these are your tasks:";
        Services.myTasksList.forEach(function (item) {
```

```
            soliliquy += item.name;
            if (item.isDone) {
                soliliquy += "(This task is already completed).";
            }
        });
    }
    Speech.say(soliliquy);
});
```

When you click the Read Tasks button, a variable named soliloquy is built up that contains the text to be spoken. The click handler loops through all of the task names to build the text. The `Speech.say()` method is called to speak the soliloquy text out loud.

I encapsulated the Windows 8.1 Text-To-Speech API in the mini-library in Listing 16.5.

LISTING 16.5   Text-To-Speech Library (\js\speech.js)

```
(function () {
    "use strict";

    function say(text) {
        var audio = new Audio();
        var synth = new Windows.Media.SpeechSynthesis.SpeechSynthesizer();

        // Use Hazel's voice
        var voices = Windows.Media.SpeechSynthesis.SpeechSynthesizer.allVoices;
        for (var i = 0; i < voices.length; i++) {
            if (voices[i].displayName == "Microsoft Hazel Desktop") {
                synth.voice = voices[i];
            }
        }

        synth.synthesizeTextToStreamAsync(text).then(function (markersStream) {
            var blob = MSApp.createBlobFromRandomAccessStream(markersStream.
➥ContentType, markersStream);
            audio.src = URL.createObjectURL(blob, { oneTimeOnly: true });
            audio.play();
        });
    }


    WinJS.Namespace.define("Speech", {
        say: say
    });

})();
```

The JavaScript library in Listing 16.5 has one public method named `say()` that says any text out loud. This method selects a voice and then calls the `SpeechSynthesizer` `synthesizeTextToStreamAsync()` method to convert the text to a binary audio blob. The audio blob is assigned to an HTML5 Audio element and played.

Notice that a particular voice is selected before the audio is played. The Microsoft Hazel Desktop voice is used with the text. This voice has a female English accent.

The `Windows.Media.SpeechSynthesis.SpeechSynthesizer.allVoices` method returns a list of all of the voices available on the machine. On my machine, I have the following voices:

▶ Microsoft David Desktop—American male voice

▶ Microsoft Hazel Desktop—English female voice

▶ Microsoft Zira Desktop—American female voice

If you don't specify a particular voice to use by assigning a voice to the `voice` property then the Microsoft David Desktop voice is used by default.

NOTE

The Text-To-Speech API also supports Speech Synthesis Markup Language (SSML). SSML is a markup language that provides you with greater control over how text is spoken. For example, you can use the `<break/>` tag to add pauses to speech and the `<prosody>` tag to control volume, pitch and rate. You can learn more about SSML by reading the W3C recommendation at http://www.w3.org/TR/speech-synthesis/.

Summary

This chapter focused on building a simple productivity app: the MyTasks app. I discussed solutions to several of the challenges that you face when building a real-world Windows Store app.

First, I explained how you can ensure that a connection to external services is available when you start a Windows Store app. The MyTasks app depends on communicating with Live Connect and Windows Azure. If connections to these services are not available then the MyTasks app repeatedly throws a Retry dialog in your face.

Next, I discussed the importance of optimistic inserts, updates, and deletes for the perceived performance of your Windows Store app. I recommend that you always insert locally before inserting remotely to provide your users with the best perceived performance.

I also demonstrated how you can gracefully adapt the MyTasks app to different screen widths. I showed you how you can use both CSS Media Queries and JavaScript to change the appearance of the app when the app is stretched or shrunk.

Finally, I talked about a new API introduced with Windows 8.1. I demonstrated how you can convert text to speech and read tasks out loud by taking advantage of the new Windows 8.1 `SpeechSynthesizer` class.

Index

How can we make this index more useful? Email us at indexes@samspublishing.com

G

H

M

How can we make this index more useful? Email us at indexes@samspublishing.com

How can we make this index more useful? Email us at indexes@samspublishing.com

X-Y-Z

UNLEASHED

Unleashed takes you beyond the basics, providing an exhaustive, technically sophisticated reference for professionals who need to exploit a technology to its fullest potential. It's the best resource for practical advice from the experts, and the most in-depth coverage of the latest technologies.

informit.com/unleashed

C# 5.0 Unleashed
ISBN-13: 9780672336904

OTHER UNLEASHED TITLES

Windows Phone 8 Unleashed
ISBN-13: 9780672336898

ASP.NET Dynamic Data Unleashed
ISBN-13: 9780672335655

Microsoft System Center 2012 Unleashed
ISBN-13: 9780672336126

System Center 2012 Configuration Manager (SCCM) Unleashed
ISBN-13: 9780672334375

Windows Server 2012 Unleashed
ISBN-13: 9780672336225

Microsoft Exchange Server 2013 Unleashed
ISBN-13: 9780672336119

Microsoft Visual Studio 2012 Unleashed
ISBN-13: 9780672336256

System Center 2012 Operations Manager Unleashed
ISBN-13: 9780672335914

Microsoft Dynamics CRM 2011 Unleashed
ISBN-13: 9780672335389

Microsoft Lync Server 2013 Unleashed
ISBN-13: 9780672336157

Visual Basic 2012 Unleashed
ISBN-13: 9780672336317

Microsoft Visual Studio LightSwitch Unleashed
ISBN-13: 9780672335532

HTML5 Unleashed
ISBN-13: 9780672336270

Windows 8.1 Apps with XAML and C# Unleashed
ISBN-13: 9780672337086

SAMS

informit.com/sams

    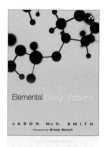

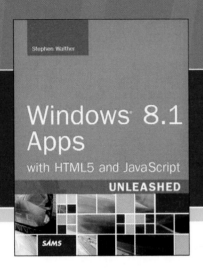

FREE
Online Edition

Your purchase of *Windows® 8.1 Apps with HTML5 and JavaScript Unleashed* includes access to a free online edition for 45 days through the **Safari Books Online** subscription service. Nearly every Sams book is available online through **Safari Books Online**, along with thousands of books and videos from publishers such as Addison-Wesley Professional, Cisco Press, Exam Cram, IBM Press, O'Reilly Media, Prentice Hall, Que, and VMware Press.

Safari Books Online is a digital library providing searchable, on-demand access to thousands of technology, digital media, and professional development books and videos from leading publishers. With one monthly or yearly subscription price, you get unlimited access to learning tools and information on topics including mobile app and software development, tips and tricks on using your favorite gadgets, networking, project management, graphic design, and much more.

Activate your FREE Online Edition at
informit.com/safarifree

STEP 1: Enter the coupon code: MMZJWWA.

STEP 2: New Safari users, complete the brief registration form.
Safari subscribers, just log in.

If you have difficulty registering on Safari or accessing the online edition,
please e-mail customer-service@safaribooksonline.com